I0762942

Also by Jack Parlett

Fire Island

The Poetics of Cruising

Same Blue, Different You (poetry)

FLAMBOYANCE

THE POWER OF LIVING BOLDLY

JACK PARLETT

Recycling programs for this product may not exist in your area.

ISBN-13: 978-1-335-94932-5

Flamboyance

Hanover Square Press
22 Adelaide St. West, 41st Floor
Toronto, Ontario M5H 4E3, Canada
HanoverSqPress.com

HarperCollins Publishers
Macken House, 39/40 Mayor Street Upper,
Dublin 1, D01 C9W8, Ireland
www.HarperCollins.com

Printed in U.S.A.

26 27 28 29 30 LBC 5 4 3 2 1

For Amy

CONTENTS

FLAMBOYANCE

THE SECRET

I AM TRYING to get better at making an entrance. I imagine being the kind of person who shows up to the party dressed like nobody else and pulling it off. Lighting up a room with sheer force of presence. It seems like a life skill, this way of carrying oneself, useful for making impressions, forging connections, flirting. A mark of self-acceptance, too, the conduct of someone who knows exactly who they are, who asserts it without fear or apology. But it could also be a sign of something else: a mask, an armor, a way of overcompensating. Some may interpret it as false or ostentatious, as indulgent or simply a nuisance, and those attitudes can reveal something about the people looking, too, their own hang-ups or insecurities. Commanding attention carries with it a demand to be seen, and this demand can be confronting. However it may be received, this art of self-presentation has a long lineage. It has been known, at least for the last two hundred years or so, by the word *flamboyant*.

I am not a very flamboyant person, although I still fantasize about one day embodying its qualities. The *Oxford English Dictionary* describes a flamboyant person as someone who attracts attention for their "confidence, stylishness and exuberance," a holy trinity of qualities often prized in contemporary life. I have had my moments: loud outfits here and there, flashes of self-belief on a stage, uninhibited movements on a dance floor, loosened by chemicals. In reality, my instinct most of the time is to move toward the background. And yet, I still find myself drawn to the glow of flamboyance, its sense of fun. I want to be the one to walk in the sun, as Cyndi Lauper once sang, with her shock of orange hair, dressed in a pink pimped-out prom dress, strutting down the street.

To be unleashed on the world without restriction may seem like an infantile desire, the stuff of child's play and adolescent rebellion. Flamboyance is often an embrace of your inner child, an unruly love of the colorful and ridiculous, a recall to the defiance of a teenage self. For this reason, it runs deep in many of our personal histories, whether we are aware of it or not, beginning as the exuberance that might be encouraged and accepted in our childhood, only to be extinguished by the responsibilities and restrictions of adulthood.

This is not to say that flamboyance, which is associated with feathers and furs, glitz and glamour, is always seen as a quality to aspire to, an index of what is fashionable or acceptable. For those largely excluded from normative ideas of respectability, the word *flamboyant* can be thrust upon us in a different way; an old-fashioned, heavy-handed euphemism for deviance, a reductive label that will not come unstuck. Many queer people, and commonly boys and men, feel discomfort around this word, perhaps because it recalls the derogatory charge that it held in our early years, when it was synonymous with femininity and same-sex desire.

Growing up in the UK in the late 1990s and early 2000s, any sense I had of flamboyance was mediated by a different word, one you were much more likely to hear used by other children on the playground or in the changing rooms. The phrase "that's so gay" has an unmistakable ring in my ears. Typing it out still makes my shoulders tense up a little. The word *gay* back then, meant limp wrists and loud, lisping voices, but also anything that was deemed lame or lackluster. As a child I felt the magnetism of these things, the boys who weren't like other boys, the men on TV who minced and preened, but I also knew that they were uncool. In fact, it paid to be suspicious of them, although I sensed they held the key to something about who I was.

I remember befriending a flamboyant boy at school because I saw him dancing in the playground, performing the full routine to Michael Jackson's "Thriller" while a group of girls clapped along. I was ten years old and drawn to his confidence and showmanship. That young friendship, although it lasted just a few years, was a formative one. I can still recognize echoes of the dynamic between us—him as the outré performer, and I the sturdy sidekick—in how I express myself today. How I felt toward him contained the stirrings of desire, but also admiration. He seemed able to transform qualities that were already coded as gay, in boys of this age, into a charming social currency. I was not unhappy or unlucky in school. I had friends and I mostly kept my head down. But this boy cast a different light. He seemed, for a while, like the main character in my world view, a portal to a different, more grown-up place.

Much of what I learned about being gay at this age I learned from other kids (a sometimes brutal education), or from pop culture. These were the dying years of Section 28 in the UK, the 1988 act which forbade teachers from "promoting" homosexuality or the "acceptability of homosexuality as a pretended family relationship." (No one was ever prosecuted under this act, and it was repealed in 2003, but the repercussions of the fearful atmosphere it created can still be felt today.)

These were also the years, at the beginning of the new millennium, when a new kind of reality television began to take hold, and talent shows like *Pop Idol* fed us with aspirational images of celebrity and pizazz. Although I often found myself as the sidekick to bigger personalities, I loved singing and dancing and daydreamed, like many children, of one day being famous myself. The premise of these TV shows, that someone ordinary could be projected to superstardom, fed my own private whimsies, and inspired me to do after-school dance classes, as well as a few later flirtations with musical theater.

There was something quite gay about *Pop Idol*, it seemed to me, although I had no language for it then, from its celebration of showbiz to the jazzed-up looks of some of the contestants. But it was mostly implicit, hidden in plain sight. The winner of the show's first season, in 2002, was Will Young, a musical theater student in his early twenties. I remember watching him avidly in the live final, singing the song he had made a mark with earlier in the series, a cover of "Light My Fire" by The Doors (in the slow-tempo, Spanish guitar version by José Feliciano). Dressed in a black sweater vest and cargo pants, he grinned warmly at the camera, pyrotechnic flames dancing in front of him. Pitched as a lounge singer with diva affectations, Young seemed less appealing to the tween demographic than the other finalist. Gareth Gates was spiky-haired, baby-faced and just seventeen, the heartthrob of the show. I definitely had a crush on him, too.

Young won the show, and when he came out as gay quite soon afterward, my ten-year-old self reacted with the force of homophobia turned inward, as if I could no longer let myself love him. I remember going to my then girlfriend's house for tea one Friday evening. The conversation over dinner turned to TV, and her mum asked me what I thought of the winner. I volunteered that he was fine, but "when I found out he was gay, it put me off." I could tell from the look on her face that I had said something edgy and uncomfortable, but I failed to register why. I thought that was the correct public take, and I was just repeating something I had heard someone on the playground say, someone who was parroting his own dad. It was the most awkward fish and chips of my life.

Pop Idol was the kind of TV spectacle that could grip a nation in the era before streaming. This was just a few years after George Michael had been forcibly outed after his encounter with an undercover cop, and Young's decision not to make a pretense about his sexuality was courageous, particularly given the consequences it might have had for his post–*Pop Idol* career. His win signaled a shift toward out gays and lesbians being assimilated into the television mainstream.

In the US in the same era, there was comedian and sitcom star Ellen DeGeneres, as well as Richard Hatch, winner of the first season of *Survivor.* None of these new TV stars were particularly flamboyant figures, in either dress or personality, which was perhaps what felt momentous. Hatch was ex-military, while DeGeneres had a certain girl-next-door appeal. When she came out as a lesbian, via an interview with *Time* magazine in 1997, she recalled a conversation with her father about this decision, in which he said to her: "You're not going to go all flamboyant, are ya?" She replied, in jest, "Yeah, Dad, I'm going to completely change, I'm going to start wearing leather vests. I'm going to get one of those haircuts they all have."

Compared with the long tradition of flamboyant, gender-bending entertainers of the twentieth century—the singers, comedians, and drag performers who were often defined by their difference—the new generation of gay and lesbian celebrities appearing on TV seemed novel precisely because they were, by straight standards, less eccentric or transgressive. Ellen could be out and famous without being flamboyantly lesbian, while Will Young could become a TV-vetted gay pop star without the expectation of being flamboyantly gay, which is to say, campy and effeminate. His sexual orientation seemed separate from having the "X" factor that Simon Cowell always talked about, neither a barrier to star power nor the basis of it. By the specific metrics of gay and lesbian representation in show business, this cultural moment could be seen as one of progress. Will Young had certainly lit a fire in me, an uncomfortable mix of desire and recognition. But wherever things were progressing was not somewhere that I, as an increasingly confused preteen, wanted to go.

In my younger years, I displayed plenty of the signs of a boy who might later come out as gay. I loved dressing up in women's clothing at friends' houses, and I adored gay icons like Doris Day, who I would describe—my older sister Louise has told me—as just "delightful" in *Calamity Jane*, my favorite film as a child. By the time I was a teenager, those traits seemed like a distant memory of innocence lost. I had vowed to myself that I would stamp them out or hide them, and my denial of my own femininity became absolute. I grew into my adolescence on high alert.

In the surroundings of my state school, it felt to me that being gay was something to be laughed at and generally best avoided. I felt repelled by the three or four boys who were out at school, the way they would queen out and boast to their girl friends about their sexual fumbles at sleepovers. Being gay was one thing, I thought, but did they have to make such a big *deal* about it? I viewed them as attention seekers, but really I think they were being authentically themselves, give or take a few youthful embellishments. I found their bravery embarrassing, but looking back the shame was all my own.

I tried to pass as straight, but I had no interest in sports or other supposedly boyish pursuits, and I sat somewhere on the effete fringes of masculinity. I had bookishness on my side, at least. When you get painted as a nerd, in high school terms, there appears a familiar and slightly sexless archetype to slip into, a distraction from the question of sexuality. I had buried my own desires deep, hoping not to reveal them in the way that I walked or spoke. I had a long-term girlfriend, who remains a great friend today. But it was difficult to bat away the suspicions of others. My parents were supportive, but outside of home I seemed to always be encountering adults who saw it as their place to speculate. I would hear remarks, second-hand, about me being camp, or gay, or in touch with my feminine side. These remarks, however they were intended, felt more like an intrusion than an invitation to openness, and I retreated further back into the closet whenever they were repeated to me.

It was a secret I carried throughout my adolescence like a weight around my neck, unsure of who I was. I was continually paranoid about being identified as something I was unable to accept. Knowing that I felt this way makes it all the stranger that I chose, aged seventeen, to enter the school talent show with a rendition of George Michael's "Faith." I had a secret love for Michael and his music, not to mention his notorious association with the forbidden adult world of gay sex. But I kept this fascination hidden, until I decided to offer a glimpse of it before a huge audience in a school assembly. The performance got a warm reception, and I got a hit from the applause (although I was robbed of the win and had to settle for second place). The whole affair was like an out-of-body experience, as if some inner force had compelled me onstage. I danced to that song in a way that felt involuntary, the expression of something latent that simply had to come out.

When I went to university, and my girlfriend and I broke up, I knew it would soon be time to face the music. So began a fraught few years of falling in love with straight boys, of binge drinking and crying in nightclub smoking areas. I was still too repressed to go searching for queer community; and passed up most opportunities to meet other gay men, or enter spaces where I might be found out, and in the process, perhaps, truly seen. When I came out at twenty-one, over a decade after those early *Pop Idol* rumblings, it was the start of a journey toward self-acceptance that I still find myself on.

I wish I could say that my awakening happened after a particularly amazing night at a gay bar, or a Pride march that changed everything. But the real shift for me took place in a more solitary way, through my exposure to queer artworks. I was most empowered by what I was reading, by books more than boys. In the final year of my English degree, I wrote a dissertation about gay poets in New York, a city that has had a particular hold on my imagination, where I thought I might one day lead a more fearless and exciting life. I was studying the way writers approached the city like a living stage, an arena of sorts, where one could shape-shift and perform as any number of different selves. I once described this literary trope to my supervisor as being quite flamboyant. She suggested I should go and explore that concept deeper, its different meanings, lighting upon an avenue of inquiry that has led me here, writing these words.

"The secret is that flamboyance *can* be so exact." On my search for definitions, I was struck by this line, from the American writer Clark Coolidge, in an elegy for his late friend, the poet Frank O'Hara. Why is this a secret? Is not the overtness of flamboyance the whole point? While we are used to thinking of flamboyance as a force that immediately makes itself known, a carnivalesque explosion of color and noise, I liked the idea that it could also be elusive. Flamboyance, I realized, holds fast to its secrets. And they are the good kind of secrets, that is, the kind you want to be discovered.

I am still processing my early experiences in the closet, and coming to accept that those years of fear and shame have left some deep scars. Was there once a more flamboyant person inside of me, a louder, fruitier self I banished from existence? Perhaps I am simply more reserved and quiet, yet able to access flamboyance in the way that any of us might, on occasion, and in particular company, or specific contexts. Personality is a strange beast, and there may be no accurate answer to these questions. What I do know is that flamboyance has been a constant in my life, contested and changeable, something I first wanted to repress, and later, after coming out, to unleash. I spent many years relying on alcohol and drugs to do this, believing that they helped me to access something real, a confidence buried so deep that only substances could coax it out. But those lowered inhibitions came at a cost, and my issues with addiction were really an extended act of avoidance, a way of never having to face myself honestly.

In the process of getting clean and sober, I also turned away, at least initially, from more outward-facing behaviors. The further I get away from the drunken chaos of my twenties, the more I cherish these quieter moments of retreat and solitude. But even as I have embraced my introverted side, I have not left behind the desire to live boldly, to tap into a louder, prouder, riskier version of myself, less tentative and self-correcting. Now I am trying to find my way back to flamboyance, while staying connected with a more innate sense of self.

How to do this remains an open question for me, and in writing this book I have sought insights from the history of flamboyance, from the changing landscape of its meanings, and its rich legacies in queer culture, to the lives of some its brightest stars. While I come at this topic through the lens of my own experience, I share this journey because I believe anyone can learn and benefit from the lessons that flamboyance has to teach us. In pausing to consider the role that it plays in our lives, there is room for us all to see ourselves, reflected back in its flaming light.

THE WORD

A BRIEF TOUR

CHURCHES

BEFORE IT MEANT anything else, the word *flamboyant* simply meant *flaming* (from the French verb *flamboyer*; to flame or to blaze). First borrowed into English in the 1830s, it became a term associated with religious devotion, and a particular kind of medieval craft. The decadent stonework that adorns the windows and facades of many Gothic churches in Europe, wavy, undulating, S-shaped curves which resemble flames, inspired the name for an entire architectural style. It was coined by nineteenth-century architects and antiquaries, who looked back upon the grand religious buildings of the past, from the vantage of an increasingly industrialized society, and saw a lost world of artisanal marvels and cultural riches. In the process, they wrote a new history of medieval architecture, divided up into distinct periods. Gothic churches of the fifteenth and sixteenth century, many of which were distinguished by these stone flames, were thus described as belonging to the Flamboyant period of architecture.

The Flamboyant period was first coined, so one story goes, when a group of three French writers were admiring the spectacular Saint-Ouen Abbey in Rouen, and one of them, Eustache-Hyacinthe Langlois, used this "happy expression" to describe the stonework. The other men present, Arcisse de Caumont and Auguste Le Prévost, were responsible for the word's first appearances in print, in 1825, where it described "components formed in the shape of flames." The English architect and writer Thomas Rickman, who met with his like-minded French colleagues during a tour of Normandy in 1832, brought the word into English circulation when he wrote, a year later, of the Flamboyant style, the most distinctive feature of which was an ornate and undulating window tracery, "alluding to the wave of a flame." The origins of flamboyance as an idea were both religious and scholarly, disseminated through a shared cultural exchange between writers in England and France.

When I first began to pursue flamboyance in earnest, I felt I needed to know more about what this architecture is actually like. It seemed unlikely to yield a smooth affinity between the quiet reverence suggested by ecclesiastical buildings and the vibrancy of contemporary flamboyant culture. In other words, I would probably not be yelling "slay" at the stonework around rural church windows.

Let's not speak too soon, though. Historically, flamboyant architecture has provoked some strong reactions from its beholders, both positive and negative. John Ruskin, one of the major thinkers of the Victorian age, stuck his neck out for flamboyant architecture when it was unfashionable to do so, given that most critics of the time viewed it as a "degenerate" style, ruined by its own excesses. He admired its stylistic richness and how the moving shapes of flames suggested animation and vitality, the drama of intricate details and intersecting parts.

A Gothic church, after all, is an ornate labor of love in the name of holiness. No other building quite aims to inspire or instill explicitly religious feelings than a Catholic cathedral. The vaulted ceilings draw the eye upward, toward (so it goes) a higher power, while large stained-glass windows flood the space with light and color. Flamboyance's lively finesse was also accompanied, Ruskin noted, by a "strange fear and melancholy" that signaled toward "the contemplation of death." The shapes and threads of "thin and nervous stonework," Ruskin wrote, were "flamboyant with a fatal glow," calling to mind "wantonness and terror." In the literal representations of purgatory and hell that adorn some church porches, could be seen a palpable fear about the "fires of condemnation."

Ruskin ultimately came to the same conclusion about flamboyant architecture's demise as its detractors. The Flamboyant style "would have lived till now," he wrote in his 1849 book *The Seven Lamps of Architecture*, "if it had not taken to telling lies." The fatal flaw of the Flamboyant style was its decadence, which was perceived as a kind of artifice. But, Ruskin argued, Gothic styles like the flamboyant did not decline simply by "becoming too florid and too rich," for all "beautiful and perfect art, literature or nature, is rich." It was rather that its stylistic excesses, in his view, became empty and heartless, had "ceased to be earnest, and ceased to be sincere." Instead, the men who designed it "had become meanly fanciful and vainly sad, or viciously gay." Suddenly this is starting to sound more familiar.

Do buildings or artworks tell lies, like people? As a personality trait, flamboyance can often be read as untruthful, all one big act. While Ruskin was using the term *viciously gay* in its original meaning of joyous and lighthearted, to contemporary ears it is a neat shorthand for the way flamboyant behavior is perceived in gay (or gay-coded) men. Even *meanly fanciful* and *vainly sad* feel evocative of these ungenerous attitudes. Whether it fronts a church or a person, a flamboyant exterior can be taken as a sign of some inner malaise, an absence of something. Depending on who is looking, it becomes a spectacle without reality, an artifice without feeling, tipping over from holiness into vice.

The French novelist Marcel Proust, one of Ruskin's biggest admirers, also reflected on the question of corrupt appearances. Writing later, at the turn of the twentieth century, Proust was eager to defend his hero's ideas from the "dilettantes and aesthetes" of the modern age. Those foppish types who spent their lives in "voluptuous contemplation of works of art . . . recognizing no other god." If there was any such thing as a religion of beauty, Proust suggested, it was about more than just the experience and pursuit of pleasure. We must cherish beauty "as something real existing outside of us," and bring to it a sense of spiritual fullness that helps us look beyond "the joy it gives us." Proust's love of the beautiful was key to his lifelong investigation into memory, which took the form of his seven-volume novel *À la recherche du temps perdu* (*In Search of Lost Time*), published in France between 1913 and 1927. The most famous moment from the novel is when the adult narrator (also called Marcel) takes a bite of a madeleine, dipped into tea, and is transported back, forcefully and movingly, to the sights and sounds of his childhood.

A different moment in the novel is just as vivid in its evocation of memory, when the young Marcel walks past a hedge of hawthorn flowers near his childhood home in the French countryside. He notices how the hedge resembles a series of chapels, how the sun shines on it as if through a stained-glass window, and how the flowers themselves, with their "sparkling bunch of stamens," looked like "delicate, radiating ribs in the flamboyant style" of church architecture. He stands admiring the hawthorns for a while, but the longer he looks at and smells them the less he is able to understand their essential mystery. This sensual encounter with the natural world is clearly an awakening of some sort, at once creative (he ponders how to describe them) and erotic (he is drawn to the flower's blush and fleshiness), but it has a religious flavor too, laced with the ready familiarity of the church. What is captivating about these flowers is their liveliness, glowing and radiating, and the same can be said for the Flamboyant style, a monument to the untamed life force of nature, fire itself.

Returning to this passage in Proust, which I first read in lockdown with my friend Joe, when we decided to tackle the whole of *À la recherche* and chat about it over Skype each week, I thought about the flamboyance of nature, something many of us were rediscovering on daily walks during that time. Indeed, flowers are not the only things that glow in Proust. In a text that is packed full of biological language and intricate metaphors, where young girls are like flowers, and flowers are like churches, light is a recurring motif. When Marcel visits a seaside resort as a teenager and first encounters his beloved partner Albertine with a group of her female friends on the beach, he observes how she is bathed in the rays of light that emanate from the girls around her. This light, we will discover, is activated by lesbian desire.

On a later visit to the same resort, he observes a solitary gay man cruising at the train station, and notes how the seemingly indifferent or disdainful looks he exchanges with other men are, for those in the know, like the "brilliant luminescence with which certain insects adorn themselves to attract those of the same species." Proust is obsessed with nature's flamboyance, the glowing matter of the animal and plant world. (This man, cruising on the platform, is also described as a shimmering jellyfish.) That he attributes this luminosity most consistently to the novel's queer characters suggests that, within the hundred years after the word was first coined to describe church architecture, this metaphorical terrain had already become associated with the emerging category of the homosexual, which had not existed in the same way in the early nineteenth century. The idea that a person's behavior could resemble something bright and glowing gave a human face to the concept of flamboyance.

The luminescent man cruising at the train station is the Baron de Charlus, one of Proust's most memorable and complex characters. Charlus is an eccentric and sociable man, regularly seen out-and-about at the most fashionable salons and society events in Paris. He is a traditional example of a flamboyant person, as blazing in his excesses and heightened aesthetic sense as he is in his desirous gaze. But Charlus is also shown to be pompous and conceited, decadent in his tastes and lacking in ethics. Regularly embroiled in tempestuous relationships and drawn toward younger men, he is also made vulnerable by his insatiable sexual desires at a time when the concept of the "invert"—the homosexual as a psychological type, a failed man turned inside out—was prevalent. Although Charlus is a less-than-subtle cruiser, and quite regularly caught in the act, he is also compelled, as the saying goes, to hide his light under a bushel.

Proust depicted queerness as a unique, even beautiful form of spectacle and light, made visible in phosphorescent women and flaming men like Charlus. But it could also be something related to one's defects, or tragic flaws. In this sense, he was anticipating a pervasive trope about what it means to be flamboyant.

Maybe it was all of Proust's talk of glowing sexuality, but I decided I had to go to France, or at least to Paris, the City of Light. I knew I might encounter there the typical kinds of flamboyance one can see every day in a city: a glamorous woman in a sheepskin coat, walking the streets of Le Marais, licking her finger elegantly as she unfurls a poo bag for her perfect dog. Or a handsome fashion gay moving stridently toward his destination, his bright green mullet just the right side of unwashed, his heavy gold earrings clanking as we pass each other and lock eyes. But I went there mostly for the churches, of course.

Disembarking from the Eurostar from London at Gare du Nord, I was barely a few minutes into my walk down the Boulevard de Magenta when a church appeared before me improbably, at a busy intersection. Its large front window, shaped in stone by flamboyant curves known as ogees, is like a medieval centerpiece in the midst of everyday modernity, looking out across the crisscrossing streets. Ticking them off like an overzealous tourist as I walked toward Notre-Dame, these Gothic buildings stood out as monuments to the past, in contrast to the worn, and sometimes run-down, elegance of contemporary Paris.

Walking on from the scrum around Notre-Dame, which was still undergoing renovations at this time following the roof fire of 2019, I was heading to a church that I had read about online, but could easily have passed by on foot. Given its more modest exterior, I was unprepared for the beauty inside Saint-Séverin. The way that it could feel dark and enclosed, even intimate, in parts, and then flooded with light in others, its vaulted ceiling a vessel for brightness. Lunchtime mass was taking place in a room off to the side, the door opened widely enough for the congregation's song to travel. This was not only a monument but a working church, a flamboyant building with a clear purpose. I half listened to the mass, a test of my French, as I walked around admiring the modern stained-glass windows, which were commissioned in the 1960s, and which acted as another reminder of this church's living quality, its clear stake in the present.

Where stained-glass windows are often pictorial, these were more abstract, made up of jagged shapes in a range of bright colors, each connected to the seven sacraments, the central rites of the Catholic faith. A window dedicated to the Holy Orders (naming the process through which priests are ordained) displayed an unmistakably fiery mix of reds, oranges, and yellows. It was a nod both to the building's own flamboyant stonework and, by extension, to the flames at the heart of the faith and the Holy Orders, the fire sent down to future members of the Christian clergy.

Just as fire can appear to people in religious visions, these buildings were also illustrating how flamboyance could confer authority. I headed on to the Musée de Cluny, just around the corner from Saint-Séverin, for a closer look. Originally a Parisian town house for the monks of Cluny Abbey, a Benedictine monastery in the south, the house was rebuilt in the Gothic style in the fifteenth century under the abbot Jacques d'Amboise, who lived there. Today it has been repurposed as France's national museum of the Middle Ages, and houses an extensive collection of medieval art and artifacts. Certain original features from the Gothic house have been retained, including the chapel, a small square room with a captivating flamboyant ceiling, adorned with curving ogees of intricate stonework.

On the walls of the chapel sat twelve empty stone ledges, topped above with imitations of flamboyant church towers. It looked like these spaces should be filled. They were platforms for individuals, it seemed; the Twelve Apostles would be traditional. But they were actually made to host statues of the twelve members of d'Amboise's family, who held senior positions in either the Church or the civil society of fifteenth century Paris. They were so important that they were equated, in miniature, with the visual grandeur of the flamboyant church. People could be like buildings.

This thought stayed in my mind as I walked west toward the neighborhood of Saint-Germain-des-Prés, named after its medieval church, a building that has been successively rebuilt over the years. The original chapel, built in the Flamboyant style, was mostly destroyed during the French Revolution, but some of the surviving arches have been preserved in the park next to the church. Shorn of their usual context, there was something sad and ineffectual about them, a small surviving trace of a larger spectacle. I was in this part of town to see more than just the church. I paused on a bench in the park and got out a book from my bag, a battered Penguin Classics copy of *Giovanni's Room* by James Baldwin.

Located in the city's sixth arrondissement, Saint-Germain-des-Prés is one of the areas most readily associated with international artists and the Parisian counterculture, its illustrious jazz bars and cafes famously frequented by the existentialist thinkers of the 1950s. It is also the neighborhood where, in the same postwar period, many of the city's gay bars were located. A stone's throw from the area's Gothic remnants, these largely clandestine spaces were sites of a different kind of flamboyance.

It was into this subculture, *le milieu*, that Baldwin landed when he moved to Paris from New York in 1948. His novel *Giovanni's Room* offered a window onto the heat and the action of the scene. But seen through the eyes of David, the novel's American protagonist, it was a view tainted by the toxicity of shame and internalized homophobia. David, we learn, has spent much of his life suppressing his desires for other men, and his move to Paris seems to offer him an escape route from the need to socially conform back in America. But he is no more at peace, nor sanguine about his sexual preferences, in Paris and finds himself engaged to marry an American woman. This does not stop him from frequenting the gay bars on offer.

In one of these establishments, a subterranean, tunnel-like space which Baldwin most likely based on Le Fiacre, a real gay bar, he meets Giovanni, a handsome Italian bartender, with whom he embarks on a passionate and doomed love affair. Not even their meet-cute is a totally happy one. Giovanni pauses their flirting while he serves other customers. Into one of these gaps walks a flamboyant omen glittering in the dark, a supposedly malevolent figure referred to throughout as the "flaming princess," who spells only bad news for David.

The language that Baldwin, or rather David, uses to describe this person is so nasty and dehumanizing that it is slightly hard to place him. He belongs, maybe, in a similar category in David's mind to "*les folles*," who he observed earlier in the bar, and a vintage type in French culture, those loud and colorful gay men "always dressed in the most improbable combinations, screaming like parrots the details of their love affair." David compares them to monkeys eating their own shit, racked with disgust that is born of his own shame.

The "flaming princess" is clearly older than David and feminine-presenting. He wears makeup, floral perfume and a multicolored shirt that "made one feel that the mummy might, at any moment, disappear in flame." This moment in Baldwin's novel is an early example of the "flamer," which, in American slang, usually refers to an effeminate, gregarious, and obviously gay man. For David, who clings onto his own masculinity for dear life, and only desires masculine men, the flamer is an abject category, viewed through the lens of misogyny and internalized homophobia.

After observing David and Giovanni flirting across the bar, this flamboyant individual has a prophetic message. Clutching the silver crucifix that dangles around his neck, he tells David: "I fear that you shall burn in a very hot fire" and gestures to both his head and his heart. "Oh, such fire!" His words are prescient. David and Giovanni's relationship will end with separation, murder, and Giovanni's execution.

After David refuses to buy him a drink, tells him to fuck off, and compares his rejected facial expression to that of a faded, tragic actress, the flamboyant messenger in the bar moves "flaming, away through the crowd." But he leaves in his fiery wake a cautionary tale. David has evidently internalized, from childhood, the belief that homosexuality is a sin, that it will only lead to eternal condemnation, which is perhaps why the warning of the flaming princess touches a nerve. In an earlier conversation with the friend who takes him to the gay bar, he dwells on the loss of innocence experienced by all humans, and how people have "scarcely seen their garden [of Eden] before they see the flaming sword." In the Bible, the flaming sword is a symbol signifying the expulsion of humans from Paradise, after Adam and Eve's transgression, and a reminder as we reach adulthood that we are all sinners. For David, the flaming sword, signifying his own fallenness, is flamboyance itself.

Baldwin himself had a more complex relationship to faith. While he critiqued what he observed as the hypocrisies of organized religion, he never forgot about his powerful experiences as an adolescent preacher in Black Pentecostal churches in Harlem. With its focus on expressive modes of worship, including singing, clapping, dancing, and spontaneous praise, as well as speaking in tongues, the Pentecostal church has long been associated with a certain flamboyance. "I have never seen anything to equal the fire and excitement that sometimes, without warning, fill a church, causing it to 'rock,'" Baldwin wrote in a 1962 essay about his early experiences. It took "a long time for me to disengage myself from this excitement, and on the blindest, most visceral level, I never really have, and never really will." Even toward the end of his life, Baldwin continued to write about those years, an uncertain period during which "my sexuality was on hold," and the "salvation I was preaching to others was fuelled by the hope of my own." He was well-versed in the punitive scenes of fire and brimstone that supposedly awaited practicing homosexuals.

Le Fiacre, the historical scene of Baldwin's Paris, was a reminder of the dark side of flamboyance, its ruinous reputation, in certain circles. But walking past Baldwin's old gay bar, which is now a fancy home interiors store, was also a reminder of the way flamboyance lives in buildings—not only in the elaborate stonework of churches, but in the furtive and libidinal queer spaces that allow those inside to act flamboyantly. When those spaces disappear, a way of being—in that time, and in that place—fades away with them.

In the space of just over a century, the idea of flamboyance had traveled vast distances, from the religious authority of a well-designed church window, to the supposedly sinful and shameful shades of underground queer life. Today, artists and activists of many different stripes continue to play with this duality. In the world of pop music, in particular, performers have gotten ample mileage out of potentially blasphemous acts. Think Madonna, plumbing the aesthetics of the Catholic Church and the burning crosses of white supremacists in her "Like a Prayer" video, depicting a love story between a white woman and a Black saint. Think Prince, the archduke of eccentric, androgynous pop, who filmed the music video for his song "Controversy," which riffed on media speculation about his sexuality, in front of a large Gothic stained-glass window. Think Sinead O'Connor, tearing up a picture of the Pope during her performance on *Saturday Night Live*, a protest against the Catholic Church's history of child sexual abuse. Where it concerns religion, flamboyance and controversy have often gone hand in hand.

Walking on through Paris, reflecting on the strange geographical proximity between the sacred architectural ruins and the traces of the subterranean city inhabited by Baldwin's characters, I was also thinking about flamboyant culture today. In particular, I thought of the contemporary queer pop artists whose expressions of identity often return to this well-worn trope, and playfully subvert biblical images. There were so many examples now that I came to think of it. I was cycling through choruses sung by Sam Smith, Kim Petras, The xx's Oliver Sim, and Rina Sawayama, lyrics about unholiness, forbidden fruit, the devil wearing Prada, and having fun in hell with your queer community.

There was one artist in particular who came to mind. Born and raised in Georgia, with religious influences from his gospel singer father, Lil Nas X, whose birth name is Montero Lamar Hill, catapulted to fame at the age of nineteen, when his self-produced country rap song "Old Town Road" went viral on social media in early 2019. He came out as gay the same year, during the song's record-breaking nineteen-week run at number one on the US charts. In 2020, still riding the wave of his new visibility, he showed up to the Grammys dressed in a bright fuchsia Versace suit and harness, a look that mixed couture, country, and Barbie.

"I've been trying to deviate from the norm that most guys wear," he told journalist Owen Myers regarding this outfit, and "to get more in touch with that flamboyant side . . . It's an ongoing journey." That journey was unfolding in real time, as his growing fan base watched him continue to tease at boundaries. "In the mix of depressingly tasteful male celebrity dressers," Myers noted, "Lil Nas X is a flamingo among barn hens." In this sense, he was also channeling pop stars past. Pop music's flamboyance "flows through Lil Nas X," wrote the music critic Sasha Geffen, citing the rich history of queer or queer-coded male pop stars—from Little Richard, to David Bowie and Prince—who showed a "similar refusal to conform to social norms, to blend in, to fade."

A year or so later, with the launch of his debut album's lead single, the horny banger "Montero (Call Me by Your Name)," the flamboyance of Lil Nas X had taken on a particularly infernal quality. The song itself splices together a range of influences: Spanish guitar plucking, Middle Eastern musical scales, and lyrical references to gay love story *Call Me by Your Name*. It riffs on a relationship with someone that Nas was seeing during the months of his early fame. This beguiling love interest parties hard on cocaine but is still in the closet, and the song itself is a raunchy celebration of self-acceptance, explicit about gay sex acts, sung by a twentysomething who had come into his power as a public figure.

In the film made about his first-ever live tour, Lil Nas X

reflected on how this song changed everything. "I went from being the friendly, likable neighborhood cowboy in people's minds, to this controversial, 'satanic' gay guy. I was able to break out of that mold that people had built for me." The uproar around the song stemmed from the music video, which makes a provocative stylistic statement about the way that homosexuality is traditionally viewed within Christianity. The scene opens in a Technicolor heaven, with the chintzy feel of a video game, and a voice-over spoken by Nas observes how we hide parts of ourselves that we do not want the world to see. The video ends with a flagrant reclamation of sexual openness. Dressed only in underwear and leather thigh-high boots, Nas slides down a stripper pole into the bright red recesses of hell, rendered in fiery Gothic detail, and gives Satan himself an extended lap dance, before killing him and taking his horns for himself, which he dons like a crown.

The video became a cultural moment and outraged religious conservatives throughout America. To promote the release, Nas performed "Montero" on *Saturday Night Live* against a backdrop of infernal red, dressed in flaming leather pants. He also announced a collaboration with an arts brand, who had created a bespoke range of "Satan Shoes," Nikes redesigned with soles that supposedly contained real human blood. The Satanic panic was alive and well in right-wing responses to this move. The Republican politician Kristi Noem claimed that the video signaled a "fight for the soul of the nation." It was the second time that Lil Nas X had captured global attention in a short space of time.

Devil imagery was perhaps low-hanging fruit, and as a provocation it did little to convince the detractors who still saw Nas's work as a gimmick. But "Montero" was also a sophisticated example of flamboyant aesthetics. Musicologists noted how the Middle Eastern–inspired musical aspects, which can be heard in the song's instrumentation, are of the sort often used in the West to signal "otherness," and were even once known as the "devil's interval." Historians similarly pored over the video's dense network of references to ancient and biblical sources, including the story of Adam and Eve and "original sin," in the Garden of Eden, and the Greek creation story from Plato's *Symposium*, which describes man as divided into two parts, each desiring his other half. More religiously literate than a mere stunt, many queer fans who had grown up in the church also found in this song a courageous and unapologetic reworking of imagery that has long been used to control and repress.

Queer visibility, of the extraordinary kind attained by artists like Lil Nas X, can be both a gift and a trap. The controversies that have characterized his career since he found fame also show that the stakes are high. Lil Nas X has carried flamboyance forward into a culture of social media virality, and his story is one of someone coming into himself, his talent and his queerness, in a very public way, which can be a precarious position to occupy as a young star. His later impersonation of Jesus in the video for his 2024 single "J Christ" stoked similar levels of conservative ire, but also accusations that it was just another flamboyant stunt, an act of provocation for its own sake. That I was listening to this song on my headphones at a cafe table in Paris, just yards away from the religious buildings that had first given shape to this concept, revealed the different historical layerings of its meanings.

The religious origins of flamboyance, carved in the stone of grand buildings, have offered one way into its story. Other cultural traditions also inform how we receive its resistant magic. It is no coincidence that the influence of one of them can be heard at the start of "Montero," as the strumming of a guitar sets the scene for the song's tale of passion and transgression, punctuated throughout by rhythmic handclaps. The echo of that sound turns us southward, to the next port of call.

FLAMENCO

A FEW MONTHS after my visit to France, I continued My Year of Gothic Churches with a trip to the Spanish city of Seville. Soaking up the last of the October sun, a welcome reprieve from weeks of rain and gray skies in London, I was in Spain to attend the wedding of my oldest friend, Lauren. I could see, soon after arriving, why it was her favorite city, with its rich mesh of historical buildings and architectural styles, and I knew that I might also learn something more about flamboyance from this trip.

Technically speaking, Seville, alongside Paris, is one of Europe's most flamboyant cities. Its showstopping Gothic cathedral, one of the largest in the world, contains many elements of Late Flamboyant style. Sharp, ornate points rise up from the center of the old town like a flame in the city's skyline, complemented by the Islamic architecture of the nearby Royal Alcazar, an historic palace with gardens full of towering palm trees. Add to this a typical sunset in shades of burning red and lurid pink, and you have a postcard picture of flamboyance both natural and manmade. But the city has another claim to flamboyance. Located in the heart of Andalucía, Spain's southernmost region, Seville is also the epicenter of flamenco, that flaming combination of guitar (*toque*), song (*cante*) and dance (*baile*).

I had actually been taught to dance flamenco at school, when I was eleven, but my knowledge ended there. Those lessons were part of a youth program celebrating different styles of dance from around the world, and it culminated with a performance by the participating schools at the newly built theater in the local city. The chosen style for our school was flamenco. I think I have attempted to block it out of my memory, this stint as a dancer, a botched bid for stardom, but I do recall a few things about it. Firstly, that the dance teacher told us boys in the group we needed to project pride and power with our movements, which felt rather foreign to me, as a kid who mostly hated sports and was not used to thinking of my body as a source of prowess. Secondly, I remember that I was jealous of the girls, whose moves involved some sprightly hand work and clicking. They got to wear red flowing skirts while doing it, which made the contribution of the boys seem boring in comparison. On the night of the performance, I was placed in the back of the group, as quite a tall eleven-year-old, which meant that I was cut out of frame of the recording. I was devastated to discover this a few weeks later when the video arrived, my dance career dead on arrival. As a metaphor for my plight, for the stark gap between my fantasies of blazing stage presence and the reality, it was a little too poignant.

I thought back to this experience again as I arrived in Seville, the city of flamenco. That evening, I dropped my things in a hotel room in the center of town, and headed straight out to catch a late performance at a *tablao* nearby. The streets were quiet but for the sounds of visitors snapping pictures of the buildings in the golden light of the streetlamps and the hum of locals catching up over tapas at the outdoor tables. It had been raining, which made the aged cobbles glisten, and I was also a little damp and worn-out myself, after a day of traveling.

When I took my seat in the venue, I made liberal use of the red paper fan they handed out to audience members on the way in. Only recently had I begun to understand the emotional power of flamboyance, a form of performance that is anything but tentative, anything but repressed. I had been reading about flamenco in the months prior, and went to see a few different performances at London's annual Flamenco Festival at Sadler's Wells, but I still felt a little out of my depth. I was anxious to see something authentic, to get right to the flamboyant source of it all. But as I had already learned from researching flamenco's history, what constitutes the real thing is a vexed, and often political, question.

Flamenco originated among the Romani community of southern Spain, the *gitanos*, in a region that was itself a melting pot of different cultures and communities. This diversity of influences can be heard in flamenco's intricate musical stylings, which recall the scales associated with Arabic, Jewish, and North African music. The exact origin of the name is unclear—many attribute it to the word *Flemish*, to refer to the heritage of its originators (who migrated to the region from Flanders). The Flamenco Museum in Seville, on the other hand, suggests that the word came from the Arabic word *fellamenghu*, meaning "fled or expelled peasant." Either way, my assumption that *flamenco* and *flamboyant* might be linguistically linked, sharing a root in *flame* (or the Latin *flamma* and *flagrare*, which also gives us *flagrant*), was not quite right. But if they are not strictly linguistic siblings, as they first appear to be on paper, flamenco and flamboyance are deeply connected in other ways.

To be flagrant is to be ardent and unapologetic, unfazed by shame or the notoriety that might be attributed to your actions. It is to have something hot and fiery running through you—the opposite of cold-blooded. From there we get the phrase "in flagrante," to be caught in the act, which informs the English phrase "caught red-handed."

Think of a traditional flamenco dancer, holding her space on the stage. Both her proud gait and her appearance, dressed in a flaming scarlet dress, adorned with waving frills and ruffles, possess an unapologetic largesse, a commanding quality. Drag icon RuPaul thinks of precisely this image in describing his relationship to the macho gatekeeping of masculine gay men as he came of age in the 1980s. "To them," Paul writes in his memoir, "I would always be a flamenco dancer, interrupting the well-rehearsed choreography of their line dance." With just a look, flamenco can stand out, or stop you in your tracks.

Flamenco has a range of different forms; some songs are light, playful, and festive. Others go as deep as the singer can possibly go, conjuring scenes of grief, violence, and heartache. In its purest form flamenco also echoes the historic marginalization of the *gitanos.* Like the similarly flamboyant genre of the blues, flamenco is an outsider art that paints hardship in vivid color.

Flamenco has its own term for the particular emotional connection that can be forged between a flamenco performer and the audience: *duende.* To produce *duende* in an audience is a matter of the skill and precision of the performer, so in that sense it is a little like the gift we might otherwise call star quality, one that exists in the same terrain as flamboyance.

To be seeing flamenco in a theatrical setting is itself some distance from the spaces where it first emerged. Although its roots extend back to the sixteenth century, flamenco as we know it today was first codified in the nineteenth century, when it became enormously popular as a form of entertainment. The creation of specialized venues known as *cafés cantantes*, increased the urban middle-class public's access to flamenco, but also created other problems. For one, like many examples of flamboyant culture across history, flamenco was subject to attacks and attempted bans from several different camps. At one time, the Catholic Church, Spanish nationalists, and working-class anarchists were all against it, each for different reasons. They attributed a whole host of social issues to the rise of *cafés cantantes*, including alcoholism, illness and disease, the decline of marriage and traditional values, and the profit-driven commercialism of mass entertainment.

This resistance to the form's infectious popularity gave rise to a movement known as the *anti-flamenquistas*, who sought to stamp out and efface the traces of Spain's oriental roots, and those vivid echoes of non-Western cultures that can be heard so clearly in flamenco music. For those who loved flamenco, on the other hand, this perceived exoticism was its own issue. It meant the form was easily romanticized by its legion of admirers outside of Spain. Among them were the European writers who wrote about flamenco as exciting and alluring in its foreignness, and a miraculous relic of a bygone age, unblemished by the drearier and industrialized aspects of modern society. Flamenco purists, many of them *gitanos*, lamented the consequences of the form's popularity, because it gave way to new iterations that watered down flamenco's fiery roots and jeopardized its integrity. In turn, they pivoted toward *flamenco puro* ("pure flamenco"), and its claim to a raw, unvarnished authenticity.

These historical complexities were on my mind when the lights went down and the performers—three dancers, a singer, and a guitarist—walked out onto the stage. As I settled into the opening rhythm, my hang-ups seemed to dissipate. My access to flamenco was of course shaped by my own limitations, being neither a local nor an expert, nor a member of the flamenco community. I found it hard to describe the performance in words without simplifying its unique effects. All I could respond to was what was in front of me, to the way the dancers stomped on the ground of the stage as if to prove its strength. What I felt was a kind of rapture, a state of astonishment not only at the incredible skill of the performers, but the emotional force that powered each step, each pluck of the guitar, and the crack of the singer's voice as she sounded each plaintive, vertiginous note.

In 1922, a festival was held in the Andalucían city of Granada, to restore some respect to flamenco's name. This gathering was called the Concurso de Cante Jondo, the "Contest of the Deep Song." Amateur performers from rural parts of the country competed in performance for prize money, and the ethos of the event could be spotted in its title, *cante jondo*, the deepest, most somber form of flamenco's song-craft.

One of the organizers was a dashing young poet and playwright, hailing from Granada, who was once described by his friend Luis Buñuel as "his own masterpiece," a remarkable person with "passion, youth, and joy," who was himself "like a flame." Although best-known as a poet and the author of classic plays such as *Blood Wedding*, Federico García Lorca was also an expert in flamenco, and a lifelong champion of its folk origins and purest forms. (His first poetry collection, from 1928, was titled *Gypsy Ballads*.) He was an ideal ambassador for the Concurso, and he would go on to write and lecture about the mysteries of *duende*.

Duende, for Lorca, is something unmistakable, without imitation, more likely to come from sacrifice, even self-mutilation, than vain spectacle. He used the example of a beloved flamenco singer from Andalucía, who on stage could resemble a madwoman. He remembered how she was "torn like a medieval mourner" and "tossed off a big glass of burning liquor, and began to sing with a scorched throat," her voice "a jet of blood worthy of her pain and sincerity." The violent howl Lorca recalls coming out of this flamenco singer is flamboyance embodied, one of its fiercest examples.

Flamboyance, as we have seen, may often be ornate, but sometimes it is raw, an uncut gem. It can be the sound of vocal cords straining, rubbing flagrantly together as though they are sticks producing fire. Listen to any of the famous Spanish flamenco singers and some version of this quality is there. The legendary Camarón de la Isla, a *gitano* vocalist who hit the big-time in the 1960s and became an international star, has a voice so beautifully harsh and visceral (while also being expertly controlled) that he often sounds as if he is on the brink of exhausting it altogether. This is no less true of beloved blues and rock vocalists like Janis Joplin, where that same fire seems to come from friction. Like Lorca's flamenco singer, gulping the fiery spirit, Joplin famously used drinks and drugs to excess during the cultivation of her own blues howl, and Camarón also struggled with addiction, as did many other flamenco stars. Both singers died young. In neither case was substance abuse merely a performative affectation. It came from a real place of deep pain, of which the voice is both act and monument.

Lorca shows us that the *real* flamenco, to the extent that such a thing could ever be agreed upon, hews close to the losses and sorrows of living. His own flamboyant life was cut short when he was killed by far-right nationalist forces in 1936, at the age of thirty-eight, in the midst of a civil war launched by the authoritarian dictator Francisco Franco. Lorca's body has never been found, and the motives behind his murder remain ambiguous, although many believe that it was related to his status as a prominent and outspoken homosexual, with socialist views. When he came to power, Franco sought to sanitize flamenco of its dissident spirit, and instead make it part of his nationalist propaganda, adopting it as the National Dance of Spain.

Some of Spain's most time-honored traditions, like flamenco and bull-fighting, are readily associated with flamboyance. The same is true of many of the country's major artworks: the paintings of Pablo Picasso, the films of Pedro Almodóvar, the performances of Penélope Cruz. This image of a flamboyant cultural heritage can easily veer into cliché, and shares space with tired and reductive tropes about Hispanic "fieriness" (both within Spain and Latin America). Like all stereotypes, this one riffs only on the surface of the thing, ignorant of complexity.

Cruz, one of our century's greatest screen actors, is compelling not only for her intensity, but the delicate interplay of passion and humor, of light and shade. In Almodóvar's film *Volver,* where Cruz plays Raimunda, a working-class woman contending with grief, sexual abuse, and the seemingly supernatural return of her mother, those nuances are awash with the indelible reds of Almodóvar's flamboyant visual aesthetic, the director's trademark. There is Raimunda, holding a knife that has just been used to kill her abusive husband, covered in thick, jammy blood. Raimunda, laughing poignantly with her sister about the smell of her mother's farts. And Raimunda, singing an impromptu flamenco *cante* about the return of the past, her face arranged into a hard-won smile, equal parts pain and joy.

Today, flamenco is everywhere, a shared point of reference across cultures. Looks inspired by traditional flamenco dress appear regularly on fashion catwalks, particularly in collections from Spanish houses like Balenciaga and Loewe. Pastiches of its music can be heard across the pop landscape, in songs by Lil Nas X, Caroline Polachek, and Beyoncé, who included a flamenco number on her ambitious, Grammy-winning country record *Cowboy Carter,* which identifies historic connections between Black musical forms and folk genres. Most notably, the Catalan singer Rosalía, a musical visionary with formal flamenco training, regularly returns to the *cante* in her radical redrawing of pop's boundaries, and finds in it a mode of profound expression for the sacred themes of love and loss, faith and betrayal.

The history of flamenco is a little like the history of flamboyance, in miniature. A cultural force is discovered and rediscovered, attacked by parties afraid of its power, and eventually typecast or appropriated by the wider culture as its popularity spreads. Like the Flamboyant architectural style, flamenco became decadent and degenerate in the eyes of its most ardent followers, who felt it had run away with itself, and even been stolen by those who had no claim to it. But this is also an instructive story, an example of a flamboyant phenomenon that travels between cultures and across time; one that is passed down, reshaped in the image of different historical moments, and somehow survives intact. In turn, flamenco's story invites us to see flamboyance in all its multiplicity; a spectacle located on a richer emotional spectrum, drawing on rage and ecstasy, sadness and joy. A fire in the blood, awaiting its expression.

FLAMINGOS

IN SPANISH, THE word *flamenco* has a dual meaning. Distinct from its definition as a musical art form, *flamenco* is also the Spanish word for a particular species of water bird, known in English as the *flamingo.* Distinguished by its long, thin legs, curved neck, and blazing pink feathers, flamingos are mostly found in warm climates. Their name translates as "flaming" or "flame-colored" (from the Latin root *flamma*), and the widely accepted collective noun for this creature is "a flamboyance of flamingos." In ancient cultures, the flamingo was associated with the sun god, and often compared to the phoenix, that sacred bird associated with renewal, and the transformation from ashy rubble into flaming new life.

The flamingo carries less exalted meanings in the modern era. In America, the pink flamingo is a symbol bound up with class and taste. Once upon a time, this bird had aspirational associations with the subtropical climes and glamorous nightlife of Florida, home to Miami Beach's iconic Flamingo Hotel in the 1920s. In the 1940s, the bird inspired a song, the jazz standard "Flamingo," which was recorded by numerous pianists and musicians including Duke Ellington. One of the largest casino hotels on the Las Vegas strip, famed for its neon logo and bright pink aesthetic, was also named after the Miami Beach original.

The symbolism of the flamingo shifted in the 1950s, the age of manufactured goods and mass production, when this pink bird's fate was sealed in plastic. Emerging from the same cultural moment that produced the Barbie doll, the plastic flamingo became a must-have consumer item.

First designed and manufactured by Union Products, a plastics factory in Massachusetts, the polyethylene bird met a growing demand for lawn ornaments among working- and lower-middle-class households. The flamingo promised to beautify the natural space of the garden with a dash of color. Dyed with a pink hotter than the shade of any real bird, these plastic creatures also became synonymous with vulgarity and the culturally "low" preference for false and eye-catching shades. *Kitsch* would be one word to describe them; something popular but not in good taste, appearing to lack artistic value, at least according to refined or respectable standards.

I have never seen a real flamingo in the wild, but I can remember the first time I encountered a plastic replica. It was on my first trip to Fire Island, the illustrious vacation spot off the Long Island coast in New York. I was visiting Fire Island Pines, one of the island's queer communities. Walking along the boardwalks at night, past the sleek modernist homes that line the oceanfront, my friend and I paused to look at a large flamboyance of plastic flamingos, arranged in tight formation, planted in a sandy clearing next to one of the houses. There was something gloriously incongruous about seeing them here, juxtaposed against the glass and gray wood of the elegantly designed houses. Also something recognizably gay, as if the flamingos were a talisman, announcing the ethos of the local community.

In fact, flamingos are such a familiar motif in queer culture that it is easy to forget how and why this is the case. The key is in their relationship to kitsch, a penchant for the plasticky and the passé that has long been associated with gay men. But just as flamingos flock together, and are most commonly found in groups, kitsch itself does not operate alone. It is intimately connected with a different yet related concept, one that occupies a central place in queer history, and also retains a unique hold on what we think of as flamboyant.

Flamingos are big in the self-affirmation space. I learned this recently on a trip to a stationery shop, while looking for a friend's birthday card. "Be a Flamingo in a World Full of Pigeons," one card read, accompanied by an illustration of the pink bird against a gray backdrop. As a mass-produced object celebrating uniqueness, I was taken with the card for various reasons, not least my newfound obsession with flamingos. But I also imagined how strange it would feel to give it to someone. The message is meant to be touching, but it is also loaded with implication. You're unique, it says, you stand out, you brighten up a gray and verminous world. But also: You're different. Call me a killjoy, but if someone gave me this card, I can predict the thought that would, at least momentarily, flash into my head: This is a nicer, more affirming way of calling me a faggot.

Maybe this is a hangover of my own shame, or maybe because I remember the birthday cards that were exchanged with other boys as a child, at school, and their different hidden assumptions. They certainly never had flamingos on them, but usually cartoon images of men in suits wearing sunglasses, captioned by some variation on "Cool Dude." That was one of two c-words I knew about then, as far as masculinity was concerned, and it was the only one I ever wanted to be called. *Cool* meant hip, well-liked, popular with girls and boys alike. *Camp*, on the other hand, also reached my ears at this age, and was code for fey, eccentric, averse to football. I was fortunate not to be bullied, but I remember being intimidated by these unspoken standards, as if I was already being accused of something.

A friend's mum once told me I was camp, a word still beyond my understanding as a twelve-year-old. I asked her what it meant, and she responded not with words but a gesture, imitating a limp wrist, ostentatiously bent. I knew very well what that meant, and I was rumbled. She was onto me, and her little impression made it seem like this truth, which I perhaps already half knew about myself, was really a silly affectation, the stuff of stereotypes. It seemed to pile duplicity on top of duplicity. I was aware enough of my burgeoning feelings to want to hide them, and I remember this interaction suggesting that even the thing I was hiding was a bit overdone. Before I knew much about flamboyance, I had learned one of the definitions of camp. It would be a long time before I grasped what either of them mean, in the bigger picture.

"Many things in the world have not been named," wrote the American critic Susan Sontag in 1964, and "many things, even if they have been named, have never been described." This was the opening sentence of "Notes on 'Camp,'" an essay that almost instantly established Sontag's reputation as a leading cultural critic. It had the distinction of being one of the first pieces of writing to explore the central concept, a mode of taste, appreciation, and humor historically associated with gay men. Sontag never arrived at a single definition of camp, and offered up fifty-eight of them instead, in the form of aphoristic jottings, in which she described camp as "playful, anti-serious," "apolitical" and "a love of the exaggerated," and also distinguished between intentional and unintentional camp. Critics have pored over and contested Sontag's ideas ever since, and camp is no less debated today, in an era when it is embraced through major museum exhibitions and red carpet events.

Camp's "favourite colour is pink," writes the critic Mark Booth, "nursery pink, sugary pink, screaming pink." And pink, as the flamboyant, magenta-haired fashion designer Zandra Rhodes puts it, is "a complicated colour." "At some point it became deeply embedded with traditional notions of femininity," she notes, "but the shocking acid versions have a more punk, irreverent feel." Pink can signal girlish innocence and conventional glamour, but it can also tip over into something more extreme, associated with both trashiness and transgression. The flamingo's hue makes it camp not only because it is coded as feminine (and thus also gay), but because it is lurid and screaming and produces a sense of wonder in those who know how to experience it.

Camp is nothing if not versatile, and it was already changing in the era in which Sontag published "Notes on 'Camp.'" Many of her historical references in the essay—including Oscar Wilde, whom we will encounter again in the next chapter—were associated with the dandyism of the past, and a certain aristocratic hauteur. "The old-style dandy hated vulgarity," she wrote in one note, "while the new-style dandy" is drawn toward it. Where the dandy of old "held a perfumed handkerchief to his nostrils and was liable to swoon," the thoroughly modern connoisseur of camp "sniffs the stink and prides himself on his strong nerves." Camp was moving from the fragrant to the flagrant.

This subversive streak, which delights in poor taste, bodily pleasures, and breaking taboos, was reflected in the avant-garde queer art being produced at the time. In her review of Jack Smith's aptly titled 1963 film *Flaming Creatures*—which she defended from the obscenity charges filed against it—Sontag praised the film for the same qualities that would inform her theory of camp, published a couple of years later. In Smith's dreamy but confrontational montage of writhing, flamboyant, gender-queer bodies, Sontag saw a sense of joy and innocence. But it was joy and innocence spun from "themes which are—by ordinary standards—perverse, decadent, at the least highly theatrical and artificial." While Sontag thought camp was politically disengaged, she also lit upon its radical potential. It could be an alternative to the choke hold of respectability, an expectation of conformity that often dovetails with the homophobic, sexist, and racist attitudes of the time.

Sontag was "strongly drawn" to camp, and "almost as strongly offended by it." She did not specify exactly why, although she saw this as the prerequisite for writing about it. Did she hold a certain disdain for gay male culture, and for the offensive representations of women often associated with drag and camp performance? Was it transgressive camp's love of the "stink," its potential for abjection? Whatever the source of Sontag's offense, camp would continue to take on riskier forms, operating at the edges of taste and morality. A decade later, in the early 1970s, a young filmmaker entered the scene, influenced by the flaming creatures of Jack Smith's films, with a love for all things trashy and flamboyant. It was thanks to him that one of the most popular pink flamingos of the twentieth century was no bird at all, but a loud, raging, three-hundred-pound drag queen named Divine.

The pink flamingo was already a symbol of bad taste when John Waters made it the title of his breakout film in 1972. It refers to the lurid pink plastic flamingos that are planted in the grass outside the mobile home of its antiheroine protagonist Babs Johnson. Because "the movie was so outrageous," said Waters, "we wanted to have a normal title that wasn't exploitative. To this day, I'm convinced people think it's a movie about Florida." It was, in fact, a movie about Baltimore, where Waters was born and raised, in a conservative, middle-class suburb of the city. He began experimenting with filmmaking in his late teenage years, and conventional morality would be his target from the beginning. With its signature blend of perversity, obscenity, and transgression, *Pink Flamingos* put him on the map, and quickly became a cult classic. Waters and his regular cast of collaborators, known as the Dreamlanders, tore through Baltimore; a place, Waters noted, that felt like it was still trapped in the 1950s. The film smashes through a laundry list of taboos: rape, murder, incest, cannibalism, bestiality, and, in its infamous final scene, the real and unsimulated consumption of dog shit. It requires a pretty strong stomach to watch, which is precisely the point.

Anyone drawn to the film by its tropical title alone might be in for a shock. But even if they are confined to the film's opening shot, the flamingos of the film's title frame the story by evoking both an outsider lifestyle and a villainous flamboyance, exhibited by the film's antagonists, a couple with dyed hairdos, the man's a deep blue and the woman's a bright red beehive, which catches fire in one scene. Then there is Babs herself, played by the actor and drag queen known as Divine (birth name Glenn Milstead, who used he and him pronouns both in and out of drag). Divine's hairline was shaved back to create more surface area for his vampish makeup and thickly painted eyebrows, followed by a mane of back-combed orange hair. In one of the film's climactic scenes, Babs takes her gun and exacts revenge on the villainous couple after they burn down her trailer, and proclaims her reign as the queen of filth. Dressed in a figure-hugging red fish-tail dress, she looks every bit the flamingo of the scorched trailer park, flaming and fearless, an iconic vision of crime as beauty, of poor taste as high fashion.

The flamboyance of *Pink Flamingos* is also to be found in the endearingly chaotic energy of its actors. Though none of the performances can be categorized as good acting, what shines through is the sense of fun and freedom, scenes of friends in their early twenties playing around, with a shared (and fucked up) sense of humor, and a commitment to their rebellious artistic ideals. The writer Cookie Mueller, an early Dreamlander, noted how "in John's films you had to exude energy, and you had to shout." This was partly to do with the low-budget sound equipment, but also because this volume was "purely a matter of style."

Divine, in particular, became a huge star after the success of the film. He was surely the first person to ever become internationally famous for consuming dog feces in the name of art, although it was his anarchic, satirical take on drag, and his trademark brand of anger and wit that garnered many fans. Waters remembered his friend as a shy and introverted adolescent at school, mercilessly bullied for his size. The blazing character of Divine was like an act of cinematic revenge against bullies and bigots alike. Divine's weight—as a man performing the part of a glamorous fat woman, a punk take on the look of a stereotypical opera diva—was an important part of his flamboyance. It showed, as the queer theorist Michael Moon put it, that it is not "wearing a wig or skirt or heels that is the primary sign of male drag performance, but rather a way of inhabiting the body with defiant effeminacy." Although he was often shy offstage, in character Divine exaggerated what everyone hated, as Waters once put it, and transformed those qualities into a winning persona.

Waters, who has his own signature look—garish tailored suit, and his trademark, pencil-thin moustache—makes films about the social forces that stop people from being themselves. In his 1988 film *Hairspray*, which went on to become a hugely successful Broadway musical and movie, he pointed at the racism and conservatism of 1960s Baltimore. It was Divine's final film before his death from heart failure, just a few months after the film's release. He plays Edna Turnblad, a harried housewife who reprimands her daughter, Tracy, for being led astray, stylistically, by the latest trends, and "ratting" her hair to make it bigger. "Tracy's flamboyant flip is all the rage," says her school friend Penny, rushing to her defense. "Jackie Kennedy, our First Lady, even rats her hair." In the end, Edna embraces the colorful and dramatic aesthetics of the new era, which are largely inspired by hairstyles and outfits from Black culture, and joins the fight for racial integration on *The Corny Collins Show*, a musical revue broadcast on the local TV network. *Hairspray* is ultimately a film about embracing and celebrating the flamboyance of countercultural energy, a message it delivers far more palatably than *Pink Flamingos*.

To find *Pink Flamingos* repulsive is part of the point. I can only imagine how path-breaking a film like this felt coming out in 1972, a flare for those who felt like freaks or outsiders. And yet, for all its transgressive power, it is hard not to notice how the film punches down. "I don't remember ever seeing a pink flamingo where I grew up," Waters said in an interview around the time of the film's release, referring to the tasteful and refined lawns of Lutherville, his upper-middle-class suburb. "I saw them in East Baltimore," he explained, the poorer part of the city, clearly an inspiration for his film about a depraved and rebellious underclass.

In our own era, it has been argued that camp can offer a way out from the bind created by social media and the increasingly polarized nature of public discourse, which compels us to make instant distinctions between good and bad, acceptable and problematic. To embrace camp, Simon Doonan suggests, is to assume a "posture of amused detachment." It allows you to "simply *enjoy the show*," to take up the depoliticized stance that Sontag described, gleefully distant from real political concerns.

Of course, camp has never been free from politics completely. As the queer filmmaker and photographer Bruce LaBruce has noted, finding Sontag's interpretation "a bit dismissive," camp was invented out of necessity by "outsiders—fags, drag queens, transsexuals, deviants, sexual renegades," and so "it was always by its very nature deeply political and committed." Nonetheless, on camp's flattened plane, where regular political distinctions are broken down and discarded, we can also see the contemporary phenomenon that LaBruce calls "conservative camp." Right-wing figures today take to the stage to enact "a kind of reactionary burlesque on the American political stage . . . wholly without substance, their views exaggerated and extremely stylized."

In this sense, camp seems less like a political vanguard than a concept starting to show its age. Although it has rarely been more visible, there is a growing sense of exhaustion around what this once-subcultural concept might mean on a broader scale. In 2019, when the theme of the annual gala at New York's Metropolitan Museum of Art was "Notes on 'Camp,'" numerous think pieces sounded the death knell, arguing that the housing of camp in a leading museum, and its mobilization as a loose theme for a celebrity red-carpet, signaled the dwindling of its dissident power. Rather than bringing the wider culture closer to understanding the significance of camp's ironic mode of theatricality, many of the celebrity looks missed the point entirely. Queer invitees mostly met the maximalism of the brief. Like Billy Porter, who arrived on a chaise longue carried by a group of men, like an Egyptian goddess, dressed in chain mail and enormous gold wings. As did many classically camp elders, like Joan Collins, dressed in a white, feathery Valentino gown with a bejeweled tiara, but some of the looks merely resembled fancy dress.

When Sontag wrote that camp was something that had barely been named, and never truly described, it may have been hard to predict that it would find its way to the heart of popular culture and the fashion industry's most important party, over sixty years later. Even then, it seems we are no closer to agreeing upon a definition of what camp is, and what it could be. If anything, its mainstream acceptance has only muddied the waters.

Although camp and I had a rocky start, I have nothing against it. As someone with a predictably gay obsession with pop divas, and a certain kind of niche female TV star (referred to in British parlance as a "hun"), I am often drawn toward camp humor. But I also think it is high time, following Sontag's directive, that we named and described other ways of seeing, particularly those that embrace what camp misses. Like *flamboyant*, it is believed the adjective *camp* derives from French, in particular the verb *se camper*, meaning to stand firm, to strike a pose, an appropriately theatrical meaning. But what happens when we look beyond camp, planted stubbornly where it is, and toward the horizons opened up by other words?

The artist-scholar and DJ madison moore has proposed *fabulousness* as one alternative. In his 2018 book *Fabulous: The Rise of the Beautiful Eccentric*, which plays upon the word's association with exaggeration and invention, moore argues that fabulousness is "an aesthetic that requires high levels of creativity, imagination, and originality," a mode of personal style that is "confrontational, risky, and largely (but certainly not only) practiced by queer, trans and transfeminine people of color and other marginalized groups." Fabulousness also refers to "art created in states of duress, and this is its political edge," something that distinguishes it from camp's complacency.

Like fabulousness, I see flamboyance as something that puts politics back into the picture, that burns with a resistant energy, where camp flames in the name of humor and spectacle. (Even though camp, as LaBruce argues, cannot help but be a political act, particularly when it is practiced by queer people and social outsiders.) Flamboyance may look big and bold, similar on the surface to the theatricality of camp, which takes difficult feelings and often pushes them to such an extreme that they are often comic, except flamboyance expresses those feelings without mockery. Like camp, it is not always on the right side of history; there are plenty of nefarious flamboyant types, figures who would seem inimical to a politics of true liberation, as we will see. But there is a difference. Where camp might see the work of politics as rather humorless, opting to dance around it, flamboyance can run hot with rage, fueled by a passion that is not burlesque but real. Flamboyance can also be something quieter and more introspective, a fire that smolders on the inside, seeking novel expressions.

Many things that are camp are also flamboyant, and vice versa. Distinguishing between the two is not an exact science, and it would not be much fun if it were. In looking beyond camp, and carving out a new path through the terrain of flamboyance, there is an example I like to keep in mind: the American national anthem. Just as a garden ornament like the pink flamingo might be used to signal a certain homeliness, only to fall into trashiness, the utter seriousness of "The Star-Spangled Banner," as a triumphalist anthem about war and nationhood, contains a certain camp potential. The kind of reverence it asks of a singer is also well aligned with the "failed seriousness" that Sontag argues is central to naive, unintentional camp, its purest form.

No one meets this brief as effectively as Fergie, who performed the anthem at an NBA All-Star basketball game in Los Angeles in 2018. Her rendition of "The Star-Spangled Banner" is inexplicable from start to finish, a rollercoaster of idiosyncratic diction, extended notes that become wails, and jazz inflections that are intended, it seems, as a kind of vocal seduction. A video of the performance is available on YouTube, which shows the players and famous members of the audience struggling to suppress laughter.

Camper even than Fergie's vocals is her triumphant grin in the pause before the song's final line, the look of someone who—like America herself, home of the brave—thinks that she has absolutely nailed it. Perhaps campest of all was Fergie's justification, when the backlash to her performance prompted her to make an apology. "I'm a risk taker artistically," she explained, "but clearly this rendition didn't strike the intended tone." Fergie's performance is glorious, and I return to it whenever I am in need of cheering up. Something about the inadvertent deflation of the anthem's overblown scale, and the vision of an artistic "risk taker" performing this sacred national text as if it were in an amateur jazz bar, is deeply funny. The ultimate camp statement, as Sontag puts it: "it's good *because* it's awful."

Whitney Houston's performance of the anthem at the Super Bowl in 1991 is a different story. Just ten days into the Gulf War, which would go on to have lasting effects on global politics, Houston took to the stage at a time when the national mood was tense, and the outlook uncertain. Ever the professional, and arguably at the peak of her commercial success, the twenty-seven-year-old singer met the moment with a soaring rendition, backed by a full orchestra, her delivery reminiscent of the blues, but also the razor-sharp precision of a pure pop performance.

Although the audio heard on the night was pre-recorded—Houston sang live, but into a dead microphone, to avoid crowd noise interfering with the feed—the sound was all her own. She forever changed the shape of the song's final "free" by extending the note into two, raising it higher than may have otherwise seemed possible. In doing so she colored the song's climax with a sense of freedom's elusiveness, as if her voice were reaching toward it.

As the writer Danyel Smith has observed, in her essay on this performance, Houston's soulful version transformed the song from a celebratory statement into a more probing question about the nation. "It's always been a question. And she sings it like the answer. People were weeping in the stands, weeping in their homes." Still remembered today as a significant cultural moment, this take on the national anthem was playful, but without irony; big and bold, but also sensitive; sweet, but with an underlying seriousness.

The performance took place in Tampa Stadium in Florida, but there was not a pink flamingo in sight, nor any hint of camp. Even Houston's outfit, a white Le Coq Sportif tracksuit with a red stripe, seemed casual and unassuming. The political sensitivity of the moment hardly called for "diamonds and furs and heels," as Smith has noted, and instead Houston looked like she could be going "to choir rehearsal on any given Thursday night at her church in Newark," eschewing the flamboyant, brightly colored jumpsuits she wore in her music videos. More patriotic than punk, this moment on the national stage may not seem, on the surface, like an example of flamboyant spectacle, compared with more ornate or transgressive examples. But in the sheer power of her performance, and the undeniable fact of her voice against a vexed backdrop, Houston offered a potent meditation on the meaning of home, and a flamboyance that was more than surface deep.

FLOWERS

THE FLAMBOYANT TREE is native to Madagascar, and cultivated in many tropical and subtropical climates. Growing around twenty to thirty feet tall, the tree is the kind to stop you in your tracks, so named for the vibrant red flowers that bloom across its branches in the summer. It is one of the most extensively planted ornamental trees in the world, and a common sight along the streets and highways of Puerto Rico, and throughout India, South America, and the Caribbean, as well as parts of North America, in particular Florida and California. A flaming symbol of natural beauty, the tree has different titles wherever it grows—it is, for example, the official tree of Florida's island city Key West, and the national flower of Saint Kitts and Nevis—and also occupies a special place in Caribbean folklore.

Like many plants, the flamboyant tree goes by multiple names, including the regal title *royal poinciana*, and the botanical *Delonix regia*, but flamboyant is its most popular name. Within the history of its naming can be seen the colonial processes of extraction, labeling, and categorization, in which plants were "discovered" by colonizers in the countries they colonized, and then cultivated as exotic novelties in their gardens and residences back home. Brightly colored and many-leaved, these flamboyant discoveries were a source of colonial pride. For those who left those countries, forcibly or by choice, they were also a reminder of where they had come from.

The flamboyant tree was often on the mind of the novelist Jean Rhys. Born in Dominica in 1890 to a Dominican mother and Welsh father, Rhys was sent to England for schooling when she was sixteen, and she remained there for the rest of her years. The image of the flamboyant tree reminded her of her early life, and the vibrant colors and tropical climate of Dominica. It also threw into relief the gray cold of her adopted home. Throughout her fiction, which she began publishing in the 1920s, after a stint among the expat literary community in Paris, and right up until her death in 1979, Rhys's characters, many of them Caribbean women living in England, like herself, return to the tree as a symbol of homesickness and disorientation. The red flowers are remembered as of a dream.

"Flamboyant trees are lovely when they're flowering," says Anna, a young chorus girl living in England, in the 1934 novel *Voyage in the Dark*, casting her mind back. This seemingly innocuous comment is also a reflection on the way Anna's own flamboyance had been stifled by relocation, her life no longer in flower. There is a similar resonance in Rhys's best-known novel, *Wide Sargasso Sea*, which was published in 1966, and brought her the kind of widespread literary acclaim at the age of seventy-six that had eluded her for much of her career.

A postcolonial response to Charlotte Brontë's *Jane Eyre*, the novel reimagines the life of Bertha, the Creole heiress and "madwoman in the attic," married to Mr. Rochester, and focuses on her youth in Jamaica, where she went by her real name, Antoinette. Toward the end of the novel, suspended between dreams of her past and her present suffering, confined to the attic and thought mad by those around her, Antoinette recognizes something familiar in the shade of her red dress, the color of "fire and sunset" and "flamboyant flowers."

"If you are buried under a flamboyant tree," she says aloud to herself, shrugged off by her maid, "your soul is lifted up when it flowers. Everyone wants that." The vivid recall of the red dress, a spiritual symbol of life after death, spotted on the floor "as if the fire had spread across the room," calls Antoinette to action in the novel's denouement. She leaves her room, candle in hand, to set the house alight, and free herself from a life that has suppressed her own inner flame.

Rhys herself hoped for a less destructive version of this fantasy, or at least for her death to be a return to the flamboyant landscape of her homeland. Twenty years earlier, trapped in postwar London, she had written in a 1946 letter to a friend that she wished to escape from the "ugliness of life in England without money," although she was learning to cope without "mountains, seas, bright colors, everything I love." Nonetheless, she expressed a wish. "I still obstinately hope I will get away to die . . . Bury me under the ole flamboyant tree every time." (In reality, Rhys was buried in Devon, where she lived for the last twenty years of her life.) The flamboyant flowers of the *Delonix regia* thus represented to her not only the spiritual traditions of the Caribbean, where they are invested with important meanings, but also, more metaphorically, the irrepressible nature of the human spirit, which can be dulled and stifled by hostile climates, but never fully eradicated.

The word *flamboyant* was first recorded in relation to plants and flowers in the 1870s. This botanical definition, describing brightly colored leaves and petals, acted as a segue between its architectural usage and its usage as a word for describing people. If comparing individuals to Gothic buildings seemed a little abstract, the connections between people and plant life were more familiar.

"Just as flamboyancy in art has marked the passing of a civilization," the American botanist Oakes Ames wrote in 1922, "so in the animal and vegetable kingdoms an excessive development of iridescence . . . indicates types of organic development that precede decadence and extinction." Director of the botanical collection at Harvard, and a particular expert in orchids, Ames noted how these brightly colored and intricately patterned flowers occupy a "precarious position in the realm of living things." There is something familiar about this death knell, like Ruskin's description of the fatal decadence of the Flamboyant architectural style. Transplanted to the botanical world, this diagnosis draws upon the moral charge of decadence, the sense that when a culture—in this case, a plant species—goes too far, or burns too brightly, decline is all but inevitable.

Ames's analysis is also a reminder that flamboyance in flowers is related to reproduction—the decadent flaw of orchids, he points out, is a "lavish yield of seed coupled with sparse distribution"—and, by extension, being seen. In the world of flora and fauna, flamboyance is often a crucial factor in the process of reproduction. The bright colors of flowers are not just a happy accident; they appear because these plants, like humans, want to get noticed. Their flamboyant colors and shapes are intended to attract bumblebees for pollination, and it is through pollination that these plants reproduce.

Proust, once again, was alive to the queer resonances of floral flamboyance. In the work that deals most directly with homosexuality, aptly titled *Sodom and Gomorrah*, Proust's Marcel observes a flirtatious gay encounter between the infamous Baron de Charlus and the tailor Jupien, which he describes as a scene of seduction and pollination. Marcel looks on as a man places his "fist on his hip with a grotesque impertinence and made his behind stick out, striking poses with the coquettishness that the orchid might have had for the providential advent of the bumblebee."

By the time this volume of Proust's novel was published, in 1921, the relationship between flowers and gay men was well established, not least because the association between flowers and femininity marked out the deviation from traditional masculinity.

Flamboyant icon Oscar Wilde was known, as historian Dominic Janes observes, for his "strategic use of flowers," such as "lilies and sunflowers" and the infamous green carnations, artificially dyed, that he instructed his gay acolytes to wear to the opening night of a play in 1892. Wilde remained tight-lipped about the exact symbolism of the flowers, but the queer resonance was hardly ambiguous. Creating "a sensation on an opening night," Janes notes, "was a favourite tactic" for a figure who was "nothing if not an attention-seeker." The association was clear enough that a satirical novel about Wilde's gay exploits—which was later used as evidence in the famous "gross indecency" trial that brought about his downfall—was revealingly titled *The Green Carnation.*

If wearing a flower seemed suspect, then acting like one, which is to say, acting flamboyantly, was even more of a give-away. A prominent queer type in the 1920s and 1930s was the "pansy," a term used somewhat interchangeably with *fairies* and *flaming faggots*, the historian George Chauncey notes, to describe effeminate gay men who adopted a "flamboyant style." Drag queens, female impersonators, and gender nonconforming queer men were increasingly visible in America in this period, on the stages of speakeasies, in Broadway theaters, on-screen in Hollywood movies, and on the streets of major cities, an era that Chauncey termed the "Pansy Craze."

Of the words used to describe gay men that I remember from my early life, "pansy" was one of the most distinctive and regularly used, the floral adjunct to "poofter." "Was the pansy pinned to us," asked the British artist, author, filmmaker, gay activist, and gardener Derek Jarman in his journal in 1989, "its velvety nineteenth century showiness the texture of Oscar's flamboyant and floppy clothes?" It is certainly still with us, this Wildean inheritance.

But if it is in the nature of labels to be imposed, pinned like pansies or green carnations to mark our difference and affirm certain stereotypes, it is also within our power to subvert their meanings and imbue them with a resistant force. One of the unexpected implications of connecting flamboyant deviance with flowers is that it invokes the processes of the natural world, a neat retort to the homophobes and moralists who try to frame queerness as "unnatural." When it comes to disrupting the picture, and seeking out nature's flamboyance in all its surprising and rebellious varieties, Jarman himself lights the way.

I said I would take pictures of the flowers myself. I had seen them reproduced many times before, in art books and on postcards, but never in person. Traveling back to London with my friends Charlotte and Sam one May weekend, following a brief seaside holiday after lockdown first lifted, we decided to make a detour to Dungeness. It was on this ominously named shingle beach, located on the Kent coast in the south of England, that Derek Jarman made a home.

A popular pilgrimage destination, Dungeness is confronting in its emptiness and eerie quiet. As we drove down a long road passing small fishing shacks, we could see the huge concrete reactors of the town's old nuclear station in the distance. And then, at closer range, the distinctive yellow window frames of Prospect Cottage, and the brightly colored foliage surrounding it. From a distance, the image of the garden, a burst of color against an unlovely backdrop, is striking.

Jarman bought the house, named Prospect Cottage, in 1986, the same year he was diagnosed with HIV, at the age of forty-four. He had first discovered Dungeness when searching the area for shooting locations for his film *The Last of England*, a title that also aptly reflects the topography of the place, poised on the south-eastern tip of the coast. Jarman began building his garden there, using flint, driftwood, and metal he found washed up on the shore. With no soil in place, and a lacerating salt-wind coming off the sea, it was an improbable place for plant life to survive. But Jarman cultivated some of the hardiest plants, which could thrive in those conditions, and created a rich and varied garden that would become a frequent subject in his writing.

Life in Dungeness was a retreat for Jarman, at a time when "my whole being has changed," as he wrote in his journal in 1989, the journal that he then published in 1991 as *Modern Nature*. The pleasures of the past, the "wild nights on the vodka," were now nothing but "an aggravating memory, an itch before turning in" at nighttime. But no "lament" for the "nagging past—film, sex and London" could dislodge his new contentment in this landscape. In the space of a single journal entry, he would alternate between recollections of gay life before AIDS, some nostalgic and others critical, and present observations of the paradise he had created around him.

In one entry, from June 1989, he muses on the pleasures and changing fashions of the city's gay scene, how "the seventies were more flamboyant," an era in which he would walk down the King's Road in Chelsea dressed in a cape from one of his films, his hair dyed a bright orange after competing in Andrew Logan's Alternative Miss World, a beloved London drag pageant, wearing "bigger, brighter earrings" and carrying a fan. "Now that world has gone," he reflects, and he tries "to look vaguely serious—as Mum would have liked—for the TV by adding a shirt and putting on suit." And then: "Midsummer and my little garden in the desert blossoms."

It is easy to see gardening as a form of retreat from the world, a pastime that is often coded as cozy and wholesome in British culture. For Jarman, the creation of this garden was no mere hobby, but an act of defiance. Defiance against both his encroaching illness and the wider political agendas of Margaret Thatcher's government, which was so negligent toward the dying. In fact, much of Jarman's work was animated by the flames of political rage.

"Can there be too much fire?" he once asked. It recurs vividly throughout his films as a symbol of resistance, from the flaming torches held by monks in the music video he directed for "It's a Sin," the Pet Shop Boys' song about religious repression, to the memorable sequence at the end of *The Last of England*, in which a bride, played by Tilda Swinton, tears apart her wedding dress next to a raging bonfire on the Dungeness beach. We need fire, Jarman wrote, because it "destroys the old, creates a place for the new," a future that becomes visible through simple yet defiant actions of creation.

"Jarman is an outsider artist," writes Philip Hoare, "who, like Oscar Wilde, became beloved by the middle classes, precisely because they like to be shocked." The garden at Prospect Cottage is, Hoare notes, Jarman's "most widely appreciated" achievement, and perhaps the most responsible for his treasured status, favored over the more controversial and obscure aspects of his explicitly political work. It has been preserved ever since Jarman's death from AIDS-related complications in 1994, tended to by his partner Keith Collins until his own death in 2018, and other gardeners today as the cottage is opened up to visitors and resident artists as a heritage site.

For the pilgrims who make their way to Dungeness, Jarman's garden lives on as a space of private beauty and communal perseverance, a sign of life in the face of loss. Jonny Bruce, primary gardener at Prospect Cottage, has observed how the plants that grow there can also illuminate Jarman's legacy. In particular the wallflower, the "short-lived, spring-flowering perennial" with brightly colored petals, whose "ostentatious display is at odds with the other common meaning of wallflower, used to describe a shy person more likely to be found at the edge of the room than the heart of the party." This contradiction is apt when considering Jarman, who embodied "the introvert wallflower within the extrovert wallflower," who thrived in London but also found peace away from it, tending privately to his garden.

These flowers could also act as a symbol of resistance; just as the "exuberant wallflowers of Prospect Cottage seem to deny the harsh conditions of Dungeness," Bruce writes, "so the irreverent flamboyance of queer culture—despite constant attempts to co-opt it—continues to exist as an act of protest." It was also at Prospect Cottage, after all, that Jarman was canonized by the Sisters of Perpetual Indulgence, an international order of gay male nuns, who reclaimed religion in the name of radical activism, while providing support to those with HIV and AIDS. Dressed in a gold sequined robe, which glittered in the afternoon sun, he became a queer saint in his own front garden.

These various images of the artist ran through my mind as we parked the car near Prospect Cottage. Moving closer to the house, I could see the careful arrangement of different flower beds, patches of white and pink revealing themselves as spring moved into summer. There was a particular spot that caught my eye, a cluster of California poppies, planted in a bed comprised of rocks and pebbles. I looked down at their orange blooms, which rose as if to meet the sun, holding the wind in their cup-like shape. I was captivated by their hue, and the feeling of their singularity among the stones and beach debris.

I had never seen poppies like these, although they reminded me of the kinds of brilliant flowers that often adorn floral prints, like those of Zandra Rhodes, a contemporary of Jarman's in the London scene in the 1970s. (They both belonged to a group of zany fashionable artists who were concerned with looking "interesting rather than sexy," to quote the cultural critics of the time.) Her signature prints, brightly colored and instantly iconic, are largely inspired by her lifelong love of flowers, from those she would sketch as a child growing up in the Kent countryside, to this "fabulously sunny" brand of orange poppy, which she discovered during her time living in California.

Seeing them here at Dungeness, planted by Prospect Cottage's contemporary custodians, who preserve Jarman's horticultural legacy through the changing seasons, these flowers appeared to represent so much. Not all of them were orange. Some were deeper in shade, almost red, and there were pink ones, too. Imbued with a spiritual significance, they were the symbol of an artist's creativity, nurtured in tranquility. But also of protest, a queer refusal to accept the drab and hostile realities offered by a negligent society in a time of crisis. And of intense feeling, something blazing and beautiful, a reminder of passion in a barren landscape. Burnished with a fiery hue, and containing multitudes, there was really only one word I could think of to describe them.

LIGHTING UP

CREATIVITY & CHARISMA

"Flamboyance . . . is at least the beginning of art."

Harriet Monroe, 1922

CREATING

OSCAR WILDE WAS fond of the word *flamelike.* As a student at Magdalen College, Oxford in the 1870s, the young Wilde "adopted it as his favorite adjective," inspired by the essayist and critic Walter Pater, who was a tutor at the university. In his 1873 book on Renaissance art and poetry, published the year before Wilde began his studies, Pater had instructed readers to stay close to the heat. For him, "success in life" was an aesthetic matter, and meant "to burn always with this hard, gemlike flame, to maintain this ecstasy." By embracing the sensual aspects of art, its most vivid and teeming aspects, and seeking to preserve the pleasures of the present moment, instead of focusing on art's moral or ethical purpose, Pater proposed a flamboyant view of the world. This ran against the grain of conventional Victorian thinking, which prioritized decorum over pleasure, and Pater's flaming maxim was an inspiration to Wilde.

Wilde is the epitome of the flamboyant writer, someone whose distinctive dress sense and charismatic wit were connected to his creative sensibility. The reason he remains a figure of cultural fascination has as much to do with the impression he made upon the world as the work he produced. During his time at Oxford, when he was pondering the ideals of Aestheticism (the broader movement of which Pater's work was a key part), Wilde was also cultivating his trademark self-styling. He wore his hair long, and threw decadent soirées in his college rooms, which were lavishly decorated with peacock feathers and exotic flowers. Perhaps his penchant for the "flamelike" was also an indication as to how he liked to imagine himself, blazing high and commanding attention among his intellectual and artistic peers.

Wilde would eventually emerge as one of the world's most famous dandies, the stylish man of leisure, a social type who moves through the world with an unhurried ease and elegance and inspires both admiration and disdain. It was not until Wilde's historic gross indecency trials, which began in 1895, when his gay relationships were publicly interrogated, that his particular brand of flamboyance came to be associated with homosexuality. Before the trials, the flamboyant qualities of Wilde's presentation, queer scholar Alan Sinfield suggests, the "dandyism, effeminacy and aestheticism," were not read as signs "that we should have guessed all along." Surprisingly, he and his peers were able to pass not, as we might expect, by "playing down" this behavior, but by "manifesting it exuberantly."

The Wilde trials marked a turning point in the history of flamboyance. The whole idea that there is something effeminate about the artistic, compared with the perceived manliness of commerce or politics, can be traced back to social changes that were unfolding in the nineteenth century. The writer Brigid Brophy has observed that, after Wilde's trials, there was an emerging view that homosexuality was a problem because "it tended toward the soppily arty, the morbidly affected, and the frivolous"; and in turn the problem with art itself was that it became "tinged with homosexuality." That word, *arty*, when it is used to describe a personality trait, is loaded with gendered implications, with the arts coded as inherently feminine (and the sciences, by extension, masculine).

Social class and a suspicion of the arts, as well as the people associated with them, are common themes in conservative political thinking.

The arty are easy targets in this regard, maligned as inward-gazing and politically complacent, hooked on aesthetics and obscure philosophical questions, and thus disconnected from the realities of everyday life. This trope perpetuates the myth of art's insularity, something intended for the privileged few, not the social whole. Ordinary working people, on the one hand, versus the arty metropolitan elite, on the other. The problem with the concept of artiness is the suggestion that certain people possess this innate capacity for creativity, or creative receptiveness, where others do not, and that artiness can always be perceived externally, through one's dress or manner.

Oscar Wilde may be an important exemplar of what we talk about when we talk about flamboyance, but the story does not begin or end with him. Qualities associated with the Wildean aesthete—ostentatious outfits, airs and graces, a leisurely lifestyle and a quick wit—have long been associated with the quality of flamboyance, but perhaps at the expense of other ways of seeing. What if we thought of flamboyance as something harder to see than an eye-catching outfit, or a finely crafted persona? As that "hard, gemlike flame" that burns inside all of us, transforming reality into something brighter and bolder? Another writer from Wilde's era, who lived long enough to observe the advances of a changing world, as the nineteenth century gave way to the twentieth, gave thought to these questions.

As a young woman in America in the 1870s, living between a strict Catholic boarding school and the hectic environment of her family home in Chicago, Harriet Monroe had big dreams.

Intellectually curious and a gifted writer, she pictured a divine calling for herself from a young age, certain that her vocation was to be a famous artist, a revered poet and playwright. From her childhood and even into her early thirties, Monroe was eager to live an aesthetic existence, whatever the cost. She would prioritize art over life, and "be happy to give up all hope of ordinary human happiness for the shining bauble of 'immortal fame.'" In 1912 she launched *Poetry: A Magazine of Verse*, which is still one of the most prominent and respected poetry publications in the world. She also published several collections of her own poetry and traveled the world as a newspaper correspondent.

Monroe's wanderlust and sense of adventure was with her until the end of her life in 1936 when, at the age of seventy-five, she set off to climb Machu Picchu in Peru, and suffered a cerebral hemorrhage, likely triggered by the high altitudes. Although her death on the way to the mountaintop might seem like a cautionary tale about stretching too far beyond your limits, it would go against Monroe's ethos as an artist to think in these terms. She was no particular advocate for mountain climbing in and of itself. It was more about what the mountaintop represented: the limitlessness of the imagination, and the capacity to conceive of extraordinary things.

Physical feats and travel might be one expression of this impulse, but the extraordinary could also be nurtured at home, within the pages of a book. As a dreamy but solitary adolescent, Monroe spent much of her time in the library, seeking companionship with the "lively and interesting people" who populated the canon of classic literature, figures she described as "friends of the spirit to ease my loneliness." This coming together of life and art can be found in plenty of origin stories about artists and writers during their early years—often described as "sensitive" and "bookish"—and it probably sounds familiar to many of us who felt like we did not fit in, or enjoyed imaginary company at least as much as being around others. What brings me to Monroe's story is the particular word she used to describe this model of imagination. For her, the impulse to look beyond the everyday was the essence of flamboyance.

America in the roaring twenties was a flamboyant place, a cornucopia of blazing spectacles and entertainments. What could be more flamboyant than the circus, Monroe pondered in a 1922 essay for *Poetry* magazine, where you could go to see the "trapeze-performer hurtling through the air," "the tiger leaping through manmade hoops" and the "painted clown, timeless type of the race, laughing that he may not weep." There was also the world of jazz music and the Follies of Broadway, the iconic flapper in an "an orange and green gown and war-paint of rouge." In the cities, there were lit-up skyscrapers; in the air, planes "skimming the clouds." It was an era of excess and technological modernity, with "extravagant, impossible frenzies of color in a world that refuses to be drab."

But America in the roaring twenties was also a place of contradictions. It seemed surprising that such frenzies of color were so vividly splashed across a society that embraced, by and large, the "exemplary three-meals-a-day-and-bed-time life." It was a nation, Monroe pointed out, known for "sitting respectably at home with its newspaper; suppressing its feelings and censoring its artists; fearing emotion as the gateway to perdition." She thought this might be a cause-and-effect scenario, these wild spectacles the product of an otherwise repressive society. The more conventionally we live, the more we seek out the extravagant.

People who are not living impassioned lives, Monroe believed, might otherwise seek thrills in darker or more destructive ways. How can we satisfy this need for flamboyance in our lives, without destroying ourselves in the process? Monroe had nothing against America's flamboyant entertainments in theory, the circuses and skyscrapers and the gaudy Hollywood movies. But in their novelty they seemed to her a distraction from a deeper need. "The imagination will not down," she wrote, "it must adorn and exaggerate life, must give it splendor and grotesqueness, beauty and infinite depth." Flamboyance might look like leaping tigers and wild flappers, but it is also an expression of faith in our own imagination, in its capacity to enlarge and enhance. Flamboyance, Monroe argues, "is at least the beginning of art."

I discovered this essay by Monroe with a certain delight. She was voicing something that I had long felt about flamboyance and its relationship to fantasy and imagination, and which still held true a hundred years later, in a vastly different cultural landscape. The 2020s started with anything but a roar, but they too began with a plague, just as the 1920s were preceded by a deadly global flu pandemic. Dwelling indoors under lockdown to curb the spread of the coronavirus, the more flamboyant shades of life, those loud collective experiences like dancing and live music, seemed a thing of the past. The quiet compelled us to imagine these things, to recall them, during that time, in the past tense. Although it grew from a place of absence and fear, the way that imagination filled in the gaps was a strangely powerful coping mechanism.

It reminded me of why I became interested in flamboyance in the first place. As a student, my instincts led me toward poetry as a space, laid out on the page, where a self could become other, could try out different guises or characters. The poet Frank O'Hara was my guiding light, someone I have returned to frequently in my writing. Heart-sore and coming into myself, the tome of his *Collected Poems* held so many riches, like a gallery of possibilities. Why, I wondered, did his poems of transformation so often draw upon the language of flames, as if fire itself were a kind of imaginative force? Across the hundreds of poems he produced in his lifetime, we see him "blazing a tirade," "set afire" by love for his friends, comparing his heart to a furnace, and inspiration to the glow of a lamp.

I was beguiled by the outward glamour of his cosmopolitan life in 1960s New York, the galleries and bars and parties, but also by the flaming theatricality that seemed to animate his writing. He showed me that flamboyance is something you could experience or aspire to alone, in quiet solitude. Late at night, reading, hoping to glow. Reading Monroe's essay cast another light over these texts, with the suggestion that flamboyance is shaped as much by fantasy as reality. Something we could turn to in private, or in moments of crisis—like "meditations in an emergency," as O'Hara once put it—to help envision other ways of being.

If flamboyance is the "beginning of art," and the artwork is the finished product, what happens in the middle? The creative process is often a mystery even to artists themselves, characterized by irregular rhythms, long pauses and bursts of intensity. Art can emerge out of extreme states, like pain or pleasure or ecstasy, as easy to glamorize as they are potentially destructive. But it also emerges from less flamboyant conditions, unglamorous states of frustration, doubt, procrastination, fear, and exhaustion. Creative work can arise in spite of these things, and sometimes even because of them.

In *A Bigger Splash*, Jack Hazan's staged documentary about painter David Hockney and his circle in London in the early 1970s, we see this process play out. Named after Hockney's most famous pool-side painting, the film depicts him creating a new work. In one scene halfway through the film, Hockney's gallerist John Kasmin, who is keen to stage an exhibition before long, grills the artist about his productivity. "You spent six months working before you achieve what you set out to do," Kasmin notes, and "often it seems to upset you. I mean you haven't actually enjoyed the six months working on the picture." Hockney responds by noting that he completed his latest painting in two weeks, working long and intense days to redo it, and that both of these stages of the process were equally important in the creation of the finished work. "I couldn't have done it in that time unless I'd wasted all that time," he says, "what I mean is the picture that took two weeks really took six months and two weeks."

Hazan shows us what Hockney got up to during the six months of gestation. It was a period of depression for the artist, following a breakup from his lover Peter Schlesinger, and we see him lying around smoking cigarettes with friends, plotting escapes to New York, California, and the South of France. He visits a friend's new exhibition of paintings, and parties with the "fashion freaks." In one scene, he attends the inaugural Alternative Miss World pageant, which was started by artist and designer Andrew Logan in his Hackney studio in 1972. Dressed in a bright red over-shirt, with his mop of platinum blond hair and thick-rimmed glasses, Hockney's flamboyant look appears relatively tame in comparison to the line-up of contestants we see walking in the pageant (which includes Derek Jarman in drag), dolled up in feathers and satin.

Hockney's six months of "wasted" time has its fair share of flamboyant activity. But while it looks glamorous, in a 1970s sort of way, the film's depiction of this period also offers a corrective to the idea that art and life correlate neatly; that the vivid colors of Hockney's signature paintings were necessarily produced in colorful or eventful circumstances. What we see instead is an artist working on a painting, inspired by the glistening waters of California, in a London that often appears gray and cold, and a place in which he spends much of his time just hanging out, and waiting for a moment to strike.

Few artists today can live and work in this way, nor live flamboyantly in the way we might imagine artists to, at their most mythic. Without economic security or the assurances of fame and success, it is increasingly rare to create work in a spirit of leisure, free from the pressures and stresses of the everyday. A more recent film, fictional but attuned to these realities, offers a different portrait of artistic life.

Picture a ceramist, early forties. She is single and lives in an arty American city like Portland, Oregon. Her one-bed apartment has a studio space downstairs, where she works on her ceramic figures. Right now, she is up against a deadline for her solo show, which is opening soon in a gallery downtown. The apartment is in a duplex building, and she rents it cheaply from her neighbor and friend, who is also an artist. Although the friend is supportive, their relationship is strained by their both working in the same field, with different levels of recognition and status, and her friend is not the most diligent landlord.

By day, our ceramist travels to the community arts center for her job as an administrator, a role adjacent to the network of respected tutors and visiting artists in residence. Outside of work, she checks in on her brother, who struggles with his mental health, and catches up with her divorced parents, who each have their own problems. Some days she forgets to buy food for her cat and has to rush out to the store before she does anything else. On another day she is forced, or compelled, to take in a pigeon mauled by her cat in the backyard, and to nurse the bird in a cardboard box while its broken wing mends. Her daily life is a series of tasks, chores, and acts of care. Her show is next week, and all she wants to do is work on her "girls," to thumb and shape and kiln and glaze her series of female figures arrested in acts of motion. If only she could find the time.

This is the story of *Showing Up*, directed by American

filmmaker Kelly Reichardt. The artist is called Lizzy (played by the always-brilliant Michelle Williams), and we watch her as the mounting frustrations of her situation, the tense personal dynamics with friends and family, the inadvertent forms of labor she finds herself roped into, seem to approach breaking point. But in the end, they do not break, and life merely continues. One of her most beloved pieces is positioned too close to the fire in the kiln and gets damaged, but the show still opens, and her friends and family show up, just as she spends many hours of her days showing up for them, in all the ways they need, and at times demand. Lizzy's feelings of envy, and her insecurities about where she is in her career as an artist, do not just disappear. But they are eased by the process of working, which is the thing, after all, that really matters. As an audience observing a week in the life of this character, we see that she is never happier than when she is creating.

Reichardt's wonderful film captures the artistic life in a way that is rarely seen on-screen. This is no glamorous hagiography of a legend, nor is it an aggrandizing account of a tortured artist creating work from a dark place. Instead, it shows us the everyday rhythms of a way of living, one in which creativity must coexist alongside other responsibilities. Even when there are many things that might seem to divert us, there is always a way. Elizabeth Gilbert calls it "big magic," a force that comes from within but is also bigger than us.

This is not to say that it always feels good, or especially magical. Creating is different from being "a creative," in the way that word has been deployed as a noun, just as making art often looks and feels different than the public expectations that surround being an artist. Increasingly, in an age where social media is often crucial for building an audience, artists must often focus on self-promotion. The scene I admire the most in *Showing Up* is a moment of quiet refusal that takes place at Lizzy's show, when the center's successful visiting artist arrives at the gallery with her glamorous friend in tow, a gallery director from New York, and approaches Lizzy to toast the show and celebrate the work. Lizzy's response is not unfriendly, but muted. Rather than seizing the opportunity to charm the gallery director, who could surely open doors for her, with stories about the pieces she is most proud of, Lizzy is a wired coil of negative energy. She complains deprecatingly about the piece that got burned in the kiln. It reads as a defense mechanism that is also a kind of self-sabotage, and although there is nothing particularly admirable about that, it is refreshing to see someone who seems unwilling, or perhaps unable, to play the game.

Where other artists in the film possess a loose and easy relationship with their own body, draped in functional but fashionable clothes, Lizzy always appears tense and hunched, dressed in floral blouses that read as old-fashioned, with pastel skirts and pop socks. She reads as the opposite of the flamboyant artist figure, but she is no less an artist, no less an admired member of the city's artistic community, even if her career may not benefit from her social skills. Lizzy's flamboyance is found elsewhere, not in her personality or her clothes, but in the works themselves.

The figures we see her making for the show (which were actually made by the Portland artist Cynthia Lahti) depict women dancing and moving, standing out and taking up space, painted with bright pinks and reds, shades more vivid than the muted tones of Lizzy's everyday life. It is as if the pieces enact a kind of wish fulfillment, a way for Lizzy to cast herself into bolder and brighter forms, expressing the flamboyant freedom she is unable to embody in her own being. If that seems a little too simplistic as an explanation for her creative practice, it is nonetheless a sentiment I recognize in myself. Words, rather than clay or paint, are my medium, but I find in them a material for remaking, for asserting that I have something to say.

Making art of any kind helps to conjure a different world, to look beyond the mundane, the cruel, the gray, the disappointing, and also the bounds of our own limitations. This is also true of consuming artworks. An inner flame burns in all of us, whether or not we move through the world striking flamboyant poses, which is, after all, just one way of expressing it. By inviting art and imagination into the space of daily life, we illuminate our interiors, and meet ourselves anew.

DECORATING

AT THE BEGINNING of the twentieth century, the author and philosopher G. K. Chesterton looked ahead, with equal parts hope and skepticism, to a future in which "human life has once more assumed flamboyant colours." Only then would it be clear that the world was turning away from "the painful greenish grey" of the industrialized Victorian age, and toward "beauty—not backwards, but forwards." If this more flamboyant world came to pass, Chesterton remarked, it would be a testament to the philosophy of its "first prophet," a "great reformer" whose gift to the world was that "he left his work incomplete," a mantle to be taken up by subsequent generations.

Incomplete is not a word that springs to mind when we think of the work of prolific artist, poet, author, textile designer, entrepreneur, and activist William Morris. Alongside Oscar Wilde, whose thinking he influenced, and John Ruskin, whose thinking he was influenced by, Morris is one of the most celebrated creative figures of the nineteenth century, and one of its most vocal advocates for visual flamboyance. While he was best-known for his fiction in his own lifetime, Morris is most recognizable today for his wallpaper, the elegant floral designs which have adorned the walls of middle-class homes ever since he began selling them in the 1860s, through his company Morris & Company. They remain ubiquitous, printed across all manner of scarves, notebooks, cushions, and other goods we would expect to find for sale in a museum gift shop.

But Morris is also remembered as a forward-thinking socialist, who believed that the fruits of aesthetic labor and artistic invention should be available to all, even if this belief was somewhat incompatible with business. Dedicated to handmade craftsmanship and artisanal ideals over industrialized labor and machine-made goods, a founding ethos of the Arts and Crafts movement with which he was associated, Morris came to realize that it was almost impossible to implement those ideals at scale, and thus make his products affordable to the working classes. It was this realization, in part, that led him to socialism. If the industrialized system could not work to offer aesthetic goods for all, regardless of class, then it was the social order itself that needed overhauling.

Born in East London to a middle-class family in 1834, and educated at Oxford, Morris turned away from his planned career in the church in favor of the artistic life. Influenced by the ideas of Ruskin and the medievalism of the Gothic Revival, which gave us the word *flamboyant*, Morris admired the Flamboyant architecture of France and carried the idea of flamboyance forward as something to be enjoyed by everyone.

Morris's dream, both utopian and highly practical, was that "some pleasure for the eyes and rest for the mind" would be found in all homes. What he saw in medieval art, as well as the Middle Eastern and Indian artistic traditions he was also influenced by, and replicated in his own timeless designs, was a love for the flamboyance of the natural world. Not flamingos, in this instance, but the luxurious hues of the peacock, and the dynamic, colorful life force of plants and flowers. Look closely at any of the wallpapers, tapestries, and textiles for which Morris is famous and you may also notice something Gothic about the ways the foliage seem to move and dance, undulating and alive, like the "delicate, radiating ribs" of the hawthorns that Proust once saw, and compared to flamboyant architecture. His designs brought the natural world into the domestic interior.

Like any artistic trend, floral wallpaper comes in and out of fashion. Morris's designs have been subject to the same whims, considered aspirational in some eras, like the 1970s, when they could be seen on the walls of many a suburban living room in England, and passé in others. In his own time, however, they were highly innovative. Wallpaper itself had become a popular commodity item by the middle of the nineteenth century, an accessible interior decoration and status symbol, but designs tended to be understated, less ornate and arresting than Morris's motifs of birds and plant life, which are both tasteful and deeply strange. They proved to be highly popular, but they were not to everyone's taste. (Oscar Wilde, who drew heavily on Morris's ideas in his own lectures on the decorative arts, once confessed in a letter to a friend that he did not believe in the "decorative value" of his elder's wallpaper designs.)

For Morris, the act of bringing brightness into the urban landscape was more than just an aesthetic matter. It was related to people's quality of life and acted as a marker of social change. Around the same time, nurse and social reformer Florence Nightingale was also observing the importance of colorful and "beautiful objects" in caring for the sick. Nightingale's perspective was drawn from her own clinical experience, where she witnessed the "rapture of fever patients over a bunch of bright-coloured flowers." While relatively little was known in Nightingale's time "about the way in which we are affected by form, by colour, and light," her observation that "they have an actual physical effect" has been borne out in contemporary research, the "brilliancy of colour" its own "means of recovery."

Decoration offers not only pleasure but respite. Morris and his peers looked back in time toward a romantic and idealized vision of the medieval period, as a time of simple pleasures and artistic virtue, and repurposed a flamboyant new aesthetic inspired by that vision. But I also sense in that backward glance something psychological, a heartfelt turn to innocence lost, and a more playful, liberated vision of the world contained in our own pasts. The particular comforts of bright and flamboyant designs speak to something deep within us, the unencumbered tastes of the inner child.

Flamboyance, after all, enters our experience at an early stage. Babies, born color-blind, develop a perception for different hues and contrasts in the first months of life. Bright colors are considered essential, developmentally speaking. Even as we grow into young children, vivid and highly saturated colors strengthen our associations, allowing us to broaden our visual perception. That we love life's more flamboyant shades in our earliest years is evident in our young enthusiasms for vibrant animations and loud personalities.

"The child sees everything in a state of newness," the French poet Charles Baudelaire wrote in 1863, a state of excited imbibing that is much like being drunk, intoxicated on the stuff of life, "a deep and joyful curiosity" in the face of "something new, whatever it be, whether a face or a landscape, gilding, colours, shimmering stuffs." Creativity, for Baudelaire, is about reconnecting with this part of ourselves. His definition of adult genius is "*childhood recovered* at will."

There are many ways we can recapture those early instincts for flamboyance, to refuse the "adult" directives pointing us toward the sensible or muted. One of them is how we choose to decorate our spaces. Morris's vision of flamboyance for all offers a model both flexible and unexpected. Flamboyance as thrift and resourcefulness. A respite from the travails of the workday. In this sense, Morris's ideas speak back to those of his contemporaries, like Walter Pater and John Ruskin, who felt flamboyance was best experienced through grand cathedrals and remote natural landscapes, and also forward to Harriet Monroe's idea of flamboyance as imagination, an inner creative drive that we all have the capacity to cultivate.

Looking back to the nineteenth century can help illuminate an equitable vision of art and accessibility, shot through with the dreams of a socialist future that never came to pass. But it was this same historical moment that shaped how we understand sexual identity, and in turn fostered a suspicion of artistic types. Today, interior design has become coded in highly particular ways, as a feminine pursuit, and the figure of the interior designer a flamboyant archetype, as if an interest in color and florals conveys inherent meanings about gender and sexuality. Flamboyance, as ever, does not remain innocent from the social meanings with which it has, over time, been enmeshed.

If William Morris—a progenitor of interior design as we know it—were alive today, he might well have his own home makeover show. Then again, he differs from the contemporary profile of a male interior designer, at least of the kind we see on television. Although charismatic, a distinguished and passionate orator in his own era, Morris cut a gruff and unconventional figure in person: bearded, disheveled and dressed, like his workers, in dye-spattered smocks. He was once described by the novelist Henry James as "burly, corpulent, very careless and unfinished in his dress." Morris was more like a candidate for a makeover, on a show like *Queer Eye*—scruffy, masculine, in need of some grooming—than a member of the Fab Five himself. If it seems at all surprising that a man so enamored of flowers and delicateness could be quite so butch, that is only because of the gendered stereotypes that have become attached to certain aesthetic pursuits.

As the historian Stephen Vider observes, in his book *The Queerness of Home*, the popular stereotype of the "effeminate gay decorator" grew out of a shift in decoration as a profession, which was initially dominated by male manufacturers in the 1870s, but later became associated with prominent female decorators like the New York socialite and actress Elsie de Wolfe (who was also queer), and thus redefined in the early twentieth century as a feminine pursuit. Having men do what is perceived as a woman's job is low-hanging fruit, comedically speaking, and this stereotype has often been "played for laughs," Vider notes, across a range of media representations over time. It perpetuates the idea that "male homosexuality" is connected to "an excessive investment in surface, style, and consumption."

It is this same stereotype that *Queer Eye for the Straight Guy* (its full title in the 2003 original), and its more enlightened 2018 reboot, are responding to. The premise: five gay men burst into the homes of normal folk to perform a glow up in five anointed areas—fashion, grooming, interior design, food, and lifestyle—and transform their lives in the process. At its best, *Queer Eye* is more interested in truths than clichés, taking as given that our decorative choices—or the lack thereof—are a reflection of our lived experiences and inner worlds. There are often complex reasons why the people featured on the show seem unable to access flamboyance as a mode of self-care, from trauma, grief, and low self-esteem to the restrictive aspects of the gender binary, which decrees that real men do not care for the decorative. The conclusions drawn at the end of each episode can verge on simplistic, the idea that all one needs to self-optimize is a fresh lick of paint, one of the dreams at the heart of capitalism. But *Queer Eye* also makes for touching television.

Flamboyance is often accepted, even celebrated, when it

has a use in this way. Many affirming narratives about queer characters offer a variation on the story told by *Queer Eye*, where a flamboyant individual (or group) helps to enrich the lives of straitlaced, stodgy, or conservative types. The movie and musical *La Cage aux Folles*, with its farcical plot about a gay couple meeting their son's conservative in-laws, and its signature queer anthem "I Am What I Am," is one example. By transforming the humdrum, making it brighter and glitzier, the flamboyant person also transforms others, allowing them to leave behind their prejudices and insecurities, and live more authentically. In this sense, flamboyance is like a magic act, a bridge across social and political divides.

What is left unexamined is the notion of the "queer eye," the idea that gay men possess a uniquely flamboyant creativity to be conferred at will. Is there really a "gay creativity gene that we all inherited?" asks the psychologist Alan Downs in his book *The Velvet Rage*. "When you think about it, is it actually plausible that our sexual orientation genetics would somehow also give us a talent for hair, makeup, and rearranging the living room?" It is a reasonable question, but one without a clear or simple answer. Downs argues that many gay men carry from their years in the closet a learned ability "to hide behind a beautiful image." To compensate for the hidden fear and shame of being gay, we "decorate the world. We decorate our lives. We decorate our bodies. And we do it all in an effort to hide our real selves from the world."

Drawn from his own therapeutic work with gay male clients, there is an uncomfortable truth in Downs's observation, although it also makes me think of a pervasive and mostly unhelpful trope about flamboyant people in general. As the legal consultant Jo-Ellan Dimitrius notes, in her book about social behavior, "extremely flamboyant people are sometimes insecure, lonely, needy, and bored and dissatisfied with their life." Peel back the floral wallpaper, this account suggests, and what we find is a lack, a fracture, a hole that needs to be hidden. In this light, the figure of the gay interior designer—happy-clappy and a dab hand with fabrics and feathers—seems rather more complex, less two-dimensional. As we will see, the tragic hue that gets projected onto flamboyant tendencies, whether accurately or not, is a common refrain in the concept's history.

Of course, not all flamboyant male interior designers are gay. Oscar Wilde's daytime television equivalent, for example, for a certain generation of British viewers, would be interior designer and presenter Laurence Llewelyn-Bowen, who first found fame on the home makeover show *Changing Rooms* in the late 1990s. With his long, flicky haircut, musketeer-style moustache, brightly colored shirts, and peacock suits, he is a walking embodiment of upper-class flamboyance, a straight man who confidently uses words like *darling* and *fabulous* in conversation. At the beginning of his television career, he recalled in a recent podcast interview, the press attempted to drag him by calling him a "flamboyant heterosexual," a label that he was happy to claim. "I absolutely *adore* the term [flamboyant]," he said (which is itself a pretty flamboyant way of putting it).

Unfazed as he was by the press discourse about him, there were a "lot of very confused people" when he arrived in the public eye. "I was *so* not twentieth-century," he continued, a time that was "incredibly controlling, in terms of society . . . there was a real definition of what was lower class, middle class, upper class . . . what was masculine, what was feminine . . . what was allowed, what was forbidden." Llewelyn-Bowen nods here to the entire century that separated him from the nineteenth-century dandies that he had clearly modeled himself on. A time, before the trials of the 1890s, when Oscar Wilde could behave flamboyantly and still be presumed heterosexual.

A hundred years later, in the somewhat unenlightened era of the 1990s, it seemed improbable that Wildean flamboyance could signify anything other than homosexuality. Still, Llewelyn-Bowen represents the type of flamboyance that is, despite some initial media discomfort, of the palatable sort, perhaps even expected of a man of his background. (There is something to the American parlor game that asks, "Is he gay, or just British?") An aesthete rather than an activist, more ruling-class than rebel, Llewelyn-Bowen is nonetheless an interesting figure, who helpfully teases at the boundaries of good and bad taste.

In one of his most recent shows, *Outrageous Homes*, we see Llewelyn-Bowen travel around the UK to observe weird and wonderful designs in people's households. The implication of many makeover shows (including *Queer Eye*) is that the aesthetic of someone's house has a lot to tell us about the person. Letting your home's decor stay frozen in time, stuck in some less fashionable decade, is the aesthetic equivalent of letting yourself go, and by neglecting it, you might be neglecting yourself. Rather than helping those in need of stylistic direction, *Outrageous Homes* instead lets us into the homes of those who already known exactly what their style is, and invest their designs with personal meaning.

The title of the show informs its basic premise: that outrageous homes are likely to be occupied by eccentric individuals, whose sensibilities are more flamboyant than that of the average viewer. For one woman in Essex, who lives in a house entirely modeled on the chintzy opulence of the 1970s, the maximalist aesthetic is a part of who she is. A living museum of loud and lurid greens and pinks, with shag carpets and pineapple ornaments, the kitschy fun of her flamboyant house is connected with her neurodivergence, she explains, a special interest that brings her comfort and joy. Also featured in the show is a mansion made up to conjure the world of *Treasure Island*, and a home inspired by the cutesy and colorful aesthetic of Japanese *kawaii* culture.

The efforts made to create these spaces are impressive, but the results are more endearing than aspirational. They are a world away from the kinds of interior design that grace the pages of magazines, color coordinated and tastefully simple. Although wealth is often associated with extravagance, with shiny objects, bright colors, and luscious textures, minimalism is its own kind of status symbol. By refraining from excess of any kind, the minimalist aesthetic—all white walls and clear surfaces—communicates a world view in which flamboyance is seen as rather gauche, even vulgar.

The artist David Batchelor recalled once attending a party at the house of an "Anglo-American art collector" in the 1990s. Upon entering, he was greeted with a sparse aesthetic that he could best describe as "accusatory," one that offered only an "assertive silence, emphatic blankness, the kind of ostentatious emptiness only the very wealthy and utterly sophisticated can afford," painted in the "kind of white that repels everything that is inferior to it." Emerging from this confronting encounter, and embarking on a philosophical survey about the history of color, Batchelor proposed the idea of "chromophobia," the idea that "colour has been the object of extreme prejudice in Western culture."

This idea may seem a little improbable, even, by Batchelor's own admission, "odd." Flamboyant colors have been part of the visual landscape of the arts for centuries. And yet, there exists a tradition of Western thought in which color has "been systematically marginalised, reviled, diminished and degraded," and "made out to be the property of some 'foreign' body—usually the feminine, the oriental, the primitive, the infantile, the vulgar, the queer or the pathological." It is an insidious belief system, perhaps not always easy to spot, but it informs unexamined notions about other cultures (the notion of bright colors as inherently "exotic") as well as color as mere surface, a cheap lick of paint, something ersatz or childish, and unrefined. When Batchelor notes, of chromophobia, that it is "typical of prejudices to conflate the superficial and the sinister," he could equally be talking about attitudes toward flamboyance.

"The color is repellent, almost revolting: a smouldering unclean yellow, strangely faded by the slow-turning sunlight. It is a dull yet lurid orange in some places, a sickly sulphur tint in others." This is how the narrator of Charlotte Perkins Gilman's 1892 short story "The Yellow Wallpaper" describes the decor of the title, perhaps one of the most famous wallpapers in all of literature. Hailed as an important work about women's rights and the oppressiveness of the Victorian "rest-cure," Gilman's story is narrated by a woman confined to a single bedroom in the decaying mansion her husband has rented for the summer, having been diagnosed with a "temporary nervous depression—a slight hysterical tendency."

The yellow wallpaper aggravates rather than alleviates her symptoms, and it is not only the color she finds sinister. It has "one of those sprawling flamboyant patterns committing every artistic sin," she notes, and "when you follow the lame uncertain curves for a little distance they suddenly commit suicide—plunge off at outrageous angles, destroy themselves in unheard of contradictions." The narrator's prejudices against this wallpaper, flamboyant both in hue and in the undulation of its patterning, evidently run deeper than aesthetic taste. It appears to figure her own mental state and lurch toward self-destruction.

The longer she looks at it, however, the more she begins to identify with it, and even to see herself reflected back in the animated lines of its design. While "The Yellow Wallpaper" could hardly be said to have a happy ending, there is the sense that its narrator emerges having truly seen something in the flamboyant surface she stares at for so long: her own repressed creative impulses, and, in turn, the seeds of her own liberation, even if freedom seems a long way off at the story's conclusion.

Gilman's haunting tale makes a clear argument against the repression of women in the home, and thus affirms, in an oblique and twisted sort of way, the sentiments of her contemporary Harriet Monroe. Flamboyance can seem an affront, a distasteful, lurid, unfashionable surface. But it can also mark a new beginning, something colorful and animated, and full of possibility. A flamboyant worldview is on friendly terms with "artistic sin," and spots the potential for freedom in things we are told are forbidden or wrong.

TRYING

YOU ARE GETTING ready for a night out, weighing up different outfit choices. You are wondering about colors and how to combine them. "Their placement, their saturation, their intensity: these are among the tensions that make art," author and fashion journalist Charlie Porter observes. "We all deal with these tensions when we wear clothes." Perhaps you are thinking of that top tucked away in the back of your wardrobe, a bright exception in a sea of pastels, bought in the spur of the moment and never worn. You were attracted to it instantly, but never quite feel brave enough to wear it. Or maybe you are out shopping, and an item of clothing stands out to you. It seems louder than you would usually choose, a little too ornate for comfort. It says something different, a distinct chapter in the story you usually tell about yourself. So you try it on.

🔥

I remember a shopping trip with my ex-boyfriend, a few years ago, the first time we were allowed out of the house after lockdown. It was a Sunday morning, and we had gone to browse at a designer outlet, on the hunt for good deals. He worked in fashion and had an instinct for exactly which shops we should go to, and what time they would put out the best pieces. I had been to this outlet many times, and lived close to it, but I was still a novice. My sense of the hierarchy between different labels was rudimentary, and my tastes when it came to outfits were a little all over the place. I had certainly never referred to clothes as "pieces" before. I learned things from him about fashion and styling, and it was one of the things I loved about our relationship. How we shared our work and interests with each other across different creative pursuits.

In the past, I had gravitated toward garishness. Colorful print shirts from thrift shops, post-ironic animal graphic jumpers, anything with overlapping patterns. An emphasis on the tacky and the naff had been there since I was a teenager. This loud-shirt aesthetic could be coded as either hipster-lad or flamboyant-gay, depending on who wears it. Although I was engaged in an act of cover-up, these clothes seemed to offer a way of still being noticed from behind the porous wooden doors of the closet. I wonder now if that "bad" taste was a kind of sublimation, the expression of something that seemed to have no other outlet.

Heading toward thirty, I was glad to move on from this particular look, if a little resentful of the narrative that I might be growing up (and the other life changes that might entail). This new fashion journey with my boyfriend was evidently about reining in some of those impulses and finding something more refined. Growing up in a suburban new town, I was familiar with the high street labels that appeared fancy, status symbols in lower-middle-class fashion, but there was a whole echelon of houses and designers I had yet to learn about, never mind aspire toward. That I wasn't sure how to pronounce the name of the Spanish brand Loewe was pretty much all I knew about it when I walked through its doors for the first time that morning.

I bought one of my favorite pieces of clothing during this shopping trip—not my most worn, but certainly the most significant. The man working in Loewe had picked this particular item out for another customer. "You could try this, sir," he said, tentatively, to the other man. "We don't have any other coats in store at the moment, but I can let you know when we have more coming in." You could tell just by looking at this customer's face that he was unconvinced. Evidently wealthy, dressed in a nice leather jacket, he had long hair, streaked with silver, sitting just above his shoulders. His look was butch, all blacks and grays, a far cry from the colors of the coat, its shades of ivy and indigo.

With more than a little disdain came his question, perfectly formed.

"This is for men?"

"Yes, most of our pieces are unisex, sir."

"Really? . . . I don't know any men who would wear this. I certainly wouldn't."

I must have been gawping at this exchange, because the guy quickly passed the question over to me, as if looking for reassurance that this was simply *not* a coat for men. "Would you wear this?" I stayed silent, but I think I smiled, as if saying that I would. He looked a little incredulous, and offered it up, with passive aggression. "It's all yours."

He and the shop assistant both walked away, and all I could think was that I had to try on this coat. In this split-second encounter it was as if this man had challenged me to try it, in the name of protecting his own masculinity. I walked up to the rack and picked up the hanger.

How to describe this coat. It is a long, white-hooded trench coat made from heavy cotton, printed with a variety of fantastic animals—peacocks, frogs, dragons, dodos—in deep blue. They are printed on the coat in large squares, like tiles. Instead of buttons, the parting of the coat was lined with pieces of white rope tied into bobbles, which could be fastened from the other side with the same rope tied into loops. It seemed like a garment from a different time. I had never seen anything like it. I got into the fitting room and took off the black puffer coat I was wearing to fend off the winter chill, and tried it on. When I looked in the mirror I did not recognize the person reflected back. My first thought wasn't even that I looked good, but rather that I looked like someone else entirely. The kind of person, I guess, who would wear this coat. There was an electricity in the room.

If the price tags on the other items were anything to go by, it was highly doubtful I could afford to take it home with me. I took a quick selfie in the fitting room mirror and then put the coat back on its hanger. My boyfriend was waiting for me outside. I told him that I loved it, and it was fun to try on, but I wasn't going to buy it. "Why not?" he said, searching for the price tag. "It's beautiful." He looked at the price tag, clearly marveling at the reduction. "You should get it." It was a good deal, compared to other items in the shop, a bargain depending on your definition of bargain. But at £300, it was still the most money I had ever spent on an item of clothing.

In French, the word *flambeur* describes a reckless gambler or a big spender, someone who splashes the cash with relative disregard for the consequences. That this name belongs to the same family of words says a lot about the regular associations of flamboyance: excess, carelessness, spectacle. I guess I was embracing my flamboyant side in more ways than one when I bought this coat. I justified it briefly in my head as an investment purchase, but evidently what I was investing in was its transformative quality, an object of fantasy over practicality. I was in a slight daze throughout this transaction, feeling a combination of wonder and recklessness, trying to imagine how often I would wear it. (The answer: only on select occasions, but I am trying to be braver.) The person who wears this coat, I thought, seemed to exist in another world, slightly apart from reality, where fashion could be about wearing something simply beautiful, or something that resembled an extravagant kind of role-play.

When I wore it to the pub a week later, my friend Mirela, an historian, told me that I looked like a medieval monk, feedback I had never received about an outfit before. Later that evening, a woman pulled me aside to admire the coat and wax lyrical about the artist it was inspired by. It felt powerful to wear this coat, as if I were tapping into some novel spring of confident expression. I also had some homework to do. It was evident enough from the craft of the coat, and the particular features of its design, the fantastic creatures printed in a deep blue, that it was telling its own tale, a story I was now keen to uncover.

"It's fantasy—but an odd sort of fantasy," said the fashion designer Jonathan Anderson, former creative director of Loewe. He was speaking about the work of nineteenth-century ceramist and artist William De Morgan. "It looks cute, but at the same time, some of what he did is kind of disturbing," and "has a sort of wizardry about it." Over several years, Anderson had been creating capsule collections inspired by the artists associated with the Arts and Crafts movement. Soon after I bought the coat, I searched online to find out how this inspired piece made it into the Loewe collection.

With its menagerie of weird and wonderful creatures, the coat was designed as a testament to the endearing strangeness of De Morgan's ceramics, which often depicted rare and extinct animals. Born in London in 1839, to a liberal, academic family, De Morgan entered the Royal Academy of Art at the age of twenty, with the aim of being an artist, although he bristled against their traditional methods of instruction. After finishing art school, he dabbled in creating stained-glass windows, but his calling as a ceramist seemed to come in the 1860s, when he began making tiles for his friend William Morris's thriving design company.

De Morgan had a studio in Chelsea, where he built a makeshift kiln to fire glass and glaze tiles. When this caught alight and set the roof on fire, he was ejected by the landlord and struck out on his own, empowered to start his own business, which soon expanded into a successful enterprise. Famous figures would come by the showroom, "newly fledged and High-art people," who used to "pose and attitudinise," while De Morgan "made a great game of their affectations." In turn, he was commissioned to produce designs for stately homes in and around London. If you were a person of means, with a large house to decorate, it was abundantly clear why you would bring in De Morgan for an injection of character and color.

Flowers and animals were the hallmark of his chosen style, and during his years as a ceramist he innovated new techniques to produce tiles with stronger and more vivid colors, which were a crucial part of his aesthetic. There were rabbits and desert rats, along with more mythical creatures like dragons and dodos. Wearing the Loewe coat inspired by these designs felt a little like owning a piece of history, or a vibrant, affectionate response to that history.

In addition to his Loewe collections, inspired by British artists from the nineteenth century and their interests in nature, Anderson is also known for the animal-inspired designs put out by his own label, JW Anderson. There you can find dark green frog-face clogs, their googly yellow eyes protruding from the shoe, and 3D-printed clutch bags that resemble hedgehogs, puffins, pigeons, and canaries. These pieces are endearing as well as chic, and a reminder that we need look no further than the deep red of a tomato, or the iridescent feathers of a pigeon, to see the flamboyance of living organisms.

As both plants and animals illustrate, there is an overlap

between the function of flamboyance among human and non-human beings. Both are about signaling, the outward expression of an inner quality. In the natural world this is often about evolutionary prowess or reproductive potential. Flamboyance as a kind of reproductive fitness can be seen in many species of birds, and some even exhibit display arenas, called *leks*, in which rival male flamboyances are displayed, sometimes in the form of dancing, singing, and strutting, and then judged by the female bird.

Perhaps the most obvious example is the peacock, whose brightly colored tail, unbridled and unwieldy and difficult to manage, signals to the female peacock that the owner of such a tail must be a strong, solid choice for the father of her progeny. It is no accident that we get the term *peacocking*—which usually describes men who go out of their way to stand out from the crowd, for better or worse—from this same process. Flamboyance can be its own kind of mating ritual among people. We use clothes in the ways a plant uses petals, or a bird uses feathers, to send out a message to the world.

If flamboyance in nature is frequently about preserving the strength of the species, and thus maintaining a dominant order of reproduction or evolution, its display among humans, in all of our messy contingencies, is rarely about prowess in quite the same way. Flamboyance has its own power, and it can make us feel powerful when we exhibit it. But this is usually because it upends, rather than upholds, the status quo. The feeling of power, or self-possession, is not to do with supremacy or competition so much as celebrating variety, of allowing ourselves and others to see the value of difference.

While the peacock is among the world's most flamboyant birds—alongside the flamingo, of course—nature also offers other metaphors. I am thinking back to that self-affirmation mantra again, about being a flamingo in a world full of pigeons. Not all pigeons are gray. Some of them are rusty red or shocking white. Many have splashes of color running through their plumage, most commonly teal or purple or pink. Are pigeons really representative of a pallid and uniform world, a symbol only of urban decay and public nuisance? The racing of homing pigeons has been a popular working-class pastime for centuries, a traditionally masculine site of excitement and competition among industrial workers, who nurture and train their birds. In Spain, where pigeon racing is a pastime of the streets, the birds' wings are sprayed with bright colors in order to tell them apart.

Anderson's clutches are inspired by city birds like pigeons and canaries. In this sense, his work carries forward the ethos of the Arts and Crafts movement, with its fixation upon natural beauty, but with a twist. One of the limitations of the movement, thought G. K. Chesterton, was the lack of "courage to face the ugliness of things." William Morris, he argued, "hated modern life rather than loving it," and thus turned to the preexisting beauties of the past and the natural world, and neglected to make the age's "humblest necessities beautiful." While they come in many varieties, city birds are often maligned and treated as an inconvenience. Anderson transforms them from vermin into a shining accessory, an object of endearing everyday splendor. Fashioned as a purse by Sarah Jessica Parker on the streets of Manhattan, and featured on-screen in the *Sex and the City* reboot, the pigeon looks positively flamboyant.

Anderson also draws upon a different animal analogy, one which reflects the theatrical quality of fashion itself, and of pieces that feel somehow risky to wear. "If you put one of these looks on the street," Anderson observes in one interview, "there is anxiety around it. It would be like seeing a crocodile in the street. That's what excites me about fashion—we are still uncomfortable about the idea of the eccentric." This definition of an eccentric sensibility points to the joy of improbable combinations, the concrete pallor of the pavement meeting with the otherworldly, even frightening appearance of the crocodile. If flamboyance is about standing out, we can think about it not just as the florid, fluttering feathers of the peacock, but something richer and stranger, an expression of our most eccentric selves.

Finding our sense of style often begins in adolescence, a time when agency over what we wear, and what we hope our choices say about us, becomes a crucial form of independence and self-expression. In the same interview, Anderson talked about growing up in Northern Ireland and shopping for clothes as a teenager. "I would go to TJ Maxx. I remember buying this orange jacket with tiger-print trousers. It was pretty hardcore, and I remember wearing it to a high school [event], and I remember being completely destroyed. I never wore it again and I went back to the rugby jersey." This is such a familiar tale, about the decision between risk and safety, and I recognize within it my own teenage yearnings to wear loud and flagrant clothes. Not as a form of rebellion, necessarily, but because they seemed to express something about me that maybe I did not know yet.

This is why I love Anderson's designs, because they seem to revive that sense of play and risk-taking, and express that impulse on an illustrious and international stage. "This idea of going back to when I first started," he said, "is, for me, trying to find naivety in clothing right now, so I can reset my own thinking." Sometimes to find the flamboyance in our own sense of style, we need to look back, in the spirit of rediscovery, to a time when the voice of reason was a little quieter.

🔥

"You must decide who you are and be it like mad." This, for the flamboyant writer and raconteur Quentin Crisp, is the simple definition of personal style. From his years as a teenage rent boy in 1920s London, to his long stint as a life model for government-funded art classes (which allowed him to name his memoir about gay life *The Naked Civil Servant*), Crisp never concealed his homosexuality, nor his love of flamboyant clothing and makeup. Only at home, indoors, would Crisp be seen in anything less dressy than his signature, a blazer and trousers with a cravat, brooches, jewelry, and a large fedora. His celebrity grew when his memoir, shocking for the time, was adapted into a British television drama in 1975, starring John Hurt as a young Crisp. We see him in the early days of his development as a flaming homosexual: dyeing his hair bright red, applying makeup, and dressing up as a woman, to the chagrin of his straight-acting boyfriend.

The success of *The Naked Civil Servant* enabled Crisp to make a career as a traveling performer and self-help guru. His popular one-man shows were full of musings, stories, aphorisms, and question-and-answer sessions, in which audience members asked him about his views on life and how to live authentically. Suddenly famous internationally, Crisp was invited to give his talk in New York, a city he soon fell in love with. He moved there in 1981, at the grand age of seventy-two, and his affectations secured his reputation as an "Englishman in New York," the name of a 1987 song about him by Sting, who wrote it after the two became friends.

Crisp's flamboyant personal style and Wildean wit made him seem rather eccentric against the backdrop of American culture and the relentless energies of his new home, which is to say that he seemed flamboyant in a peculiarly English way. "Modesty, propriety, can lead to notoriety," Sting sings of Crisp, defying the usual logic of infamy. The song's chorus sums up with a line that sounds almost like a proverb—"At night a candle's brighter than the sun"—describing a light that is small but luminous, if you catch it at the right time.

Crisp, as a public persona, combined old-fashioned gentility and flaming faggotry, and it was this intriguing mix that constituted his style. His flamboyance was received differently in his new home. "People have always imagined," he wrote in one of his magazine columns, that "I seek to provoke hostile attention. This is rubbish. What I want is to be accepted by other people without bevelling down my individuality to please them . . . I want love on my own terms." In London, he remembered, people "stood with their faces six inches from mine and hissed, 'Who do you think you are?' What a stupid question. I didn't think I was anybody else." Whereas on the streets of New York, he countered, the so-called freaks could pass by unnoticed, or received affirmation from strangers for their looks.

Style is personal and political. As academic and curator Monica L. Miller notes, the difference between the "fop"—a derogatory term for one who is "foolishly attentive to dress"—and the "dandy" is rather like the distinction between the concepts of "fashion," which "can be bought," and "style," which "can be earned." In his account of fabulous style, madison moore outlines that one of the basic traits of fabulousness is that it "does not take a lot of money. You can achieve creative brilliance with very few resources." More than that, moore suggests, great style is not about "parading financial status or posturing heightened social position" either, but rather looking beyond normative ideas and regular hierarchies. To dress fabulously is to look "beyond the expanse of the believable," to rediscover naivety and in the process find something new. Style, in this light, as something earned and created, is also about taking a risk.

In the case of the Loewe coat, the most flamboyant thing I own by some distance, it was a purchase that did involve a lot of money, although what was powerful to me were the other ways in which this was not a "sensible" purchase. I was buying into the fantasy of something different, beyond what I had considered "believable," and when I wear the coat now, it brings up a range of different feelings. Fun and pleasure, for sure, and the sense that I am expressing something about myself, although I am sometimes unsure whether I can really pull it off, this self-expression. There is also the nervous sensation of being on alert, conscious that this garment might reveal something about who I am, in a way that could make me vulnerable, or at least more open to unpleasant interactions.

Walking down the street in it, I have received some slightly inscrutable looks, more blank than explicitly negative, but a little unnerving all the same. I know this coat is not the safest of choices, that it makes me look gayer than anything else in my wardrobe. When I wore it to go and see a different ex-partner's gig, they described it as "faggy," a word that felt strangely like a hug, the adjective I had perhaps been aiming for all along.

After my boyfriend and I broke up, the coat also became a souvenir from our relationship. I reentered the world of dating and hookup apps. Leaving the warm bed of a four-year relationship, as the world began to open up after several successive lockdowns, I was more than a little rusty, and forced to face the world in a new way. I had also just turned twenty-nine, getting on a bit in gay male years. I decided to put the mirror selfie of me in the coat as my profile image on Grindr. Partly because I liked what it said about me, and partly because I hoped it might stand in for a bit of personality, not always easily conveyed across the interfaces of apps.

I was struck by the responses. Someone messaged, sweetly, with the opener: "I love your style!," a novel compliment for me. In another conversation on the app, where I had initiated contact, I got a terse reply instructing me to tread no further: "Sorry not into femmes." Given that we had not uttered a word to each other, he could only have been going on the coat in the picture, and what it seemed to suggest about how I might act or talk.

Part of the pleasure of flamboyance is the risk that it requires. Not caring about whether your outfit pisses someone off, or might make you less superficially attractive to a stranger, is a more enjoyable feeling than I had ever realized. Of course, it is not equally safe for everyone to push at the boundaries in this way. To lean into flamboyance in spite of censure, or even the threat of violence, is part of its resistant power (the theme of the next section of this book). That dissident spirit can also be found in the sense of play, what Anderson called "naivety in clothing," the act of choosing something because you like it, not because it is sensible or proper.

When I was a teenager, donning bad animal prints and imagining a more glamorous adult self, I do not think I ever expected to be walking down the street in an ornate designer coat decorated with wild animals. Looking, in the words of my friends, like a faggy medieval monk. But I am glad I did. When I wear the coat, it feels like I am letting flamboyance in, or perhaps letting it out. Either way, it feels good.

STYLING

THAT COATS CONVEY our dreams is something I learned, as a child, from the world of musicals. Andrew Lloyd-Webber shows seemed particularly fashionable in the 1990s, having made their way from West End stages to VHS recordings. Vibrant in hue, didactic in scope, and zany in execution, I would watch them endlessly over school holidays. From these surreal and sentimental takes on Christianity's founding narratives, I learned about some of the most flamboyant biblical figures. Like Joseph, the shepherd who becomes a star, marked out as special by his opulent, multicolored coat.

Before I really knew what it meant to be flamboyant, or to be famous, I gathered that it looked something like Donny Osmond, who plays Joseph in a filmed production, walking down the aisle of a school hall full of children, backed by a smoke machine, singing something soothing about dreams in the musical's opening number. As the curtains on stage open to a cartoonish backdrop of a desert, we are transported into the bizarre and brightly lit world of *Joseph and the Amazing Technicolor Dreamcoat*, and Bible study begins.

One of the lessons of Joseph's story is that flamboyance is both a blessing and a curse. Unlike the drab, sleeveless sheepskin work coats he and his brothers would wear for herding animals, the coat given him by his father is long-sleeved and ornamental. A dazzling, finely woven patchwork made up of many colors, it is an outward manifestation of Joseph's unique charisma and exceptional status within the family, a sign that he is the favored son, and not like the other boys. He is so delighted with his garment, swishing and twirling around in it, that modesty eludes him.

"I look handsome, I look smart," he sings, "I am a walking work of art." It is little wonder that Joseph's brothers are jealous. When Joseph reveals a vision he saw in a dream, one in which he will rule over them all in the future, they decide to take action, and their punishment is harsh, very Old Testament brutal. They hatch a plan to kill him, but later decide to dispense with him by throwing him down a well and then selling him as an indentured servant to merchants who are headed toward Egypt.

Before his long years spent in servitude, Joseph's flamboyant status feels nominal, an expression of his father's love. During his years in Egypt, however, a unique skill set emerges. People recognize his charisma even as he occupies lowly positions within the hierarchy. His capacity to interpret people's dreams takes him to the highest echelons, including to the right hand of the pharaoh. Joseph's irrepressible goodness allows him to survive hardship, but there is clearly something more than virtue that makes him a remarkable figure. He is an icon in the modern (rather than just religious) sense, someone who is able to hold, explain, and embody people's dreams, to peer into the future and see which way the wind is blowing.

Like *Jesus Christ Superstar*, Lloyd-Webber's other musical based on a Bible story, *Joseph* makes a clear case for religious figures as the earliest celebrities, adored by their followers and immortalized by scripture. There is a point somewhere behind the gaudy aesthetic of these shows, and a reason that the pharaoh in *Joseph* is dressed as Elvis Presley, an ancient Egyptian ancestor of the

"King" (of Rock and Roll). These echoes with popular culture call to mind the quasi-religious status of celebrities in modern life, deified as religious icons once were, as well as a theological concept that also applies to famous personalities in today's world.

Charisma is an ancient Greek word for a person gifted—by the gods—with a special grace, and the ability to court favor and move an audience. Christianity similarly reworked this idea as something God-given, an extraordinary gift of grace, or wisdom; the capacity to heal and the capacity to dazzle with speech. In the New Testament—which the writer Jamaica Kincaid once referred to as "that celebrity magazine"—charisma was no longer reserved for prophets, heroes, and anointed leaders, but could be harnessed by believers of Christianity.

In an increasingly secular world, celebrities are the readiest embodiment of charisma. With access to the finest resources, to designer collections, stylists and glam squads on call, they offer glimpses of the divine amidst the noise and clamor. They, like Joseph, are walking works of art, their flamboyance scrutinized and imitated, and imbued with a symbolic power.

"One should either be a work of Art," said Oscar Wilde, in one of his many memorable aphorisms, "or wear a work of Art." This line perfectly captures the ethos of the dandy, a figure who also anticipates the modern celebrity in his embrace of pure style. Joseph, who appears to us today like an Old Testament dandy, divided opinion, inspiring not only awe in his followers, but jealousy and suspicion among his critics and enemies. He has been studied by religious scholars as a queer figure, a flamboyant ancestor in extravagant and gender-bending garbs, just as the dandy's love of fashion has historically been read as queer-adjacent and therefore suspect. An interest in the sartorial has traditionally been coded as feminine, in contrast to the functional quality of much of men's clothing across history, cut from military cloth. Because dandies are fashionable in this way, and concerned with the art of self-representation, throughout history they have also been written off as vapid or artificial, as if their flamboyance conceals some inner lack.

The dandy aesthetic is versatile, and was first exemplified by Beau Brummell, a man widely considered the original dandy. An influential socialite in Regency England in the early decades of the nineteenth century, Brummell was known for his signature outfit, a dark blue coat over a waistcoat, with a white linen shirt and fitted trousers, a precursor to the suit as we know it today. He was also famous for his cleanliness, for his impeccable grooming and well-tied cravat.

Brummell's dandyism was an exercise in exactitude, a look that was fine rather than frilly, correct rather than camp. Although it was a type of social currency, one that commanded attention and fueled Brummell's celebrity, this look was not obviously associated with gender play or sexual otherness. Oscar Wilde and his fellow aesthetes took the dandy look to an extreme by pushing it beyond this less-is-more aesthetic, and adopting feathers, fur-trimmed coats, and the distinctly queer symbol of brightly colored flowers. At the same time, the look also connoted one's status as an artist.

The dandy may be neither gay nor elite, by definition, but the flamboyant aesthetic of dandyism usually places its wearer at an intriguing intersection. As the Wilde scholar Alan Sinfield puts it, the dandy is as much a cultural construct as a particular person, a "site upon which issues of class, culture and sexuality" have been illustrated and contested. In many cases, the dandy looks aristocratic but hails, originally, from a lower social class (as is true of Wilde and Brummell, both originally middle class). The dandy may be heterosexual, or not, but either way his look confirms that he is different from other men. Resonating throughout the centuries, from the Regency courts to contemporary hip-hop scenes, the dandy is defined by the transformation of masculinity into something that exceeds the functional.

The rich history of the Black dandy illustrates not only the political implications of this style, but its continued relevance today. Monica L. Miller, co-curator of the exhibition *Superfine: Tailoring Black Style* at New York's Metropolitan Museum of Art, which informed the theme of the 2025 Met Gala, argues that the dandy ethos "mounts a critique against the hierarchies that order society." This is one reason why the style of dandyism has notably been adopted within Black communities throughout history, and offered a "negotiation of the transition from slavery to freedom in America in the nineteenth and twentieth centuries." Style, in Black dandyism, becomes a protest against the legacies of dehumanization, and an exuberant reworking of tailoring, street fashion, and design trends that are not only Western, Miller observes, but "Afro-Caribbean, Afro-European," and "straight up African."

Dandy subcultures have flourished in a number of African countries, in particular among working-class Zulu men in South Africa, known as *swenkas* (from the English word *swanky*), who compete in amateur fashion show and choreography competitions, and the *sapeurs* in the Congo, a name that puns on the French slang verb *se saper*, "to dress well," and the community's full title, La Sape (the Society for Ambiance-Makers and Elegant People). In the cities of Kinshasa and Brazzaville, *sapeurs* and *sapeuses* of all genders transform the basics of European tailoring (which was introduced to the country during French colonial rule) into a dapper style that is all their own, with an emphasis on bright colors, textured accessories, and stripes, patterns, and prints.

The Black dandy style encompasses an enormous range of

flamboyant looks, from the "elegant, well-appointed formal attire of, say, Duke Ellington, Nat King Cole," Miller observes, to the "more ostentatious, funky, over-the-top hyperfashion of Little Richard, Sylvester, and Prince." Singer and actor Janelle Monáe, regularly one of the best-dressed on the Met Gala red carpet each year, has drawn upon these different Black stylistic traditions throughout her career. From her early Afrofuturist android aesthetic to pink silk disco pants in the shape of a vagina, and a 1920s zoot suit, Monáe's daring looks have ranged from androgynous to high femme, a display not only of her remarkable versatility as a performer, but the flexibility of the dandy figure (traditionally represented as male) across the gender binary. In the guise of a queer icon like Monáe, the dandy emerges as a preeminent flamboyant figure in contemporary culture, an embodiment of its most shape-shifting qualities.

In 2000, a posthumous single by the Harlem rapper Big L called "Flamboyant" was released, a year after he was killed in a drive-by shooting at the age of just twenty-four. A New York peer of Jay-Z and Nas, who once described being "scared to death" by his talent, Big L is still remembered in hip-hop circles as a prodigiously talented freestyle artist who had a bright future ahead of him. The song was titled after his independent hip-hop label Flamboyant Entertainment, of which he was the CEO. The phrase "flamboyant for life" is repeated as a refrain across this and many of his tracks, and in his musical world the flamboyant lifestyle equates to style, status, and extravagance: drinking champagne, driving 100K cars, to wearing jewels.

These are familiar themes in hip-hop, a form that often celebrates bravado and rags to riches narratives, with fashion looks and styles to match. As Jeffrey Boakye observes, "Afro-Caribbean cultures are often typified by a flamboyant stylishness designed to showcase wealth and status," which can be seen in the "flamboyant furs" of the early "post-Disco" era of hip-hop, and "the shiny empowerment of gold chains." From the late 1980s to the early 2000s, the Black dandy was more likely to be seen dressed in branded sportswear and extravagant jewelery than in a suit. Harlem itself was an epicenter for this style, home to couturier and tastemaker Dapper Dan, another important dandy figure, who made his name appropriating the logos of high-fashion labels and printing them onto tracksuits, bomber jackets, leather jackets, and baseball caps, the outfits favored by athletes and hip-hop stars. This look was valued, Miller notes, for its "communication of oppositionality, its deliberate advertising of hip-hop culture as urban, working-class, ghetto," a way of communicating your authenticity, as well as your achievements.

Big L framed his flamboyance in relation to the creative talents that put him in the spotlight in the first place, his inventive play with language and rhyme, his capacity to improvise with panache, "always writin' poems / I can write it or recite it off the top of the dome." Flamboyant Entertainment, similarly, was about more than just money. It gave Big L creative freedom, free from the influence of music industry executives with no relationship to the streets, where hip-hop was born, as he noted in a 1999 magazine interview, the "A&R people" who "want you to be a copycat of whoever's selling the most records at the time." Flamboyance, in Big L's view, was about the assurance that accompanies true independence, and the belief in your own singularity.

A few years later, in 2003, another song called "Flamboyant" hit the airwaves, one that also explored celebrity, charisma, and masculinity, from a slightly different perspective. Long before they released a song with this title, the Pet Shop Boys were well-versed in the flamboyance of pop. Having met serendipitously in a hi-fi shop in Chelsea in the early 1980s, the British synth-pop duo came up through the London dance music scene, and paired Chris Lowe's maximalist beats with Neil Tennant's arch, witty, and yearning lyrics. Their songs convey both a comic and tragic view of the world, populated by larger-than-life characters and memorable scenes. They skewer and celebrate the glamour of urban subcultures, the grit of city life, and the offbeat theater of the British suburbs, all dog races and puffed-up hairdos.

Listening to a Pet Shop Boys song often feels like the moment you cross a threshold, stepping into a bar or a club, and enter into the heady story of the night ahead, so full of potential and significance. They did not publicly acknowledge their status as a gay band until the mid-1990s, when Tennant came out in an interview with *Attitude* magazine. By that point, during their self-described "imperial phase" in the late 1980s, they had covered the Village People, released a duet with Dusty Springfield, produced an album of reworked show tunes for Liza Minnelli, and addressed rent boys, Catholic guilt, and HIV/AIDS in their lyrics. Their flamboyance hardly needed an explanation.

In "Flamboyant," Pet Shop Boys look at the concept through the flashing lens of the paparazzi's cameras. Neil Tennant sings to a flamboyant individual, someone whose "sole employment" is garnering attention because of the way they look. On first listen, the song sounds like a critique, describing a world of excess, where more is always more, but also decay, where performance conceals a falsehood. Like Joseph swishing around in his ostentatious coat, the person in this song seems like an object of awe, fantasy, and envy all at once, a figure consigned to play before an adoring but volatile audience.

When he talked about the inspiration for the song, Tennant name-checked many of the people who have already featured, or will feature, in the pages of this book. It is a song "about the importance of flamboyant people in our way of life," he observed, "people like Oscar Wilde and Quentin Crisp, Boy George and Marilyn, Elton John . . . Anyone with a bit of sparkle."

Tennant also cites David Beckham, the footballer also known

as Golden Balls for his prowess, and perhaps even better known as a fashion icon and international celebrity in his own right. Look at any of Beckham's red carpet looks from the 2000s—a leopard-print shirt with velvet trousers, an all-white suit with a ponytail, an all-black leather ensemble inspired by *The Matrix*, a bedazzled tracksuit worn with one of his signature hairstyles, flicky with frosted tips—and you can see that sparkle in abundance. When listened to as a song about Beckham, "Flamboyant" sounds immediately of its time, a reference to the tabloid obsession with footballers, their wives, and their glamorous lifestyles. This was also a time when football had ballooned far beyond its origins as the working man's game, and become a circus of the rich and famous, populated by styled and stylish players who were paid eye-watering sums for their very public labors on the pitch.

I find it intriguing how the word *flamboyant*, so frequently used as a way of othering queer people through implication, can also be used interchangeably about famous heterosexual men. All without appearing to inspire speculations about their sexuality, or to threaten their ironclad grasp on masculinity. Beckham's red-carpet prime overlapped, not accidentally, with the rise of the "metrosexual," loosely defined as a man who not only understands the basic tenets of grooming and fashion, but indulges in them. A guy who knows how to take care of himself, the metrosexual is no stranger to skin care, or a mani-pedi, or regular appointments to get his hair cut and colored. He might even choose, instead of a rucksack, to carry a bag over his shoulder, or to hold it like a clutch. With a riff on every possible stereotype, the implication is that really he is just like a woman, in straight male form.

During sessions spent down tabloid rabbit holes, I have noticed how frequently the word *flamboyant* gets used about metrosexual male football players, perhaps more than any other category of celebrity. It is also commonly used to describe a style of play in football itself, a way of distinguishing between footballers who play it safe, and those who take risks in the game, and show off their finesse with the ball. This flamboyant masculinity is not taken as a mask, but rather a comfortable expression of charisma, status, and sexual attraction. You can see it all kinds of places, from the dapper, ostentatious, and highly groomed aesthetic often associated with Italian men, to the styling of male contestants on reality shows like *Love Island*. It is a kind of flamboyance, paradoxically, that seems to reassert gendered norms, and fix the boundaries of masculinity by teasing at them.

Although it seems outdated rather than transgressive today, I found the idea of the metrosexual tantalizing when I was younger and lacked any real language for my sexuality. As I remember it, my real sexual awakening arrived when I watched the British soap opera *Footballers' Wives*, not just because of the graphic sex scenes (some of them between men), but because the men in it were hunky but also a little off, somehow, a little fey in their showiness and flamboyant outfits.

Lusting after straight men who looked gay was like a gateway drug, or perhaps a less intimidating way to come to terms with my sexuality, as if their heterosexuality could be an alibi for the fantasy. In turn, I think this is why many footballers, but also male rock singers and rappers, are referred to frequently as "flamboyant" without their masculinity being thrown into question. They are protected by the macho associations of their chosen form, whether it is football, or guitar music, or hip-hop. There is a kind of freedom here, an invitation to play with fashion in controlled conditions.

The Pet Shop Boys song is alive to this. In one of the later verses, Tennant describes the flamboyant protagonist at yet another preview, posing with the artist on show. "To look so loud may be considered tacky," he sings, particularly when the "collectors wear black clothes by Issey Miyake." As well as being a fun rhyme, this moment is a good reminder that, like camp and kitsch, tackiness is another concept flamboyance dances close to. Compared with the chic monochrome simplicity of a Miyake look, say a cashmere sweater with plissé trousers, an obvious flamboyant look could appear tacky, out of place, even vulgar. But this is its appeal, perhaps even its value. At least it could never be accused, to quote another Pet Shop Boys song, of being boring.

The tacky fun of flamboyant masculinity is also turned on its head by Dorian Electra, a gender fluid singer and songwriter, who in 2019 released a song and an album called "Flamboyant." Electra wrote the song explicitly to reclaim the idea of flamboyance, to wrest it from its historical usage, they noted, as a "derogatory term" for queer people who choose to present as "obvious as opposed to secretive, which is what you're supposed to be in a world that doesn't embrace you." Electra wanted to build on the word's more positive meanings, as a way of "describing something colorful or flame-like that you couldn't look away from," both "people's personalities and other pieces of art." For Electra, whose work often skewers masculinity and gendered archetypes, personality is itself a work of art, a consciously created persona that catches the eye.

In the music video for "Flamboyant," which is dense with cultural references, Electra takes on multiple characters. There is a seductive lover reclining in front of an open fire in a red satin dressing gown, with slicked-back green hair and come-hither eyes, a subversive play on the Hugh Hefner playboy archetype. There is a keyboard player in a gold-sequined tuxedo and frilly collar, clearly modeled on the campy extravagance of the beloved entertainer Liberace. An androgynous model sits before a mirror in an all-white suit. A slick host in a 1970s brown checkered suit and roller neck, martini in hand, and a pop star in a frilly white collar and fur jacket, his hair cut into a pair of exquisite curtains. Not all of these characters point to explicit references, but they each convey a different strain of flamboyant masculinity, and the sense that we know exactly who these men are and what they are like.

As for flamboyant icons, Electra had an extensive list of names in mind when writing the song, a familiar lineup including Oscar Wilde, Liberace, Prince, and goth legend Alice Cooper. Also, Austin Powers, the fictional character created by actor Mike Myers, in a series of satirical spy comedies in the late 1990s. Loosely based on suave agents like James Bond, Austin Powers wears loud colorful shirts and ruffled collars, and espouses "groovy" free love sentiments straight from the 1960s. When they watched the films as a child, Electra recalled, they had no idea that "the whole joke of the character was that he was supposed to be grotesque and humorously unappealing." They were drawn instead to his velvet ensembles and paisley print mod suits, and Austin Powers became their reference for the "masculine ideal," and one of the most "inspirational flamboyant icons ever."

Electra's characters are stylish and arresting, and make good on the song's opening line, "I'm a very flaming flammable guy." Flammable, of course, can also mean unpredictable, volatile, and one of the most intriguing aspects of Electra's performance is the slight glimpse of angst beneath the sparkling aesthetic. As they gaze intensely into camera in their different guises, lit by candles and flames, holding a glass of champagne or making themselves up in the mirror, it is like they are seducing us, and denying our ability to turn away. While the song operates as a campy, tongue-in-cheek celebration of exaggeration, there is also something slightly unnerving about the refrain "I go all the way," Electra's voice modified by electronic distortion so that it sounds not so much male as otherworldly.

In the world of this song, flamboyance reads as sexy, strident, lecherous, and even a little frightening, all at once. "No taste for subtlety," they sing, "and no time for restraint." But there is also something earnest at the song's heart, a queer refusal to tone things down for the appeasement of others. If being flamboyant means going all the way, it also means transgressing the usual boundaries of good and bad taste, and offering up a fantasy vision where no fucks are given. That image of a more empowered self—hard to reach, perhaps, but bright and vivid in the hands of artists—is one of the pop music's greatest gifts.

EMPOWERING

THERE IS ONE more coat I want to talk about, if you will indulge me another chapter in the wardrobe. A symbol of flamboyant lore, it too has a story with a lesson, found not in the Book of Genesis, but the songbook of a country singer with a religious sensibility. Unlike the tale of Joseph, with its fraternal violence and social jockeying, this is a tribute to flamboyance that grows from need, and is nurtured by love.

Raised in a large working-class family in the Great Smoky Mountains of East Tennessee, in the late 1940s, Dolly Parton's childhood was one of poverty. But from these years of hardship she gleaned that "if there's one positive thing about being poor, it's that it makes a person more creative." She enjoyed playing dress-up with different hand-me-downs and sack dresses made from flour bags by her mother. She preferred bright colors and foraged the landscape for natural beauty products, like berries whose colorful juices could stain your lips like lipstick. Her mother also once made her a multicolored winter coat, woven from different fabric scraps in the manner of a patchwork quilt.

Parton named it the "Coat of Many Colors," after Joseph's, and immortalized it in her 1971 song of the same name, a nostalgic ode to maternal care and resourcefulness. It would become a central part of the Dolly Parton story, the tale of a young girl from the mountains, dressed in a Technicolor coat more beautiful than the sum of its parts, who would go on to become not only one of America's most beloved entertainers, but a particular kind of fashion icon.

In the song, Parton remembers how other kids made fun of her coat when she wore it proudly to school, with its mismatched patches of color. Like the inverse of Joseph's opulent number, it seemed to bestow on her a lowly status, a clear sign of her family's financial situation. But the message of Parton's song is to separate status from luxury, and to focus on the more important components of its construction, the "love / my momma sewed in every stitch," which made it worth "more than all their clothes." Wearing that coat, even if the material was cheap, and the different colors a little tacky, made her feel like she was rich, empowered by the tenderness of its making.

The coat provides an apt origin story for a star who famously said, regarding her own fashion choices, that "it costs a lot to make a person look this cheap." When it came to choosing her signature style, Parton was never interested in appearing refined, however much her ensembles would cost to produce. She first began performing country music at local venues in her early teens, and moved to Nashville to pursue her career after she graduated from high school. She was inspired by the rhinestoned outfits of some of the scene's biggest stars but frustrated by the otherwise conservative and old-fashioned expectations about what wholesome country women should wear on stage.

Equally important to the origin story of Dolly Parton was the style icon she used to see on the streets of her hometown, a woman ungenerously known as the "town tramp." She wore tight skirts, high heels, painted her nails and her lips, and lightened her blond hair with peroxide. The young Dolly found her beautiful where others called her trashy, and this woman's example would form the basis of her aesthetic.

Like most teenagers, Parton got in trouble for pushing the boundaries of what she was allowed to wear. Her grandfather and her parents were none too keen on her wearing tight-fitting clothes and short skirts, with their perceived suggestion of sexual availability. Similarly, when she signed with RCA Records, the head of the label told her she needed to change the way she looked, to leave behind the big hair and gaudy outfits, if she wanted to be taken seriously as an artist. Luckily, the young Parton did not take these attitudes to heart. Her looks only got gaudier as time went on, and she only became more herself.

"I have my own idea of what beauty is," Parton shared recently. "I try to take my negatives and turn them into positives, and I always feel better being more flamboyant." She ignored the people who told her to dress down when she started wearing "that big hair and my flamboyant clothes and my boobs sticking up," and those who told her "you look more like a hooker than you do a singer." Parton's commitment to flamboyance made her feel more confident. But it was also a middle finger to received ideas about how female singers, and particularly female singers in the traditional world of country and western, should present themselves.

All the while, her musical talent has never been in question, so enduring are her songs of yearning and envy, of perseverance and self-affirmation. Parton's legacy is imprinted widely around the world, from her museum theme park Dollywood in Tennessee, to her philanthropic work, and a book-gifting program intended to inspire a love of reading among children. Parton is known for being glamorous but also humble in her outlook and socially conscious with her money. Some may consider her high-femme looks over-the-top, but her lyrics are earnest and their messages generous. She holds these contradictions, makes them part of her endearing persona as the country girl made good, a flamboyant public figure who is able to unite disparate groups of people.

As an artist she "has embraced all of everyone," said one of Parton's admirers recently, a young singer who follows in her footsteps. "That's the beauty of Dolly," an inclusive ethos that can be glimpsed at her shows, attended by a broad array of people, a sign that despite the genre's traditional associations, "there are lots of gay people and trans people at country concerts and they love country music." Rhinestoned to the nines, her hair a platinum blond, the singer imparts a simple and flamboyant tenet to anyone and everyone: Here I am.

🔥

In the months when I was first writing these words, I needed some musical encouragement. I found myself in a slump, unable to pinpoint exactly why. In the same period of time that I moved to London, committed to a career as a writer, and tried to move on from the heartache of past relationships, something in me had dulled. Going freelance in a big city meant I could no longer buy Loewe coats (or much of anything!) on a whim, but I was already losing my interest in aesthetic things. Maybe it was all the ups and downs, the string of bad dates, the no-shows and the nonstarters. Without the escape of drugs and alcohol, I was also beginning to face myself more honestly, and the shame and insecurity that had taken root within me in my teenage years.

While I was thinking and writing about flamboyance on a daily basis, in myself I was feeling anything but flamboyant, more like a "plastic bag" than a "firework" (to borrow Katy Perry's turn of phrase). I realized I would need to work a bit harder to feel hopeful, to find pick-me-ups wherever I could. While I am partial to melancholy music, guitar-led and bittersweet, and to staring out of train windows while something slow and gentle plays, it was loudness that would help to guide me out of this hole. As a genre that expertly blends longing and elation, having pop on full blast was a way of leaning into joy when it otherwise felt absent. All of this is to say that Chappell Roan came into my life at exactly the right moment.

When I first heard "Pink Pony Club," an early single from her 2023 debut album *The Rise and Fall of a Midwest Princess*, I was captivated by its flamboyant balladry, a pulsing, piano-bar tale of a girl pining for home, both the small-town world she has left behind and the glittering alternative offered by queer spaces like The Abbey, a bar in West Hollywood. It offers an imagined dialogue between the singer, who dreams of a new life in LA as a "pink pony girl" on stage in high heels—another flamboyant animal to add to the menagerie—and her concerned mother back in Tennessee. Clearly autobiographical, the song, Roan has said, "came from me wanting to be a go-go dancer in LA," but lacking the confidence to do that, "so I wrote a song about it." A four-minute daydream of a more flamboyant life, "Pink Pony Club" also sounds like a mission statement for Roan's career.

Born Kayleigh Rose Amstutz in 1998, Roan was raised in a conservative Christian community in Missouri in America's Midwest. She has spoken repeatedly about feeling stifled by the traditionalism of her hometown, an environment barely more tolerant of vampy or outré feminine fashion than Dolly Parton's Tennessee upbringing decades earlier. Spending time in cities like LA and New York allowed Roan to discover her showmanship in a way that felt true to her queerness. She developed an onstage aesthetic that she describes as "very loud and provocative," trashy and immodest, characterized by leotards, bodysuits, and her signature hair, wavy, voluminous, and flaming red.

In the years since the song was first released, in 2020, it has become harder to recognize the reticence Roan describes about being the center of attention, at least on stage. (She has spoken defiantly about her difficulties with the spotlight, and the encroachment of fan behavior when she is trying to live off duty.) Her massive breakthrough in 2024 was down in no small part to her powerhouse vocals and magnetic presence. Here was an artist who knew how to put on a show, but one who also appeared to find a certain freedom through performance. She has described "Chappell Roan" as her drag persona, an outlet for a more open and sexually empowered version of herself, and she has affirmed her stake in the art form of drag, as a woman performing hyper-femininity.

At every opportunity, Roan's theatrical vision onstage transforms perceived negatives into something bold and affirming, in direct resistance to attitudes that made her feel fearful about her identity before coming out. "I was scared of flamboyantly gay people," she said in a *Rolling Stone* interview, because she was taught to be, and she attributes this cultural aversion to flamboyance to misogyny. Flamboyance often "exudes femininity, and people hate women." In response to another high-school sentiment—the idea that flamboyant gays are "clowns," who are "so loud, dress so obnoxiously . . . and have to be the center of attention"—she has chosen to embrace a similar aesthetic. For her triumphant performance of "Pink Pony Club" at the 2025 Grammys, a crowning moment in her rise to fame, she was accompanied by a troupe of dancers made up as clowns.

Roan's persona draws upon a wide range of flamboyant touchstones. Lay out the staples of a typical Chappell Roan photo shoot—towering wigs, hairbrushes, powder-puff makeup, and other high-femme accoutrements—and you could easily imagine they were meant for Dolly Parton. She has taken specific pointers from her country forebear: the long red nails, big hair, and blue eye shadow, which has often been stigmatized as "sex worker drag." Divine has also been on her mood board. At one particular show she paid tribute to *Pink Flamingos* with a red fish-tail gown and drawn-on eyebrows, her face painted high with bright blue eye shadow. "Everything I do," she noted, "is a fuck you to the box I was so pressured to be put in, and a reference to people who came before me."

I listened to *Midwest Princess* incessantly when I was feeling low, inspired by its "fuck you" ethos. With songs about the chaotic joys of nightlife, sexual experimentation, and renouncing men in the process of realizing her true desires, the record paints a daring portrait of self-actualization, of the kind that had started to feel elusive in my own life. I was becoming increasingly morose about love and intimacy. I was sober but continually thirsty, craving new experiences that might take me out of myself. As corny as it may sound, I really found myself in these songs, sung by a lesbian in her mid-twenties who was living out her wildest dreams on the public stage. To me, the great subject of *Midwest Princess* is precisely this: the role of fantasy in our inner lives, how it helps us picture more vivid and liberated versions of ourselves.

By the time Roan's debut headline tour made its way to London, I really needed what her show had to offer, not least an opportunity to dress up and feel something. My friend Becca and I went to see her at Brixton Academy, a venue that felt relatively intimate given the scale of Roan's star power, and booked before her massive breakout. Becca and I had been on a journey together. We became close right at the beginning of university, when we lived in the same corridor, and came out to each other at different times over the subsequent years. It was exciting, going to see our new musical obsession together, and meaningful. Roan's queerness was center stage, explicit and unapologetic, something that felt less imaginable even a decade earlier, when we had been students.

The show was everything we hoped it would be. To stand in a sea of pink cowboy hats and double denim, as everyone sang the words to "Pink Pony Club" in unison, was a deeply moving experience. It reminded me of those nights early on, when we first went out to gay bars, and looked out on the tableau of bodies dancing to the biggest, trashiest tunes, and I felt some of that shame and loneliness, built up over many years of hiding, begin to melt away.

"Pink Pony Club" is now a number one hit, culturally ubiquitous and a regular fixture on wedding dance floors and radio stations. It is catchy and earnest, a heartfelt pop pastiche, with an infectious, sing-along quality that accounts for its success. It has made me cry each time I have seen Roan perform it live, as the show's closing number. But it would be an error to hear in it only a sentimental narrative about self-acceptance, wrapped neatly in a bow. The song may be framed as a maternal dream, two voices caught between Los Angeles and Tennessee. But behind its wall of sound, its solemn piano chords, and campy hair-metal guitar solo, and the longing in Roan's voice, something else can be detected. Difficult memories, banished like the ghosts of past selves we have left behind, and a bigger picture, a glimpse at what we are still up against in the quest to live freely.

As a pop star with a huge platform and a clear vision, Roan also meets the anti-flamboyance of the contemporary moment. While conservative lawmakers pass repressive legislation, ban drag performances, and repeatedly target trans people, Roan's show foregrounds drag culture and all forms of femininity. When she performed at the Governors Ball in New York in 2024, dressed as a drag version of the Statue of Liberty, complete with a flaming torch, she recited the words etched on the bottom of the statue: "Give me your tired, your poor; your huddled masses yearning to breathe free." She invoked these familiar lines to make clear her own stance on contemporary issues, calling for the freedom and rights of trans people, women and oppressed people living in occupied territories, and revealed that she rejected an invitation to perform at a Pride event at Biden's White House. "We want liberty, freedom and justice for all. When you do that, that's when I'll come."

In her captivating play with queer aesthetics, and her lyrics about self-acceptance, sexual confidence, and community, Roan embodies the essence of a flamboyant pop star. She delivers her inclusive message with a charisma that is equal parts sincere and provocative. Rooted in the pop culture of the past, as well as its more contemporary waves, her work also offers an important reminder. Flamboyance, then and now, is an act of protest.

FLAMING

PERFORMANCE & PROTEST

"I must mold and direct that fiery cool mass of angry energy—use it before it uses me."

Joseph Beam, 1984

PERFORMING

ONE FRIDAY NIGHT in December 1966, the American film director Shirley Clarke invited a friend over to her apartment in New York's Chelsea Hotel. She had known this man, Jason Holliday, for several years, through her partner Carl Lee. He would sometimes come around to clean her house, uninvited, and in return she would give him money to support his nightclub act. Holliday, in his own words, was a hustler with more than one hustle: a cleaner, a sex worker, and an aspiring performer. Clarke had long hoped to make a film about performance, and when she bumped into Holliday again in the street, having not seen him for some years, she knew she had found her subject.

Holliday's birth name was Aaron Payne, and details about his early life are scant. He trained as an actor and lived in various cities, including San Francisco, where Jason Holliday was created. A charismatic speaker, with some wild tales to tell about his experiences as a Black gay man, Holliday was happy to accept Clarke's invitation to make a film. With a few others present, including Lee and a small film crew, Clarke filmed Holliday for twelve hours, well into the early hours of the next day, and interviewed him about his life.

In its edited final form, *Portrait of Jason* comes in at under two hours, but it successfully captures the breadth and force of Holliday's presence. On camera, we see him recline on the sofa, stretch out on the floor, and walk around the room. He chain-smokes, sips spirits from the bottle, and performs many bits. He sings wistfully, first a few lines from an old Lena Horne number, and later a bracing rendition of the torch song "My Man" from the musical *Funny Girl*. At one point, he grabs a lady's hat and a feather boa from his prop bag and impersonates screen icons like Mae West, Scarlett O'Hara, and Dorothy Dandridge. His act is steeped in the divas of Hollywood and Broadway, as well as the drag queens he knows from the streets of Harlem, who catwalk along the avenues in their wigs and fur coats. He also recalls being inspired by the "fabulous people" he met while "on vacation" in Rikers Island (meaning when he was in prison), where the queens clapped back to police officers with a click of the fingers, and declared they would never reveal what this gesture means.

"I'll never tell," Holliday says, multiple times, in homage to his prison mates. And also, "I've got to tell." His disclosures seem torn between these two refrains: caginess, on the one hand, a desire to withhold, and total candor on the other, a need to reveal these parts of himself. Each story he tells leads unpredictably toward some kind of punchline, and he delivers even the darker episodes—about his abusive father, homelessness, racist encounters, and brushes with the police—with a full-throated laugh. As a raconteur, he is many things: charming, spiky, mischievous. Flamboyant.

Portrait of Jason is an uncomfortable and astonishing film, in no small part because its subject, who is so compelling to watch, is captured by Clarke in a naturalistic style, giving us intimate access to the workings of his charisma. But toward the end of the shoot, things starts to come apart. As the night turns to morning and Holliday gets progressively drunker on the liquor Clarke has provided, her questioning becomes more antagonistic. She and Lee begin probing him, questioning the veracity of his stories and calling him out on alleged lies he has told and things he has done in the past. It feels like an ambush, as if Clarke is puncturing a balloon that has been steadily blown up in the preceding hours, becoming larger and more colorful as it fills with warm air.

In the final moments, we see Jason not in a climactic blaze of glory, swishing his feather boa, but exhausted and vulnerable, muttering incomprehensibly behind drunken tears and manic laughter. This unsettling conclusion has been interpreted as a sign of the film's exploitative production, and also a commentary on the ethics of filmmaking, a questioning of what honesty looks like when someone sits before a camera. It remains ambiguous whether Jason was in on it—the last thing we hear him utter, as the screen turns to black, is the line "I'm very happy with how this all turned out." Either way, what the film strongly implies is that Jason, beneath the flamboyant front, is a tragic and dishonest figure, hiding his pain with the bells and whistles of performance.

This destructive climax was always planned, in the hopes that it would create a sense of revelation. "I was going to let Jason do whatever he wanted for as long as I could," Clarke recalled in an interview years later, "and then I was going to challenge him to come clean, to tell the truth." That aim sounds noble enough for a documentarian, except that it leaves unexamined the power dynamics at play. Clarke was aware of the discomfort around her own position as "white lady director," a position of power in this particular scenario, but less so in the wider world and the male-dominated film industry of the 1960s. But that did not stop her admitting that she "started that evening with hatred, and there was a part of me that was out to do him in, get back at him, kill him." While she came to love her subject eventually, and "changed a lot of judgmental ideas by really getting to know Jason," the presence of those judgmental ideas in the first place is revealing.

What is it about flamboyance that makes people smell blood? By conducting this attack on Jason, Clarke zoomed in on the more negative qualities that are often associated with the idea of a flamboyant person: a love of drama, a need for attention, a penchant for excess or artifice. "Look at me," Jason seems to say, directing attention away from what is happening offstage, behind the scenes, even if it cannot help slip into view sometimes. By allowing him to be queen for the night, and enjoy his moment in the spotlight, Clarke saw a fantasy that needed tearing down. As viewers, we are invited to view Jason as if he were a doomed heroine in a play by Tennessee Williams, who was in fact one of the audience members at an early screening of the film. A character, perhaps, like Blanche DuBois, the aging Southern belle from Williams's classic play *A Streetcar Named Desire*, who lies, cheats, drinks heavily and, at the play's denouement, clings onto her fantasies even as she is being taken away to a mental institution, and utters her immortal closing line about depending on the kindness of strangers.

Which truths did Clarke hope Holliday would face under her gaze? The same so-called truths that had been served up to him by a hostile, homophobic, and racist society, which cast him in the role of outsider? Maybe some of Holliday's stories were unreliable, embellished with exaggerations, or amplified by booze. But his delusions of grandeur also possess their own truth value as a mode of survival, a means of resisting the unpleasant realities of a life that had evidently been a difficult one. Flamboyance may be a kind of armor, but it is not always protective. When you are excluded from society's idea of normal, acting flamboyantly also puts you at greater risk of hostility, even outright violence. In this sense, the events captured by *Portrait of Jason* reveal something about attitudes toward flamboyance, the idea that it is all an act, surface deep or masklike. Perhaps it is easier to believe that someone is a tragic fantasist, or a trickster, than to believe that someone maligned by society could possess this much gumption. That despite their pain, they still refuse to blend in, or fall in line, even at the cost of their own safety. Strangers are unpredictable, and not always kind.

I first watched *Portrait of Jason* when I was in my early twenties. The film had recently been restored by Milestone Films and brought to public attention again, after the original print, thought lost for many years, was discovered in an archive. At that point in my own life, I was trying to consume as many films about queer people as I possibly could. I had only recently come out, and moved to London after graduating from university, my first time living in a big city. I was eager to explore my sexuality, but cinema seemed like a more accessible way to learn about queer culture than venturing out myself, into a scene that still felt unknown. Needless to say, these films from decades past hardly painted a romantic or idealized picture of queer life, but I was captivated all the same.

Jason Holliday, in particular, struck a chord. Although his schtick seemed partly recognizable, having filtered down into problematic cultural stereotypes about sassiness as a Black gay trope, he also seemed like a true original, the kind of flamboyant person I had never met in real life, and one I would have loved to spend an evening with. The question of performance was on my mind. Studying flamboyance as an academic subject for my final-year dissertation, I had been thinking about theatricality and its enemies, and reading around the subject.

Since its first airing in Plato's *Republic*, the Berkeley professor and historian Jonas Barish argues in his book *The Anti-Theatrical Prejudice*, there has been a widespread and culturally pervasive discomfort around the notion of the theater, with its emphasis on playacting over reality. While Barish's study mostly focused on the form of theater itself, and the role it has played in societies across history, he also observed how this aversion to theater's perceived falsity and moral dubiousness inflects the language of our daily lives. Unlike other words borrowed from the arts to describe our experiences (like *poetic* or *epic*), terms "borrowed from the theater—*theatrical, operatic, melodramatic, stagey*, etc.—tend to be hostile and belittling," and so do "a wide range of expressions drawn from theatrical activity expressly to convey disapproval," like "*putting on an act*," "*making a scene*," "*making a spectacle of oneself*."

Acting flamboyantly, as a related concept, could easily be added to this list. Although Barish never explicitly drew a connection between anti-theatrical prejudice and queerness, the connections seem clear. Prejudices, after all, have a tendency of appending themselves to each other, and long-standing ideas about queer theatricality—from drag as a theatrical art, to the clichéd associations of gay men with the theater—would seem to position queer culture uniquely in the firing line of these attitudes. I was reminded of this because so many of the films I was watching in my early explorations, *Portrait of Jason* included, seemed to be about performance, both what it does, its imaginative potential, and how it is received by those who care to look.

Twenty years after Clarke's film, a more famous, and no-less divisive, documentary about the figures of the queer subculture was being made in New York, also by a white female director. This too was a film about race, and the relationship between fantasy and reality, but it opted to tell the story not just of an individual, but a community, one with its own unique customs and strategies, which had until this time remained largely invisible to the straight world. Rumblings of that culture could be heard in some of Jason's observations about the queens he encountered on the streets of Harlem. In the late 1980s, it had become well-known enough to reach mainstream attention.

By the time Jennie Livingston's film *Paris Is Burning* hit the film festival circuit in 1990, drag balls had been a fixture of New York nightlife for over a century. They could be traced back to the first masquerade balls, which took place in storied venues in Harlem in the late nineteenth century, a space where same-sex couples could dress up and dance with each other, and also to the highly conspicuous drag balls associated with the Harlem Renaissance. Langston Hughes once described them as the "strangest and gaudiest of all Harlem's spectacles in the '20s." When Livingston decided to make a film about the Black and Latino ballroom community, she was entering a flourishing scene with a long history, although the balls associated with that community first began to emerge in the 1960s. Many of the city's drag balls, at that time, favored white drag queens, or drag queens who could make themselves appear most convincingly like white women. In response, queens of color decided to throw their own balls and create their own spaces, which became known as "houses." The houses doubled up as alternative family units for young queens, many of whom had been forced to leave home at an early age, and they were named after, and presided over by, drag mothers.

Paris Is Burning is named after an annual drag ball that took place in New York throughout the 1980s. (The 1986 edition is captured in the film.) The ball was named by its founder, the drag artist Paris Dupree, Founding Mother of the House of Dupree, one of a number of alternative family structures that exist in the ballroom community, with house mothers who mentor and protect their drag children, who compete in the balls, which are a cross between a pageant and a dance competition. But the title of the film feels resonant in other ways. It conjures images of change, revolution, and the Eiffel Tower on fire.

A ball takes some of its cues from Parisian influences. The drag houses are named and grouped like classic fashion houses. The fashion center of Paris represented something establishment and unattainable, a "bastion of standards of Western beauty," as one viewer of the film, the poet Essex Hemphill, put it. It seemed a far cry from the milieu of the balls, where many of the queens were living in poverty, with limited resources or access to high-fashion labels. Ballroom, with its model of community as spectacle, looked to destroy the barriers between the inaccessible glamour of Paris and the more vexing realities of New York. It is in the business of setting things on fire.

Voguing, which first emerged in the 1980s, is one of the dances that distinguishes these flamboyant performances. It is often attributed to a night when Dupree, one the form's early innovators, began a spontaneous dance holding a copy of *Vogue* magazine, and imitated the fashion poses that could be found within its pages, holding each one for long enough to be photographed, like a model on set. Inspired by the broader fashion industry, early voguing was also distinguished by its non-Western influences, including African art and the shapes of ancient Egyptian hieroglyphics, which inform its angular and exaggerated hand gestures. (Another theory suggests that voguing grew out of a dance devised by inmates at the prison on Rikers Island, the place where Jason Holliday recalled meeting some "fabulous people.")

This dance is defiant, dramatic, and technically intricate, not a routine you simply pick up on a night out. (Not that this stops people trying.) It is traditionally grouped into different historical categories (the Old Way, the New Way) and particular styles, like Vogue Fem, a physical performance of femininity that is comprised of five key elements, including the catwalk, the duckwalk, and spins and dips (known popularly as "death drops"). Much of voguing is centered around walking, and it reveals the immense power and theatricality that everyday motions can be charged with. Done "well enough, and at a fast enough clip," notes the writer and critic Ricky Tucker, voguing "means walking into the room followed by a trail of flames."

As a form of physical storytelling, voguing's fiery quality also comes from the heat of throwing "shade," with moves directed competitively or antagonistically toward others. There is also the associated practice of "reading," a verbal mode of critique. (In breaking, another urban dance craze that emerged within the Black community in New York at roughly the same time, these physical gestures of insult are know as "burning.") The reads exchanged between queens and ball participants can be pretty penetrating. They might even seem to complicate the sense of solidarity offered by these spaces. But shade and reading also helpfully resist clichéd or overly pat ideas of togetherness, a reminder that saltiness can be its own kind of recognition and belonging. In ballroom, shade and reading also serve to raise the stakes of the competition—they are a way for certain standards to be upheld in the pageantry of the ball. The secret is that flamboyance *can* be so exacting.

This drama of the ball is illuminated by the concept of "realness," which describes how effectively queens can exhibit different qualities, and perform different characters and social types when they walk a runway. Realness is a marker of quality: of the convincingness of a queen's outfit, the brio and charisma of their movement as they perform different identities and walk down the runway as if it were a sidewalk. That relationship between the street and the runway, the public and private, underpins the other function of realness. When the streets are unsafe for queer and trans people, and particularly queer and trans people of color, the capacity to "pass" (as straight, as male etc.), to temper the flamboyant self of the ballroom, to hide it beneath more conventional garbs, is not just a competitive feat. It is a practical reality, a mode of survival.

"You've got to be real," sings Cheryl Lynn on the iconic 1978 disco track that closes out *Paris Is Burning.* Realness may be ballroom's primary philosophy, but it has also been a divisive idea, both among critics responding to Livingston's film and also within the community. The late bell hooks famously critiqued *Paris Is Burning* for the power dynamics of its production. She argued that Livingston, a Yale-educated white filmmaker entering a marginalized space, offered up an unquestioning portrayal of the desire for conventional status in the white heteronormative world. Could the ball really be celebrated as a space where people embraced their difference, when one of the main competitions was about crafting realistic illusions of those more powerful?

Gender theorist Judith Butler responded by arguing that "realness," as conveyed in *Paris Is Burning*, was not about actually attaining the markers of normality, but was instead a form of radical play, exposing the theatrical quality of gender itself. If establishment social types like "executive realness" (the suit-and-tie look of the corporate world) and "town and country" (rich, WASPy look of the Hamptons) could be performed by the ball's flaming walkers, many of them visibly queer and trans, the distinctions between these groups are revealed as false and arbitrary, a set of inherited attitudes that society unthinkingly reproduces. A satirical attitude to the straight world is characteristic of queer culture, and this breakdown of received categories is one of the premises of drag itself. Drag, in the words of pioneering trans writer Kate Bornstein, author of the landmark book *Gender Outlaw*, is "the runway at the heart of postmodern gender theory," the "proudly flamboyant performance of a broken binary." An act of resistance.

And yet, despite the efforts of gender outlaws, those categories remain stubbornly intact. The gender binary is held as sacrosanct among those who proudly claim the title "trans-exclusionary." In this unequal landscape, the struggles of those who are simply fighting to live can be misunderstood, romanticized, and appropriated, even by those who seem well-intentioned. This was exactly what bell hooks was concerned about in relation to *Paris Is Burning*, noting how many of the white middle-class viewers in the screening she was at responded to the film with laughter, a reaction that seemed, at best, misplaced, going against the grain of what was being shown on-screen. In their negotiations of realness, many of the queens appeared to appropriate the trappings of straight society and mainstream culture to their own ends, a bid for safety and their own form of stardom. The material realities of their lives, for the most part, did not change. When the script is flipped the other way, and stars of the dominant culture take their cues from ballroom, things tend to turn out differently.

"I thought it was a really cool dance," Madonna recalled, of voguing, "very presentational, elegant, all about vanity." When she released the single "Vogue," her homage to the form, in 1990, voguing had reached peak visibility, in no small part because of Livingston's film. With a music video choreographed by and starring esteemed dancers from the community, Jose Gutierez Xtravaganza and Luis Xtravaganza Camacho, Madonna's disco-inflected house track involved some of the individuals from inside the scene. The singer herself was no stranger to New York's dance circuit, having spent the early years of her career as a regular and performer at the city's discotheques in the 1980s. When she hit the big time as a mainstream pop star, she was also one of the most vocal advocates for the queer community, and raised awareness about HIV/AIDS at a time when few in her position did. The world of voguing was not far away from the one that made her. All the same, voguing was not truly her world.

"Vogue" may be a certified banger in Madonna's back catalogue, still sampled and riffed upon in contemporary pop. But as an homage, it defanged voguing's political edge. Most egregiously, it included a rap section that name-checked a long list of iconic Hollywood actors, while neglecting ballroom's homegrown players, or indeed anyone who wasn't an established white star from the 1950s. (Beyoncé redressed this in her 2022 sample of "Vogue"—released alongside her own homage to ballroom and the house music that grew from it—with a spoken-word list shouting out Black musical legends like Nina Simone, Lauryn Hill, and Janet Jackson, as well as multiple drag houses from the contemporary scene.) Madonna brought the flamboyance of ballroom to the masses for a brief moment in the early 1990s, but not without effacing some of the form's origins in the process.

Much ink has been spilled on the concept of cultural appropriation, the way that particular symbols, aesthetics, and lived experiences are mined for parts by those who have no immediate or given relation to them, and who are usually more visible and powerful than the people they borrow from. Whether it is done respectfully or poorly, an act of avowed appreciation or straight-up copy, appropriation has long been a divisive issue, and contemporary pop culture is never short of examples. Black aesthetics, as critic Lauren Michele Jackson notes, have frequently been imitated by non-Black artists, from Christina Aguilera to Miley Cyrus, as a way of signaling sexual availability and maturity. Queer culture, similarly, has been a treasure trove of looks, phrases, and moves that are regularly extracted from their original contexts, and tried on for size, to provide a dash of color, a sense of vibrancy, or left-field edge. The ubiquity of the phrases "Yasss queen" and "slay"—originating in the flamboyant vernacular of ballroom, and brought to popular attention by *RuPaul's Drag Race*—is just one example.

The related concept of "queer-baiting" belongs to this same arena, a charge often placed at the door of a contemporary pin-up like singer Harry Styles. He wears stylish, gender-bending looks, in magazine editorials and on red carpets, but has never labeled his sexuality or relationship to queerness, with many presuming (not unreasonably, given his public dating history) that he is straight. Few argue that Styles is not *allowed* to wear these things; more often than not, the issue of appropriation is not one of permission. Only in the case of outright plagiarism or uncredited imitation does the law take a position, and while the court of public opinion is an increasingly potent forum when it comes to reputational damage, artists continue to copy and paste regardless. Some even argue that appropriation of some kind is an intrinsic part of the creative act. Even true originals, like the boundary-pushing icon David Bowie, a clear reference point for Styles's fashion, took cues from the queer subcultures he orbited in the 1970s. Influenced by the freakish, confronting aesthetics of the trans performers he knew in New York, like punk rocker Jayne County, who reflects on the star's borrowings in her memoir *Man Enough to Be a Woman*, Bowie saw the power that androgyny could have for his own image.

What appropriation actually lays bare are the stakes at hand, the unequal social structures that separate the powerful and the marginalized. Much of the discourse around this issue is rooted in the wider injustices it exposes. "I'll put on something that feels really flamboyant, and I don't feel crazy wearing it," Styles once commented in an interview about fashion, "it's like a superhero outfit." For him, "clothes are there to have fun with and experiment with and play with. What's exciting is that all of these lines are just kind of crumbling away." Sounding less like a cynical appropriator than a positive role model, Styles has a point, one that is hard to argue with. Why should anyone be boxed in by the boundaries of menswear and womenswear? The premise of queer-baiting can quite easily be argued the other way: In some respects, the flamboyance of a Harry Styles seems like a net positive. In his role as a celebrity, he expands our sense of how it is possible to look and dress as a man, seemingly free of toxic hang-ups about masculinity.

In truth, however, those gendered lines are not simply crumbling away. The impulse to praise an enlightened relationship to fashion, unless it is matched by a commitment to uplifting those for whom choosing what to wear has real consequences, should be tempered. The sense of playfulness that Styles enjoys about contemporary fashion, the experimentation and dress-up of donning a "superhero outfit," is often weaponized in contemporary discourse against trans people, and used to question their true gender and the reality of their experiences. The tidy narrative of historical progress, based on advances made for women's rights, gay rights, and trans rights, is not borne out in our political reality.

Visibility alone only takes things so far. It may change minds, but it cannot, by itself, create better conditions for marginalized people. Nor does it necessarily pay the bills. While Madonna scored a number one hit with "Vogue," before moving on to her next reinvention, many of the form's innovators, and the main players of *Paris Is Burning*, continued to lead precarious lives, without access to the cachet and the cash that began to flow during voguing's moment in the spotlight. Several of them were HIV-positive and died from AIDS-related illnesses in the years following its release.

Livingston's film is alive to these harsh realities, even if, by most accounts, the aftercare of its participants was insufficient, and their hopes of a breakthrough went unmet. Like *Portrait of Jason*, the film probes at the line between fantasy and reality, although from a different perspective, with greater awareness that performance is, in the end, not merely dishonest, but a way of life. (Jason Holliday, for that matter, never did become a star, although Clarke's portrait gave him a cult status in the world of independent cinema.) At the film's conclusion, Livingston leaves us with a final shot of the young queen and sex worker Venus Xtravaganza, lighting up a cigarette by the Hudson River and looking out into the distance. In this moment of immortalization, a voice-over by her drag mother, Dorian Corey, reveals that Xtravaganza was violently murdered by one of her johns. It is a harrowing revelation, one that dispels any audience illusions about what we are witnessing on-screen. The voguers of *Paris Is Burning* are not living in a fantasy world, nor are their acts of self-expression or realness merely performative (another word with a derogatory charge). In their commitment to flourishing, they can hardly afford to deny the reality of life outside the ballroom.

Performed in real time and space, flamboyant acts entail wildly different risks, depending on who is doing them, and who is looking. It is worth distinguishing, then, between the different forms this performance can take. There is fantasy as play, the capacity to dream things up, to try something out, to don a different costume for a night. Fun and frictionless, as in a child's game. Then there is fantasy as a protest, a lived experience, which may draw upon the same strategies of invention in its flamboyant refusal to accept reality as given. It is a demand to be recognized outside of the preexisting categories we are born into, and a performance of something true, a way of subverting those categories and keeping it real, whatever the consequences. While the ball conjures a space of community and theatrical excellence, a space where realness can be practiced, and flamboyance nurtured, out on the streets, before uncertain audiences, there is nowhere to hide the flame.

WALKING

WASHINGTON, DC, THE late 1980s. One summer's afternoon, a man, Black, late twenties, stepped off the bus in his home neighborhood of Mount Pleasant, in the northwest of the city. He had spent his day running errands downtown, passing the officials and the suits who populate the White House and the surrounding corridors of political power. He was not dressed in a suit, but his own kind of uniform, signaling his vocation. A bright fireball-red T-shirt, tinted with a little orange. Unmissable in the afternoon sun, the color was as confronting as the text visibly emblazoned on his T-shirt. Thick, white letters, spelling out the words FAG CLUB.

He had expected his choice of day wear might ruffle a few more feathers when he boarded the bus, or walked along the downtown streets. But it went unremarked upon, besides a few surprised looks from passersby. By the time he returned to Mount Pleasant and stopped off at the supermarket for groceries on his way home, he had practically forgotten that he was wearing it. It came as a surprise, then, when he heard someone by the supermarket doors shout: "Look, everybody, there's a faggot in the store!" There was something curious about the phrasing, the man thought, as if the "faggot" in question might be some kind of superhero. Was it a bird, a plane, or some otherworldly force the oblivious shoppers needed to spot, and take shelter from?

What happened next did not shift the tectonic plates of history. The man showed no particular resistance to this comment, gave no blistering retort. Nor was there any grand act of solidarity from any of his fellow shoppers. It was rather a quotidian encounter, complicated and surprising in the ways that everyday life can be. When he turned around to recognize his antagonist, the man noticed that it was not a fully grown adult, as he might have expected, but a ten-year-old Black boy. A boy who later approached him at the checkout till and asked him questions about the T-shirt, and whether he could buy one locally for his gay cousin.

The man explained that he bought it in San Francisco. The boy followed up his questions by affirming that he liked the T-shirt, or rather that his cousin would like it. He did not think you could buy a T-shirt like that in DC. It is then that this exchange came into focus. Although it might have seemed, at first, like a verbal attack, of the sort that the man was used to, there was no fear or animosity here. When the boy hailed him with that all-too-familiar f-word, it was not shouted in hate. It was an expression of genuine curiosity, maybe even a sense of affinity.

The man in this story is the poet, performer, and gay activist Essex Hemphill, a beloved member of Washington DC's Black arts scene in the 1980s. Growing up in the working-class neighborhoods of the city's southeast, Hemphill well understood the pressures on boys, and particularly Black boys, to uphold the received norms of masculinity. "I had to carefully allow my petals to unfold," he wrote of his early adolescence. "I was already alert enough to know what happened to the flamboyant boys at the school who were called 'sissies' and 'faggots.'" The threat of violence and humiliation was always around the corner, and exhibiting flamboyance was risky. He had girlfriends in high school, a temporary cover for his sexuality, but he was not into sports like the other boys. Instead, the young Hemphill found solace in words, and began writing poetry when he was fourteen, a kindling of later fires.

Hemphill had a clear picture of what a life of uniformity would look like for him, the masculine ideals and inflexible identities that Black men were supposed to grow into. "I didn't want to strike cool poses on the corner and father numerous children to prove my manhood," he once wrote. "I didn't want my anger to disfigure me with various kinds of self-abuse and self-hating behavior. I could not use exaggerated bravado and butch drag to smother my homo yearnings." Rather than fall in line, Hemphill chose to live truthfully in his flamboyance. He attributed this decision to the influence of an older Black man with whom he had a love affair as a teenager.

While flamboyant behavior was verboten, Hemphill recalls that many of the boys he grew up around also had discreet sexual relationships with each other, and with older men who lived in the neighborhood. George was thirty years older, a former boxer and volunteer at a local Episcopal church, physically imposing but gentle and high-minded, intellectual and well-read. Although he lived in the closet, and could not bear to come out as gay, George's example showed the young Hemphill an alternative model of adult life, shaped by the flamboyant pursuits of literature and art.

Unlike George, who belonged to a different generation of gay men, Hemphill pursued his flamboyant life openly and without apology. He was fully aware of the risks this entailed, day-by-day, and in particular at night when, as he wrote in the poem "In the Life," he would wear tight-fitting jeans and gold jewelry to cruise the street for sexual partners. Dressing in a style that was legibly gay was a way of being noticed, of finding his kin, but also posed the risk of being noticed by the wrong people.

In another, unpublished poem, Hemphill recounts a lonely small-hours walk to Meridian Hill, a once-verdant park that had fallen into destitution, an epicenter of the crack epidemic that swept through DC, and which also doubled up as a gay cruising ground at night. As a police patrol car comes into view, Hemphill ponders whether the officers can see the flames of desire in his eyes; when the car passes without stopping, and the predicted police encounter does not transpire, he wonders if they have assumed that he only poses a danger to himself. These two facts of his existence, his racial identity and his desires, make him hypervisible, vulnerable not only to the police, who would often target and mistreat Black citizens, but to the acts of street violence that may await him around the corner.

As a performer, Hemphill possessed great theatrical flair—many of his poetry readings were conceived in collaboration with theater makers and musicians—and he was fierce and uncompromising in his political convictions. Not just gay as in happy, but flamboyant as in angry. There was a lot to be angry about in his era, from inaction about HIV/AIDS and the crack epidemic, both of which disproportionately affected the Black community, racist and exclusionary attitudes within the white gay community, and the oppressive actions of politicians and lawmakers in his own city. When he was awarded funding for his work by the federal arts commission and invited to perform at their ceremony, the director asked him to omit the word *corruption* from his poem "Family Jewels," about the racist inequalities of daily life in DC, for fear that it would upset the city's mayor, in attendance that night. He agreed in the moment. But when he got up on stage, he read the poem as written, which was met with thunderous applause from the audience.

When Hemphill walked into the supermarket in Mount Pleasant that sunny afternoon, dressed in his FAG CLUB T-shirt, it was an act of everyday defiance in itself, a protest of one. Boldly announcing his faggotry, he was spreading the word about his people, a club whose members were dying from the still-mysterious disease. But it was also a lesson in the politics of style, simple but effective. When we imagine a flamboyant outfit, we might first think of the extravagant world of fashion, the eccentric figure of "crocodile in the street," or the "superhero suit" donned by a celebrity in couture. But sometimes all it takes is a simple red T-shirt with a provocative slogan, worn casually with jeans.

Hemphill walked away from this encounter with a simple mantra in his mind. *If I simply wanted status*, he said to himself, *I could wear Calvin Klein and strike a pose. That's safe.* Logos confer status, but also a sense of safe familiarity. They are designed to make a brand or a label or a company recognizable, but also to offer a glimpse at what it offers, what it feels like. By wearing a logo, you might also be cosigning what a particular brand stands for. In that way, logos and labels resemble being part of a club, an imagined community pledging (and wearing) their allegiance to the same thing. At either the low- or the high-end, there is a certain comfort in brand recognition and group membership. In refusing the call of Calvin Klein, the trendy underwear brand that was heavily associated with gay men in its promotional campaigns in the 1980s, Hemphill was refusing the uniformity of conventional fashions associated with the white gay world. In turn, he was announcing that he wanted something more than simply status—you could call it honesty or acceptance, a flamboyant authenticity. When you do not see yourself in the labels on offer, you have to find your own way.

"He pointed out a different way to me," Hemphill remembered of his older lover George, "hinting at others who had gone before us, suggested a tradition, ways of being." Perhaps Hemphill did something similar for the boy at the store that day, if only in passing. Given his own experiences with older men, and the wider moral panic around gay men and young people in this period, it was not surprising that Hemphill felt self-conscious talking to the boy in the supermarket, aware of the connotations that might be read into their interaction. Whether the boy was gay himself, or simply empathetic and interested, in that moment Hemphill acted as a walking symbol of a way of life. By choosing not to hide, he left his young audience member something to remember, to learn from, or imitate. He was, in his own words, "truly voguing."

When I try to picture this afternoon in Essex Hemphill's life, immortalized in his 1991 essay "If I Simply Wanted Status, I'd Wear Calvin Klein," I like to imagine what his walk was like. It is a way to bring him to life in memory, to envision the shapes he made as he stepped off the bus, crossed the street, and entered the supermarket, "truly voguing." Voguing, after all, is a form of walking, and the stories we convey about ourselves in public are found not only in what we wear, but the way we move. "I remember Frank O'Hara's walk," the American writer Joe Brainard once recalled of the poet's "light and sassy" movements along the sidewalk. It was a "beautiful walk. Confident. 'I don't care.' And sometimes 'I know you are looking.'" A flamboyant walk can communicate several things at once, both an armor and a disclosure. Sometimes it protects us and sometimes it gives us away. That gay men walk quickly, mincing or raging down the street with an iced coffee, is a pervasive online trope with a kernel of truth in it, a joke masking something sincere about the image we project in public.

The way women walk is hardly less remarked upon. Amidst the heady mix of unapologetic hedonism and vulnerability that characterized Brat summer, the cultural phenomenon surrounding Charli xcx's 2024 record of the same name, a guest verse by Lorde struck a particular chord. Responding to Charli's admission of complex feelings about their friendship, Lorde reflected on the self she presents to others and the world. "Girl, you walk like a bitch," she recalled someone saying to her at the age of ten, a girlhood grievance that became an instantly iconic line, shouted back with joy and fury by crowds at *Brat* concerts. Tapping into an experience clearly shared by many, Lorde reflected how a bitchy walk often begins, in our younger years, as a form of self-defense. Until it takes you over and you find yourself "building a weapon," armed and ready against the gaze of others. Performed with enough gusto, this stride conveys a projection that becomes believable.

Observing these projections, and trying to reconstruct their meanings, is one of the pleasures of people watching. "Everybody is quite peculiar now and then," the poet, dance critic, and travel writer Edwin Denby, a friend of Frank O'Hara's, once observed. He was talking about the great variety of life in a big city—in his case, New York City in the 1960s—and how you can see "everything in the world here in isolated examples." As a professional dance critic, Denby knew how to see the beauty and power in the way people occupy space and identify the precision and effect of dancers' movements. He also encouraged his students to apply this way of looking to the everyday.

In a lecture titled "Dancers, Buildings, People in the Street," he advised his audience to look out for the presence of dancing in daily life, the "pretty movements and gestures people make." Well-traveled, and deeply curious about the world beyond New York and the United States, Denby found different cultural variations of walking on the streets on the city. From the way "American young men loll . . . resting on a peripheral point," to the "Italian *contraposto*," characterized by small turns and "shorter muscles, more complex in their plasticity," and the "miraculous stroll" of men and women from the Caribbean.

Although Denby's grouping of walks by national heritage feels reductive, he is right that we often perceive others culturally, consciously or unconsciously. For him, a walk exists on a larger continuum of beautiful things you can see in the daily life of the city, from a stranger who moves a little like a dancer, to the wonders of architecture, "the peculiar ways buildings end in the air" and the "fantastic differences in their street facades." As we know, buildings and people can both be accurately described as flamboyant. When we encounter flamboyance in another person, we fall into this odd slippage between life and art, person and object.

I always knew that I was "a little light in the loafers," to quote an old-school euphemism commonly used about gay men. But I had never given much serious thought to the way I walked until I read Denby's essay for the first time, at university. Around the same time, I was also getting into student theater, which gave me a slightly more practical education in movement. In my final year, I was cast in a small role in a production of Arthur Miller's *A View from the Bridge*. I was playing a longshoreman from Brooklyn in the 1950s, one of a group who had to walk on and exchange a few words with the main character at the play's midpoint. The conversation was about another of the play's characters, a flamboyant Italian man with dyed blond hair and a "funny" (as in gay) way of walking and talking.

My character, however, was supposed to project a tough, masculine self-confidence. In the movement rehearsal, my gay ass could just not get the hang of walking butch. I found it hard to connect my shoulders, which seemed to be the part of a body where a walk like this emanates from, held firm in a kind of aggressive tension, without it seeming like a parody of masculine movement. More than anything else, this probably spoke to my limitations as an actor, but it also made me see my own, somewhat effete movements in a new light.

Some years later, on a cobbled street in the same university town, I saw my walk reflected back at me through the actions of others. I was leaving a poetry reading to go and meet my sister for dinner. I had a few white wines earlier that evening and I could feel the way they had loosened up my body. I was walking down the street quite slowly, languorously, in a way that felt almost involuntary, my defenses down. It was like an expression of exactly the state of mind I was in at the time, leaving a gossipy voice note to a friend about a boy I fancied.

I noticed a white van parked up the street. As I sauntered closer, the engine started and it moved toward me. It stopped as it passed me, and a man and a boy who did not look much older than ten, pulled down the window, their faces arranged in cheeky grins. Before I had a moment to clock what was happening, the boy grabbed a bottle of Fanta, half empty, and threw it at my face, clearly egged on by the man as they both shouted "Poof!" out the window, and drove off.

By this point in my life, in my late twenties, I had come out of my shell a bit. I had moved to Manhattan and back, fallen in love for the first time, made new friends in nightclubs. I could feel these changes begin to reveal themselves in the way I walked and talked. This moment felt like a reminder that showing ourselves fully, expressing it even in small or everyday ways, can still cost us a sense of safety or comfort. As acts of street harassment go, it was mild. The fact that it was a remarkable event for me was itself a sign that I had lived most of my adult life unbothered by the hostility of others. Nonetheless, it had an effect on me.

My own self-defense had never been to walk like a bitch or move like a flame. Quite the opposite: I had always hoped to blend into the background, to evade detection. After that moment, I vowed to stop capitulating. That if I felt like walking with an extra flounce, I would do it. I have not always stuck to this. But the history of flamboyance is populated by those who have refused to dull their flame, who have made their walk both an art and a weapon.

Sometimes it takes the parameters of a visual artwork, the homing in and zooming out, to notice what Zadie Smith calls "the performance art of everyday life." Smith made this observation about a 2005 video work by the American artist Mark Bradford, a four-minute film that I remember being totally transfixed by when I saw it in the American Pavilion of the Venice Biennale in 2017. The film is simple in scope—an exterior shot of a street in South Central Los Angeles, with the camera resting at ground level on the sidewalk, flanked by chain link fences on one side, and lampposts and parked cars on the other. In the foreground of the shot is Melvin, a young Black man. He has his back to us—he is walking down the sidewalk, away from the position of the camera. But we have a clear visual of his clothes from behind: a gray tank top, tucked into buttercup-yellow linen shorts, with white sports socks pulled up to his shins, and black shoes.

It is a fairly casual outfit, not particularly flamboyant besides the pop of the yellow shorts. Instead, the eye is drawn to the flamboyance of his walk, the way his arms swing rhythmically through the air, and his hips sway from side to side with each step. As viewers we know almost nothing about Melvin. The film gives us no access to either his face or his interiority. All we have to go on is his strident, captivating walk, and the way it interacts with the visual landscape of the shot, the cracked sidewalk and the weeds growing up through the concrete. A certain defiance is at play here. We may not know much or anything about Melvin, but from the perspective of an onlooker, he seems very much like someone who knows himself.

Melvin was artist Mark Bradford's former neighbor in Los Angeles, a figure often seen walking around the neighborhood near his studio. The personal connection might make the film seem like candid footage, captured on the hoof. But Bradford carefully uses the techniques of cinema to allow us to see Melvin differently. For one, the film unfolds in slow motion, a visual artifice that allows us to admire his dramatic movements. But it is also framed as a visual homage to Marilyn Monroe.

Bradford's video is not named *Melvin* but *Niagara*, after the 1953 film noir in which Monroe starred. The film contains a famously extended shot of her character, a femme fatale named Rose, getting out of a car and sashaying down the street, beyond the camera's frame. The scene is often celebrated as the "longest walk" in cinematic history, one that helped to solidify Monroe's status as a star by capturing the sheer charisma of her movements, strident and suggestive. Maybe Bradford's film serves a similar end—it gives Melvin the star treatment.

But there is more to the Marilyn Monroe reference. Although this scene from *Niagara* is an iconic one, in the context of the film it is full of dread, as we observe that Rose's walk is leading to a violent (and fatal) confrontation with her husband. So there is something morbid and vulnerable, too. A queasy sense that, by the dramatic logic of the film, Monroe's Rose will be punished for her transgressions, figured here by that unmistakable walk. Bradford's film also captures a sense of threat, the uncanny feeling that Melvin's street spectacle might bear consequences. The danger is implicit, beyond the frame, but there is an unpredictable quality to the eerily empty urban scene he walks in. As an audience, we do not know who can see Melvin, nor who may be around the corner: a homophobic tough, a racist police officer. He seems fearless, even when there is plenty to fear.

"Think about a man, walking down a street in South Central, swishing, or swaying back and forth," Bradford noted. "What does that mean, for a man to take public space and own it for himself, and use it as a runway?" These are some of the questions his work poses. *Niagara* trains our eye on Melvin's "fearless embodiment of flamboyance in an especially tough public sphere," as Bradford puts it, an act which belongs to a longer tradition of queer people of color reclaiming space. As far back as the nineteenth-century "cakewalk," performed by formerly enslaved Black people after emancipation, and all the way through the history of ballroom, there has been a rich seam between walking and dancing for marginalized people.

These forms of movement have allowed communities to parody and rewrite the hostile terms of the cultures they live in, to act out against the ways they are seen by their oppressors, and to create joyous or liberating performances in the process. Zadie Smith calls it the "nuclear option of the disenfranchised"—making something out of very little—through steps that possess the "political urgency of street-level grace." In this light, the flamboyance of dance shares common ground with the flamboyance of walking, each of them ways of moving with radical potential. They are practiced, on a daily basis, by fearless individuals, the lone rangers of the sidewalk, and, more communally, by groups seeking pleasure and camaraderie on street corners and dance floors. But also, most urgently of all, by those who gather en masse in the spirit of resistance, who place their bodies in the streets and the firing line, and give the word *protest* its name.

RESISTING

"THE TIME FOR flamboyance is behind us and ahead of us," wrote David B. Goodstein, publisher of gay American magazine *The Advocate*, in 1977, "not now." The years following the Stonewall riots of 1969 had been an era of flourishing for many queer people, characterized by a newfound openness, sexual freedom, revolutionary fervor, and great parties. But by the late 1970s there was a clamping down on homosexuality in parts of the country, an anti-flamboyant backlash in the political sphere. Goodstein was referring in his forecast to two recent developments: Anita Bryant's "Save Our Children" campaign in Dade County, Florida, which aimed to repeal the rights of gay and lesbian teachers, allowing them to be fired on the basis of sexual orientation, lest they "recruit" children, and Senator John Briggs's Proposition 6 in California, which also sought to ban gay and lesbian teachers from teaching in public schools. Building support for the campaign to resist Proposition 6, Goodstein argued that flamboyance would have to take a back seat. "If we do not project a non-threatening, very ordinary image," he wrote in his editorial, "we will blow it."

Goodstein represented a particular sect of the gay community, whose advocates expressed a certain caution about how gay people behaved and were perceived in public. They perhaps did not believe that true liberation—the acceptance of all queer people, however flamboyant or rebellious—could be achieved. It was a pragmatic approach, but also a pessimistic one, and it no doubt mostly served the interests of the circles Goodstein moved in, populated by gay professionals who could blend into the social life of the establishment more easily than others. An investment banker turned activist, Goodstein bought *The Advocate* magazine in 1975 and relocated it from Los Angeles to San Francisco, in the hopes of making it a major and respectable publication. The projection of a "non threatening" image on the gay community's part was a touchstone of his activism, and he advocated for assimilation over spectacle, political lobbying over street-level demonstrations.

As a public gay figure, Goodstein was a foil to the flamboyant San Francisco politician Harvey Milk. The first openly gay elected public official in California, Milk used his platform to resist Proposition 6, and famously played a major role in defeating it, although he achieved his ends using rather different means. Not content to project a "nonthreatening" image as a way of garnering votes, Milk was a bold and theatrical presence, and a charismatic public speaker. He advocated above all for visibility, and encouraged people to come out and take to the streets. In Milk's view, flamboyance was exactly the right source to be drawing upon in the face of homophobia, a means of fighting fire with fire. His flamboyant advocacy is one of the things he is most remembered for. Milk was murdered, at the age of forty-eight, by conservative city official Dan White in November 1978, less than three weeks after the defeat of Proposition 6.

While the events of the late 1970s stoked tensions within the community about the most effective methods for achieving social change, flamboyant protest had long been a hallmark of liberationist movements, and had often divided opinion. Earlier in the decade, the "zaps" performed by gay, lesbian, and trans activist groups were a particularly potent method. Inspired by the radical civil rights and anti-Vietnam movements of the 1960s, demonstrators would interrupt gatherings and confront public figures, suddenly and without warning. They often did so with a theatrical flair, dressing in flamboyant costumes and drag, and mocking their political opponents. As a form of street theater, a zap was intended, primarily, to attract attention, and to encourage people to join the movement. At first, the gay activist Arthur Bell argued, people might be "vaguely disturbed at demonstrators for 'rocking the boat,'" but "when they see how the straight establishment responds, they feel anger." Flamboyant actions could be a useful tool for winning over skeptics, because they exposed the brute force of an anti-flamboyant society, the policing of demonstrations that were disruptive but, for the most part, nonviolent.

There is a famous photograph from the Christopher Street Liberation Day in New York in 1970, one of the first Gay Pride marches, to commemorate the events at Stonewall Inn a year earlier. The photograph features the lesbian artist and activist Donna Gottschalk standing in the street, facing the camera with an inscrutable but uncompromising look, and holding up a sign. It reads: "I Am Your Worst Fear. I Am Your Best Fantasy." It is pithy and defiant, perfect for a protest placard. It communicates the double-sided fear that informs prejudice, in this case the prejudices directed at queer people. The fear *is* the fantasy.

What instils fear about a lesbian living openly and defiantly, against the grain of social norms, particularly in the 1970s, is the threat she poses to those things we are taught to think of as normal. Domesticity, compliance, the choke hold of respectability. It may be churlish to say that all homophobes want to be us, to fall back on the cliché that they are secretly gay. And yet, there is a palpable sense of exposure among them when queer people are flamboyantly themselves, and embody both the nightmares and the dreams of the straight world. When one person colors outside the lines, when a thousand people choose to stand out en masse, it sends a message to whoever is watching. You could do this, too, and have fun doing it. Forsaking the solemnity of a sit-in, a march, or more peaceful forms of direct action, the sting in the tail of flamboyant protest is the sense of joie de vivre, the centering of play and pleasure as a response to injustice.

Flamboyance remained divisive during the political in-fights of the 1970s, and attempts within the community to suppress it inspired countermovements within the movement, protests within protests. The visibility of drag queens and transvestites at Pride—figures who had played an important role politically ever since Stonewall, and who we would today more likely describe as trans women—revealed a political fracture. The 1973 Christopher Street Liberation Day was a perfect storm, in this regard. It was in that year that the parade committee sought to ban drag queens from appearing in the march, lest they give the movement a "bad name," and the feminist lesbian group the Radicalesbians called for the same thing, because they viewed drag and female impersonation as demeaning to women, a parody based on gendered stereotypes.

In response, the trans activist and Stonewall veteran Sylvia Rivera stormed the stage and took the microphone. In her impromptu speech, she spoke about the pain and suffering she had experienced in her life, compounded by her attempted exclusion by gay men and lesbians. It was a howl of rage, a demand to be seen and heard that marked an important moment in queer history, but was met with boos and hisses from the crowd, and some applause by those who believed in Rivera's cause. Nonetheless, drag queens did appear at the 1973 parade, including queens who performed at the East Village establishment Club 82, a mafia-owned drag bar with a mostly straight clientele. When they marched along Christopher Street, they carried a banner emblazoned with Club 82, a walking advertisement for the bar itself. The seeds of numerous contemporary issues—from the politics of respectability and the commercialization of Pride, to the precursors of TERF ideology among gay men and lesbians, and the ban on drag performers in the US—can be found here, at an historical moment when the question of who was allowed to be flamboyant, and visible, was being contested.

The unique power of flamboyant protest was thrown into relief in the 1980s, when the onset of the HIV/AIDS epidemic, and the government's inaction, called for collaboration, and for groups that were trans-inclusive and intersectional. The fight ahead certainly called for something stronger than a well-behaved picket line. The loud, theatrical protests of ACT UP (AIDS Coalition to Unleash Power), with their arresting black and pink visuals and signature "die-ins," which saw demonstrators drop to the ground and play dead, in homage to the deceased, were a hallmark of protests in this era. While these actions brought a sense of levity, and a dash of bright color to the streets, they were also deadly serious. The social grievance being resisted—the neglect of the government toward people dying of AIDS, and the gatekeeping of medical information by the pharmaceutical industry—was a matter of life and death. ACT UP's methods were carried forward, in the 1990s, by groups like the Lesbian Avengers, who performed actions that were "fabulous, original and witty," as their protest handbook put it, using a wide range of visuals including flaming torches and, most famously, "fire-eating."

The Lesbian Avengers first ate fire in 1992, following the murders of a Black lesbian and white gay man, Hattie Mae Cohens and Brian Mock, who were killed by a white supremacist firebomb attack at their apartment in Oregon. The Avengers established a shrine for the deceased, emblazoned with the words "Burned To Death For Being Who They Were," and the activists involved sought to "transform the image of their deaths by learning to eat fire," in the words of co-founder Kelly Cogswell. Having learned the art of fire-eating, a precarious choreography involving a rag, lighter fluid, and a well-timed exhalation, the Avengers performed it by the shrine as a "circus trick transformed into a sacrament." They recited lines about taking "the fire of action into our hearts," and transforming the fire of their enemies in order to "make it our own."

These flamboyant actions were forms of embodied activism, mourning rituals in which the bodies of participants were placed front and center. "The bodies that say 'I will not disappear easily,'" notes Judith Butler, of contemporary protest movements, "or, 'My disappearance will leave a vibrant trace from which resistance will grow,' are effectively asserting their grievability within the public sphere." In unequal societies, Butler argues—which is to say, all societies—not all citizens are considered equally grievable. In the 1980s and 1990s, this was particularly true of people with AIDS; many queer people who died from the disease were forced back into the closet by their families, after death, their lives shrouded in a shameful silence. In our own era, differences in grievability, Butler notes, are demonstrated by the modern state's violence toward marginalized groups, including migrants and refugees, trans people, and people of color. The flamboyance of embodied activism remains a powerful tool of resistance across different struggles and communities, and among those whose bodies do not conform to society's imagined norms.

"It was the old handcuffing ourselves to London buses, Westminster Bridge, or wherever," remembers Liz Carr, the Olivier Award–winning actor and disability activist, protesting the inaccessibility of the city's transport system. For her, the vocations of acting and activism go hand in hand: "it's about getting attention, flamboyance, exhibitionism, getting in the press, having an audience." It is ACT UP protesters marching down the streets of Paris, dressed in bright pink, performing a dance routine with pom-poms. It is fake blood thrown across the clinical white surfaces of a negligent pharmaceutical company's New York office. It is bright red paint thrown at a Van Gogh masterpiece by climate protestors, the brightly colored liquid separated from the artwork itself by a protective screen. Flamboyance, at its most political, takes what might be perceived as a character flaw, an excessive desire for attention, and turns it into a collective force. It is both incandescent and inconvenient, an affront to the polite regularities of the status quo, and the violence it perpetuates against those excluded.

🔥

Plenty of people who describe themselves as sympathetic to the cause of a given movement are turned off by flamboyant protests. This speaks to a difference in opinion about how politics should be done, but also, I think, a deeper fault line, a cultural and social aversion to flamboyance as an act. A revealing example of this attitude can be found in a feminist sci-fi film from the early 1980s, which feels reminiscent of today's headlines in numerous ways.

Picture, for a moment, a society after an economic revolution, which has established a system of equality, freed from the dominant logic of capitalism and the market. No longer governed by wealthy charlatans or neoliberal ideologues, the country is now steered by a social democratic government, with a clear focus on provision for all. This is the kind of utopian image that has long fueled leftist political movements, an idealized vision of a more just society, always on the horizon, never quite achieved. What would happen if it were achieved? If the inequities of contemporary life were cut off at the root, and society were reorganized within, would peace finally be possible, in a world without discord, without the need for protest or resistance?

This is one of the questions posed by *Born in Flames*. Shot by director Lizzie Borden (born Linda Elizabeth Borden) over five years in New York, on a shoestring budget with nonprofessional actors, the film's perspective seems radical even by today's standards. It is both of its time, inspired by the activist fervor of the feminist and gay liberation movements, and ahead of it. It envisions an imagined world that feels neither utopian nor dystopian, and one that bears some resemblance to the world we live in today, with several important differences.

The film begins with news broadcasts celebrating the anniversary of a social democratic revolution, which took place in America ten years earlier. But all is not well in this new society. Despite the economic sea change, inequality persists, and racism and misogyny are no less a part of daily life. A number of feminist collectives, from the radical activist Women's Army, to two different pirate radio stations led by white punks and Black lesbians, are preparing to fight back against the violence and discrimination that women continue to face in the new world order.

Not all women in the story are sympathetic to the activist cause. The middle-class white women who work as editors for the nation's socialist newspaper regularly patronize these radical groups live on-air, in radio and television interviews. Toeing the party line, they suggest that the activists are acting out because of their "gratuitous desire for excitement and romanticism, and the idea of revolution." These women had once been at the forefront of political change, on the frontlines of the revolution ten years previously. But now they show little empathy for the struggles of the present day, and suggest that the contemporary activists merely feel "a certain amount of envy for experiences that you and I had," as if the youngsters are just cosplaying the revolutionary movements of yore, and distracting from the political progress that has been made.

Generational conflict is a hallmark of many political movements. This scene in *Born in Flames* also shows how power and respectability can change people's outlook, in the case of these privileged white socialists, now distanced from the things that they once held dear. It is a classic example of an anti-flamboyant attitude, the suggestion that the protest has no meaning behind it, fed not by radical thinking or a genuine desire for change, but an attention-seeking affectation, a romance for the aesthetics of revolution. In the end, the editors come around to the cause. They are radicalized once more by the murder of a Black woman and Woman's Army activist, and collaborate with the different movements to stage an intervention on the airwaves.

The act of resistance that concludes the film—the blowing up of the antennae on top of the World Trade Center, a symbolic explosion of the media and its propaganda machine, but one that crucially is not intended to harm any human life—of course feels shocking today for different reasons. It is haunted by the shadow of 9/11. But in its original context, it strikes a revolutionary note, a sensationalist fire that sends a clear and unambiguous message from the future.

Working with limited resources when making the film, director Lizzie Borden created this final image using a miniature model of the World Trade Center's twin towers, and the illusion of the fire was created by shooting glitter above it in slow motion. (As one critic has noted, "in an obscure way, this film even anticipated glitterbombing," the flamboyant protest tactic and sometime prank, where glitter is thrown over the intended target.) This creative, behind-the-scenes method feels apt, a political fire made of something cheap and chintzy, a sparkling material with its own associations to queer culture. What the final segment of the film affirms, above all, is that coalition is the most effective asset to any resistance movement. It arises from women coming together across racial and class lines, and each bringing their different resources, skills, and cultural backgrounds, which allows for their flamboyant, symbolic acts to have the maximum impact.

"For women, the need and desire to nurture each other is not pathological but redemptive," the poet, activist, and feminist icon Audre Lorde argued, "and it is within that knowledge that our real power is rediscovered." Interdependency, the acknowledgment that we are not all siloed individuals, but groups depending upon each other for our well-being, could be a form of freedom. Race had long been a problem within the feminist movement, and Lorde argued that space should be given over to meaningfully consider racial differences, and the different lived experiences of white women and women of color, rather than pretending they did not exist. Difference, Lorde notes, must not be "merely tolerated, but seen as a fund of necessary polarities between which our creativity can spark." That is what makes fire. "Images of women flaming like torches," she wrote at the beginning of her memoir, *Zami: A New Spelling of My Name*, "adorn and define the borders of my journey." It was their differences, and their defiant spirit, that warranted the term *flaming*, as a collective force.

In the absence of a truly coalitional feminism, many Black feminist groups were compelled to create their own spaces for resistance. These groups were made up not by the mass movements of the streets, although they too marched in protests and launched actions, but a more particular demographic, private and curated. Creating safe spaces for those on the margins of the dominant culture has long been a radical act, an act of separatism as solidarity. The emphasis in these groups was not only on self-care—the political and personal practice first coined by Lorde, but which has today been bowdlerized into marketing copy for scented candles—but of care for others, and mutual understanding of shared experiences. The freedom to act flamboyantly, or authentically, which is too rarely granted in public life.

When Borden's film previewed at a feminist film festival in New York in 1983, it was followed by a live performance from a group called The Flamboyant Ladies Theater Company, a Black feminist collective set up by Alexis De Veaux and Gwendolen Hardwick in 1977. The company produced theatrical works and performances, but it also organized brunches, dances, and protests, and held a regular Saturday Salon at De Veaux and Hardwick's

Brooklyn apartment. The salon setting was a throwback to the flamboyant era of the Harlem Renaissance. It recalled the "rent" parties and private soirees, where the neighborhood's Black luminaries could socialize, for the most part, away from the gawping white tourists from downtown, who quickly caught wind that Harlem was hot.

The new generation of Flamboyant Ladies in this era were mostly younger than Audre Lorde, but the influence of her thought and her work as an activist was clear to see. Alexis De Veaux, a poet, playwright, and friend of Essex Hemphill, was also the author of the first published Audre Lorde biography. The collective's aims was to highlight the artistic work and experiences of women of color in Brooklyn, and the concept of flamboyance was, naturally, of great importance. The name itself was defiant, the scholar Kate Davy has observed, because "ladies" by definition are "not elaborately showy" nor "behave excessively," while the category of the "ladylike" had itself long excluded Black women. Both flamboyance and ladyhood was being reclaimed, and De Veaux saw flamboyance as a form of "outrageousness—a sexual, racial, beautiful extreme" that flouted the "limitations of having to identify as either butch or femme" in Black lesbian culture.

The group's flamboyance could be witnessed in the heightened sensuality of the performances they programmed, with explicit lesbian content that ran against the grain of right-wing homophobia and anxieties within the mainstream feminist movement about the expression of sexuality. As Davy notes, in her history of lesbian theatrical culture in New York, there is a tendency to think of feminist movements of the 1970s and the 1980s as a little dour and humorless, focused on serious political matters at the expense of fun and more playfully subversive tendencies. But as the Flamboyant Ladies showed, there was also a flowering, at this time, of exuberant and rebellious queer performance by lesbian groups, who took something traditionally associated with gay men and drag queens, flamboyance, and remade it in their own image.

The Flamboyant Ladies collective featured a number of esteemed writers in its time, including June Jordan, Jewelle Gomez, and De Veaux herself. Their influence at the time could be felt widely, and they traveled to Europe in 1982 to perform and run workshops at a grassroots women's festival in Amsterdam, an important fixture for feminist groups internationally. It seems no coincidence that a few years later, a feminist and queer organization run by Black and migrant women was founded there, simply named Flamboyant. While the name of De Veaux's New York collective recalled the glamorous and gender-bending years of the Harlem Renaissance, the Amsterdam group looked specifically to natural flamboyance: the bright red tree from the tropics, whose leaves, when flowered, look like they are on fire. For this group, as the scholar Chandra Frank has shown, the tree's flaming defiance of European mores was the perfect metaphor for their organizing. "Contrary to other trees / plants from the tropics," many of which came to be used as houseplants, "the Flamboyant tree has not been tamed and would prefer to die instead of shrinking in the Dutch living room."

The important work of these groups continues to be celebrated by queer and feminist scholars today for the lessons they have to teach us about resistance. Sometimes it looks like a march on the street, and other times the cultivation of a community committed to the flourishing of its members. In claiming a space, they were also reclaiming a concept, expanding its possibilities, and wresting it from the limitations of familiar meanings, the definitions that still today possess a derogatory charge. As many of the flamboyant rebels from this history well knew, one of the places where violence is commonly played out, and in turn resisted, is language itself.

RECLAIMING

"MAYBE YOU'RE A *flambé*," says a character in a 2006 episode of *The Sopranos*, the acclaimed HBO show about a New Jersey crime family. It is a euphemism, capping off a list of slurs. The characters are speaking to head honcho Tony Soprano about the outing of a *capo* (or "boss") in the organization, who is married with a family. He was recently spotted dancing in a gay bar in New York, dressed up in leather "like one of the Village People." As the news spreads throughout the organization, the messengers can barely contain their disdain. They use words that are familiar (*fag*) and particular (like *ricchione*, its Italian slang equivalent), along with innuendos about taking it in the back, cocks up asses, and weight loss associated with AIDS. At no point does anyone say the word *gay*. When one of the men reveals that he is unfazed by this rumor, the accusation is turned back on him, as if being tolerant makes him gay by association. It is then that he is accused of being a "*flambé*."

The scene feels like a round of word association, as if the characters (and maybe also the screenwriters) were thinking up as many insults as they could muster. It is funny that this parlor game ends up at *flambé*, which sounds closer to a dessert you would order in a fancy restaurant than it does a type of person. Unlike the other labels we hear, *flambé* is unrelated to gay sex acts or the cultural taboos around them. It says more about how someone appears—flaming, delicate, ostentatious—than what they do in bed, even if the connection between those things is implicit.

As any extended watch of *The Sopranos* shows, these same men who are freaked out by the idea of flaming gay men are pretty flamboyant themselves. They greet each other with kisses on the cheek. They are impeccably groomed, with slicked hair and tailored suits, loud shirts, and silk dressing gowns. One of them openly gets manicures. As mafioso who mutilate and kill, and hold regressive views about women and gays, these men seem to embody masculinity at its most violent and brutish, all while displaying a precious aesthetic sense traditionally viewed as feminine. Qualities that may seem surprising, as far as masculinity goes, are par for the course in the Italian American enclave of the show, a place with its own value system and set of expectations about how men should look and act. In the world of *The Sopranos*, there are right and wrong ways to be flamboyant. This is also true, of course, of the world outside of it.

Here's another euphemism. On August 3, 1986, *The New York Times* ran an obituary for a powerful man who died the day before, in a Maryland hospital. "ROY COHN, AIDE TO McCARTHY AND FIERY LAWYER," read the headline, "DIES AT 59." During his lifetime, Cohn was well-known as a lead prosecutor in the McCarthy hearings of the 1950s, and for his cruel and unflinching treatment of Ethel and Julius Rosenberg, a married couple who were convicted for being Soviet spies and sentenced to death.

The courtroom, as Harriet Monroe put it, is one of the most flamboyant spaces of American life. The nation "finds the flamboyant in the courts," she wrote, and "listens to every passion-molded word uttered to judge and jury." While the space is known for order and formality, what actually plays out is often highly dramatic. Attorneys draw upon theatrical techniques to convey their arguments, using emphatic gestures, rhetorical flair, and emotive delivery to instill particular feelings in an audience and, most importantly, the jury. The courtroom has long been a source of fascination to those outside the proceedings, from the televised celebrity trials of our own age, which only amplify the sense of theatricality, to the splashy trial reports in newspapers during Monroe's era in the 1920s. Famously ruthless and impassioned, as a prosecutor, Roy Cohn thus built his career in a profession where flamboyant self-presentation was an important skill, although his flamboyance as a figure also went beyond his legal prowess.

While he was famous as a charismatic public figure, with celebrity friends and an expensive lifestyle, Cohn was also infamous as a liar and a crook, who represented mobsters and would stop at nothing to win a case. (Shortly before his death, Cohn was disbarred from the profession for unethical and unprofessional conduct.) In Ali Abbasi's 2024 film *The Apprentice*, where Cohn is played hauntingly by Jeremy Strong, we are shown the long tail of his influence, as the mastermind behind young Donald Trump's rise to prominence. Taking meetings from his ultraviolet sun bed, where he tops up his tan and drinks Paloma cocktails, Cohn seems every part the flamboyant villain. The young athletic men who wait on him hint at the sexuality his conduct barely conceals.

"Why not say 'flaming' and be done with it?" wrote the queer theorist Eve Kosofsky Sedgwick, in her analysis of Cohn's *New York Times* obituary. The loaded meanings behind words like *fiery* and *flamboyant*, she argued, barely hid the "sniggering" accusations about the open secret of Cohn's sexuality, which he vehemently denied, even as he was flagrant about his other transgressions. Just as Cohn insisted during his final days that he was dying from liver cancer, rather than AIDS, despite all the obvious signs, the way he was written about after his death leaned heavily upon euphemism, as if to expose the fragility of the illusion.

Sedgwick studied this obituary not out of sympathy for Cohn, who she described as a "poisonous" figure, but because the fiery language about his legacy exemplifies what she describes as "the spectacle" of the closet, where the implicit reveal about someone's sexuality becomes embedded in public discourse. The implication, in *The New York Times*, was that the homophobia and bigotry of a villain like Cohn might be explained by the fact that he was closeted, which made him abnormal and warped his sense of right and wrong. The readers of the newspaper, presumed straight, perhaps broadly liberal, could rest easy. He was not one of us.

A figure like Roy Cohn was the product of a society that had long repressed queerness and remained squeamish about its expression. Words like *fiery* still did the heavy lifting. At times, it seemed almost like Cohn was testing the boundaries. His lifestyle was hardly subtle, and included summers spent in the gay resort town of Provincetown, and glitzy nights at Studio 54. But without an explicit admission, a singular out-of-the-closet moment, Cohn's flamboyance could only be viewed obliquely. It was a force that was made to seem ominous, contagious, even destructive.

The "flamer" covers a range of social types, a multitude of secrets or sins. While it is often used to describe a transgression of gendered or sexual norms, like the trope of the effeminate gay man, or the unspoken, deviant associations of the "straight" man who has gay sex, it has also been used to describe people who amplify the normative expectations of their gender. In American slang, the "flamer" most often refers to the feminine gay male "queen," but it also has an archaic definition stemming back to the late nineteenth century, meaning "sexually expert," or a "ladies'" man. These are opposite ends of the masculine spectrum, and by the 1960s the word's gay meaning had usurped its straight counterpart, a compliment about a man's sexual prowess and attractiveness that is rarely, if ever, used today. But they have more in common than may first appear.

As the psychoanalyst Erich Fromm put it, often if the stereotypically "masculine *character* traits in a man are weakened because emotionally he has remained a child, he will try to compensate for this lack by the exclusive emphasis on his male role in sex," and the result is often the "Don Juan" figure, who needs to "prove his male prowess in sex because he is unsure of his masculinity." While the flaming queen's flamboyance is an extension of his failure to embody masculinity, the loud and ostentatious sign of a perceived deficiency, the flamboyant swagger of the straight flamer might also be coded as suspicious. What these flamers, gay and straight, have in common is a shared performance, an overcompensation. The proximity between them, as social types, is a source of intrigue but also squeamishness, if only because it reveals a fine line between seemingly polar opposites.

As I watched *The Apprentice*, a few weeks before the 2024 election, there seemed to me few more naked examples of a flamboyance forged from distorted masculinity, and feelings of insecurity, than Roy Cohn's protégé himself. The flamboyance of President Donald Trump may seem counterintuitive and confounding. I feel averse to even describing it, to confer upon a figure so regressive a label so rich with resistant potential. But nor can we pretend that flamboyant bad actors do not exist, and in Trump's case the examples are plain to see. Trained as a reality TV star, as a public speaker he is brash, bold, and unpredictable. There is a flamboyant quality in his aesthetic, too, from his fake orange tan, which resembles stage makeup, to his extravagant makeover of the Oval Office, which is everywhere painted gold, one of many crass references to his (inherited) wealth and new-money empire.

Most disconcertingly, Trump's flamboyance entails a comic performance of masculinity that fails. His physical gestures onstage or at press conferences—the wagging fingers, limp wrists, and pouty lips—hardly scream fit-for-combat. He reads as bratty tyrant rather than a martial leader. Walking out to the Village People's "Macho Man" at rallies does not a macho man make, nor did the choice of "Y.M.C.A." as his 2024 campaign song read as anything other than campy (despite the band's surviving members claiming, disingenuously, that the song was never intended as a gay anthem).

A curious mix of bullish and effeminate, Trump's persona has been a clear and tempting target for parody. It is a form of parody itself, a moneyed parody of cheapness, as Bruce LaBruce identifies in relation to "conservative camp," a heavily stylized and crude "spectacle that mocks the unwashed masses by pretending to be one of them." (LaBruce also identifies Sarah Palin, Newt Gingrich, and Bill O'Reilly as other examples of this phenomenon in US politics.) Since Trump first came to power following the 2016 election, comedians and drag queens have got plenty of mileage out of impersonations that riff upon his flamboyance, while many works of protest art have poked at his gender and sexuality, like the graffiti motif that depicts him and Vladimir Putin locked in a kiss. All too meme-able, there is a shared, colloquial sense of Trump's proximity to gayness.

There were variations of this sentiment circulating online in the weeks leading up to the election, memes that depicted Trump as a bit of a flamer, in his own way, a gay diva in alt-right form. It may have comic potential, this trope, except it masked a reality that is now anything but funny. Trump's continued onslaught of policies targeting trans people, and his attacks on diversity, equality, and inclusion initiatives, are evidence that there is nothing to be gained from viewing him in these terms. These jokes might be intended to belittle him, by inferring something about his masculinity, itself a regressive form of humor, but the last laugh belongs to the clown himself.

While easy to make fun of, Trump's flamboyance is powerful. He has used the significant resources available to him—wealth, power, media attention, visibility—to harness flamboyance as a political strategy, a deliberate way of drawing people in. That it seems so nakedly egotistical and often immature has not diminished its effectiveness. His success as a figurehead for the far right attests to the theatricality of contemporary politics, but also the formidable quality of flamboyance. Even as he works to suppress flamboyance among the queer and trans people for whom it has long been a vital form of expression, Trump is living proof that such expressions are potent, and in a sense right to be afraid of.

There is no denying the danger Trump poses, as a demagogue determined to make life harder and more frightening for anyone he has cast as dissident in his reactionary imagining of society. But he cannot simply legislate flamboyance out of existence. The fresh hell of his second presidency is not without historical precedent. In Trump's America, the right to flamboyance has once again become a part of the struggle. To reclaim it, holding fast to its power, is an act of dissent.

In the 1970s, the "flamer" had another valence in the gay community. As well as describing a particularly queen-y gay man, it was also used to refer to unflinching activists and revolutionary types, those who were politically active and unapologetic. (In contemporary parlance, "flaming" also refers to heated online discussions and conflicts between anonymous users on internet forums.) The "flamer" may seem no more flattering a word in this light, in that it implies someone is behaving excessively, but it does serve to recover a more radical meaning, oriented toward a greater good. It locates the heat in flamboyance, the righteous anger which often ignites it. That anger can often be traced back to the word's other meaning, and the way it is wielded as a reductive stereotype about femininity. Taking back the word, and redirecting its meaning, is one way this anger finds its expression, laced with a subversive humor.

In the second issue of the gay anarchist newspaper *Fag Rag*, which came out of Boston in the early 1970s, the writers of the Fag Rag collective offered a resonant explanation for the paper's name. They explained that the inspiration came from a leaflet handed out at the Christopher Street Liberation Parade in New York by a group called the Flaming Faggots. That group clarified their stance by arguing that "brazenly calling ourselves faggots keeps us from denying our oppression." Whereas the word *gay* had once been a word chosen "to affirm our right to be free, unashamed, and joyous," it had "outworn its usefulness," having become a way for "The Man [. . .] to trivialize us." The word *faggot*, on the other hand—another term with flaming roots, originally a medieval word for a bundle of sticks used to light a fire—could not be co-opted in the same way; it was already an insult. As the Fag Rag collective then noted in their editorial statement, "when a straight man calls us faggots," he is "showing his contempt for us because we don't fit the stereotyped definitions of manhood."

What the straight man perhaps could not bank on is that "we're PROUD of the fact that we don't fit those definitions because they are essentially anti-human," and "proud to admit, flagrantly, that we don't fit or want to fit" them. Humor, along with pride, was important in the Fag Rag vision of the world. As Michael Bronski, author, activist, and one of the original Fag Rag collective remembers, these reclamations would also be expressed in the songs chanted and sung at protests, with lyrics including "we are faggots, flaming faggots," and "if our flaming brings you pleasure / Come out now, be a queen, be a fiery femme." The repurposing of the word *fag* in these lyrics, and the paper's title, was an example of a gag that possessed a real political force. Adorning the cover of the paper's second issue was an eye-catching drawing of a long-haired man, surrounded by bright-red tongues of fire. A flaming faggot, a statement of intent.

There is something inherently flamboyant about the act of reclaiming. Words that once held a violent power are brought back into playful, subversive circulation, their bigoted connotations mocked, their ability to hurt or diminish now undercut. The sound of a repurposed slur in polite conversation has the potential to shock, but it is also an expression of authenticity, of an unfiltered relationship to the world. It says: I know how you see me. And also: You do not own me. To use a reclaimed slur is to also choose one set of meanings over another. *Gay* and *faggot* are not direct synonyms.

I reflected on the distinctions between these words watching Jordan Tannahill's 2025 play *Prince Faggot*, in New York, a bold contemporary take on this discussion. The show is partly a speculative account of what might happen if Prince George, son of William and Kate, and the likely future King of England, grows up to become the first openly gay monarch. (Speculations about George's possible sexuality arose, controversially, after a set of photographs of him as a six-year-old, captured in a queeny-looking pose, were published in 2017.) By imagining this scenario in the not too distant future, and the royal drama that would no doubt unfold, Tannahill's play illustrates the limited impact that such progress would have on queer liberation more broadly, across class, racial, and gendered lines. Given the monarchy's historic status as a patriarchal and colonial institution, it allows little room for difference. And what if, the play asks, King George were not simply gay—smiling, neutered, respectable—but a flaming, kinky, hypersexual faggot? In one of the play's numerous sex scenes, we see George tied up in bondage gear, screaming at the top of his voice, and claiming this word for himself at last, with equal parts defiance and desire.

Prince Faggot is narrated by six queer and trans performers, who take on different roles in the play-within-the-play, and comment on what the action brings up for them about their own experiences. This deeply personal commentary observes how certain structures, like the monarchy, or the nuclear family, were not made to accommodate the flamboyant potential of queerness in all its glory. When you are excluded from those structures, you have to stake your own claim to royalty and status, to being seen in all of your glory, and reclaiming the projections that are foisted upon you. In this blistering work of theater, Tannahill activates the meanings of faggotry, and its radical potential, in smart, thrilling, and moving ways.

The reclamation of the term *faggot* more broadly still remains a matter of personal choice, and thus disagreement. Reclaiming language continues to be a divisive issue, just as it was in the 1970s. For those who have been on the receiving end of insults, at a time when they held the power to inflict fresh wounds, it can sometimes be difficult to hear them used another way. This is also true of the word *queer*, which has traveled the distance from homophobic slur to a catch-all term covering the spectrum of the LGBTQIA+ community. It is a word used regularly in polite conversation, and one that comes as second nature to many of us today as a self-identifier (myself included). Reclaimed as a political term by activists and queer theorists in the 1990s, *queer* occupies a curious position in contemporary conversations. It is seen as offensive and retrograde by some, particularly among older generations, who remember all too well its original meaning. But also, as too vague or vanilla by others, who feel that the word's political edge, and its broad definition as rebellious or unorthodox, have been diluted by its ubiquity.

Reclaiming, as a flamboyant speech act, extends beyond communities centered around gender and sexuality. In the disabled community, there has been a long-standing, though not uncontroversial, reclaiming of the word *crip*. An abbreviation of *cripple*, which refers by definition to those with mobility impairments, the word has been taken up by people across a broader range of mental and physical disabilities. As the crip theorist Robert McRuer observes, the word has been used by many disabled activists and artists "to mark a flamboyant sense of collective identity," characterized both by humor and "defiance against able-bodied norms." It can be both "flamboyantly identitarian (as in, 'We are crip and you will acknowledge that!')" and "flamboyantly anti-identitarian (as in, 'We reject the capacity of your ableist categories to describe us!')." Either way, *crip* has offered some disabled people a radical alternative to the language of an ableist society, a way of speaking back to walls of silence and patronizing stereotypes.

In its dredging up of offensive tropes, the word *flamboyant* can, as we have seen, operate as an insult. "Flamboyant was a word that was used to marginalize me and pigeonhole me and keep me in a box," notes the American actor Billy Porter. Renowned for his work on Broadway, his Emmy-winning role in *Pose* as an emcee in the ballroom scene, and his showstopping red carpet looks, Porter has spoken frequently about the phenomenon of being typecast. "Flamboyant was code for 'You're a faggot, and we don't want you' [. . .] You get in the room, you give them flamboyant, and then they come back to you with, 'He's too flamboyant.' And that's when I started to want to murder people." Call someone a "flamer" enough times, whether directly or through implication, and it should come as no surprise when they fight back.

Porter's experiences illuminate the derogatory charge still held by this word, and his response to the industry's cold shoulder offers a lesson. No matter how many times he heard he was too Black, too gay, too loud, too extra, too flamboyant, Porter refused to dull his flame. He chose not to repress those aspects of himself that were being rejected by casting agents and taste-makers. Instead, he doubled down, and waited for the world to catch up, or at least for the often-fickle trends of the industry to change course. Stories like Porter's affirm flamboyance as a way of taking up space, and finding a way to flourish even within the confines laid out by the unimaginative.

For the men of *The Sopranos*, the flamer could mean only one thing, a man whose sexuality makes him a traitor in their midst, a villain among villains. Yet from this word's vexed history, the flamer also emerges as a figure of many guises. They might be someone who embraces and proudly expresses the different aspects of their gender. Someone who shows up for their community, driven by principles they adhere to passionately. Or someone who is simply sick of the bullshit, who can remain silent no longer.

At this moment in our history, flamboyance is ripe for reclaiming along these lines, not only from the hands of its political enemies, who might also, paradoxically, exhibit a certain flamboyance, but from the meanings that have congealed and ossified around it, obscuring its radical core. Shot through with the verve of liberationist action, and the charisma of contemporary stars carving out their own space, *flaming* no longer sounds like an insult to me, laden with baggage as the word may be. Enriched by the lineage of a queer ancestry, the flamer is a figure to embody and aspire to. Someone I would like to be brave enough to be.

REMEMBERING

"I'VE ALWAYS BEEN called flamboyant," recalled the writer Richard Bruce Nugent, in 1986. At the age of seventy-nine, Nugent could claim to be the last living figure associated with the Harlem Renaissance of the 1920s. He had also been one of the first, perhaps *the* first, to write publicly about Black gay sexuality, when he published his controversial story "Smoke, Lilies and Jade" in the short-lived journal *Fire!!*, in 1926. Nugent consciously set out to shock readers with the story, which alludes, in a stream-of-consciousness style, to a sexual tryst between Alex, a young artist, and a man he refers to as Beauty. It made good on the promise of this flamboyantly named publication, which was intended, in the words of Nugent's friend Langston Hughes, poet laureate of Harlem, to "burn up a lot of the old, dead conventional Negro-white ideas of the past."

In publishing this story in the 1920s, Nugent had staked a claim to Black queerness as a literary subject, and illuminated a more radical and exciting future. Now, in the 1980s, he was something of a hero among the younger generation of queer artists and writers for whom he paved the way. In conversation with the journalist Charles Michael Smith, he reflected on his flamboyant life as a writer, artist, and someone who had always worn "his bohemianism and his homosexuality as a badge of honor," regardless of how others might judge him.

"Smoke, Lillies and Jade" also inspired a dreamily erotic sequence in British filmmaker Isaac Julien's groundbreaking 1989 film *Looking for Langston*, which set out to rediscover the queerness of Langston Hughes, who never came out in his lifetime, but whose sexuality had long been an open secret. Combining archival footage with artistic reconstructions, shot in monochrome, Julien's film drew explicit connections between the world of the Harlem Renaissance and contemporary Black queer culture, which included ballroom, the house music scene, and a thriving new literary culture.

The 1980s saw a flowering of flamboyant political art made by Black and queer artists in America, of a kind comparable to the Harlem Renaissance sixty years earlier. It is a vital moment in the history of flamboyance, and one which fully engaged its potential as a mode of fiery creative resistance, as we have already seen in the work of Essex Hemphill, Audre Lorde, and the Flamboyant Ladies. In cities and urban enclaves throughout the US, Black gay men and lesbians were not only communing with flamboyant icons of the past, but fighting back against the racism and homophobia of Reagan's America. These problems were only compounded by the specter of HIV/AIDS, and many of the artists associated with this movement were HIV-positive themselves, living and working on borrowed time. Anger, unsurprisingly, was a common theme.

"I must mold and direct that fiery cool mass of angry energy," the writer Joseph Beam declared in his 1984 essay "Brother to Brother: Words from the Heart," and "use it before it uses me." A close friend of Hemphill's, Beam was best known for putting together a 1986 anthology of Black gay writers called *In the Life* (in which Richard Bruce Nugent's retrospective interview had appeared). The first collection of its kind, *In the Life* grew out of Beam's frustration at the lack of visibility afforded to contemporary Black gay writing, compared to works by white gay men.

Beam's own reflections, included in the anthology, offer an intriguing insight into anger and the creative process. How "angry energy," often figured as hot in the cultural imagination, must be both fiery and cool in order to find its expression. Just as the materials of art must be molded and shaped, the anger that drives creativity must be cool enough to handle, to work and rework into coherent form, while retaining some of its resistant heat. Anger that goes unexpressed, repressed, or squashed down, may eventually consume you. But flamboyant art can contain it, transforming it into something that can be consumed by others.

Joseph Beam died of AIDS-related complications in December 1988, at the age of thirty-three. His friends and collaborators picked up the baton, compelled to remember one of their own by carrying forward his work. The same year, Hemphill moved from DC to Philadelphia (where he would live for the rest of his life), in order to edit a second anthology titled *Brother to Brother*, at the request of Beam's devoted and supportive mother, Dorothy, who was determined to see her son's unfinished work completed. Hemphill also gave new life to Beam's work when he spoke it aloud on-screen, in the 1989 film *Tongues Untied*, a landmark for Black gay representation. Directed by Marlon Riggs, the film is a candid and poetic meditation on race, identity, and masculinity, shot through with flamboyant anger. Heavily inspired by Beam's writing, *Tongues Untied* commits his words about homophobia in the Black community, and anger as a weapon, to a pulsing rhythm. "Anger unvented becomes pain unspoken becomes rage released becomes violence, cha cha cha," Riggs and Hemphill chant over and over, singing a tune that is also a cautionary tale.

Anger is often an unsociable and confronting emotion, the expression of an inner pain that is easier to turn away from than face head-on. It is treated as a force to be quelled or denied.

Anyone who has been told to "calm down" during a domestic tiff or a political debate, has probably felt the force of this unspoken decree. It is often racialized too, unfairly ascribed to Black people and fed by offensive stereotypes about aggression. In a world that seems rigged against your every move, where and how do you direct your anger? How do you express your resistance without being belittled, or misunderstood?

Riggs grappled with these questions in his work, which was widely shown and received international acclaim, but was also, at one point, pulled from American television channels because it was deemed "obscene" by right-wing pundits and politicians. Even certain of his peers were unsure about his approach, at least at first. "I remember thinking at times that Marlon was rather outré," noted the cultural critic Michele Wallace, when she saw him deliver a talk in the late 1980s, "a bit too dramatic and flamboyant." "Why was his flame turned up so high," she wondered. This was before she knew that Marlon was HIV-positive, at a time when that was a death sentence. "If you hadn't known he was dying," she wrote, of a talk he later gave at her 1991 conference on Black Popular Culture in New York, "you might have thought his words too bitter, too drenched in black sarcastic humor for anybody who was all of thirty-four."

In that same talk, titled "Unleash the Queen," Riggs had called out academics for living within a self-created "illusion of safe, sage detachment," an illusion he could hardly afford in the cold light of his mortality. Riggs suspected that his welcomeness in the world of academic theory was proportionate to how well he could master and mimic the complex language of the "crit queens," and less to do with any genuine interest in Black gay identity. He imagined a question the room may be asking of this rookie "conference queen": "Can she, in a word, *really* read?" In this witty and unflinching provocation, Riggs certainly read his audience—in a ballroom sense—and rejoiced in "rhetorical gender-fuck," his "preferred expression of drag."

His flamboyant stage presence, even as his body was being consumed by disease, spoke to the scale of the catastrophe presented by AIDS. A sign of life in the face of death.

Before the life-saving protease inhibitors that were discovered and rolled out in the mid-to-late 1990s, the HIV virus developed, in most cases, into AIDS, an immunodeficiency disease that attacks the body and leaves it vulnerable to life-threatening illnesses and infections. Healthy individuals, living flamboyant lives in every sense of the word, became frail, bed-bound patients with severe symptoms, failing bodily functions, and limited mobility. How could life be lived flamboyantly, against the grain of a regressive society, in a body no longer fit to fight?

Riggs remained prolific even as his health deteriorated. He spent the last years of his life making *Black Is . . . Black Ain't*, an ambitious meditation on the history of Black culture in America, featuring interviews with Black intellectuals including Wallace, as well as Angela Davis, bell hooks, and Essex Hemphill. He also used archival clips featuring none other than Jason Holliday, who is identified in the film as a trailblazing ancestor. Interspersed within the film are clips of Riggs laid up in hospital, gaunt and depleted, but determined to complete the project.

"I fell in love with the resiliency of Marlon's spirit, with his passion and courage," Wallace remembered, of the shoot. She came to see his work as a flamboyant tribute to a way of life, a heavily autobiographical and highly emotional refusal to conform to expectations, to critical fashions and artistic trends. It was also a way of saying goodbye. "That's why his flame was high and his art was not cool," she reflected, citing that other term often associated with (straight) Black male aesthetics, denoting calm and composure. Riggs harnessed its elemental opposite, flamboyant heat, for a simple reason. "He was burning up." Marlon Riggs died of AIDS-related complications in April 1994, at the age of thirty-seven.

Essex Hemphill was also in the process of saying goodbye.

He spent his final years in Philadelphia, writing when he could, sometimes leaving to tour, give readings, and take up short residencies in other cities, as much as his ailing health allowed. His final poem, "Vital Signs" is a sweeping meditation on a range of familiar subjects. The thrill of anonymous sexual encounters in gay bathhouses, the healing qualities of love and intimacy, as well as homophobic violence, and the vulnerability of the fearless queens who walk the streets. But the poem is also a portrait of his own fragile body, a call upon the strength required of him to move from one state of being to another, to be cared for in a state of extreme transformation.

Hemphill charted his dwindling vitality, the dulling of the "lucent flames" in his eyes, the fiery "balls of energy" he used to shoot from his hands. No longer a "wand waver," the flamboyant showman he used to be, he hoped to let go with grace, even in the midst of "my grand queen conflama," a gay slang term combining conflict and drama. His departure from the world was not about denying his rage, the political conflict, and the righteous drama, but finding a way to leave it behind, to mold it into something that others might hold on his behalf, carried forward like a torch. He hoped his gestures might provide a "broader lesson" to apply to the ongoing battles faced by so many like him, the "daily civil war." Essex Hemphill died from AIDS-related complications in November 1995, at the age of thirty-eight.

🔥

In the process of exploring this flamboyant artistic moment, I visited the Schomburg Center for Research in Black Culture, a branch of the New York Public Library. The center is located on Harlem's 135th Street, the heart of cultural life in the years of the Harlem Renaissance. A hundred years earlier the library would regularly host readings and discussions with the luminaries of the scene, at a time when many libraries in the country were segregated and closed off to Black patrons. The archives of many of the Renaissance writers, like Langston Hughes, are stored in the Schomburg's collection, as are those of the writers and artists from the 1980s.

I was there to visit Essex Hemphill's collection. On a blazing hot day in late spring, I deposited my belongings in the locker and entered the study room, temperature controlled and serenely quiet. I checked in with the staff, who directed me to a trolley of boxes waiting beside one of the desks. I knew from the inventory that Hemphill's collection contained personal and professional letters, programs of his performances, alternate versions of his poems, and fragments of unpublished work. As I opened the first folder, I was stopped in my tracks by a program for Hemphill's funeral, dated Thursday November 9, 1995, just a few days after his death, at an African Methodist Episcopal church in Temple Hills, Maryland. It was printed simply in an A5 booklet. On the front page, alongside explanatory details about the time of the ceremony, was a small headshot of Hemphill, close-up against a brick wall, a large hoop earring in one ear, beaming a toothy, irrepressible smile.

Looking at this image, so candid and endearing, I began to tear up. I had been reading and teaching Hemphill's work for some time. Over the years, I came to see him as a presiding figure in my research, a model for what flamboyance could be, on an artistic and political level. But the reality of his death, and the injustice of it, like so many of those who died young from AIDS, had never hit me quite like this before. Alongside this swell of emotion was a sense of intimacy that felt almost inappropriate, as if often the case in an archive. It seemed strange to be handling a document like this, a dispatch from the time and place of his passing. He was an icon, but also a person in the world, a friend and a lover, a son and a brother, mourned by those who raised him and remembered him as a child.

Hemphill was distinct among his peers in affirming the sense of home offered by family. He advocated for Black people to maintain relationships and promote understanding with their biological families, even when some of those family members struggled or failed to appreciate their queer identity and their plight. He wrote, movingly, that "our mothers and fathers are waiting for us," and "they will remain ignorant, misinformed and lonely for us, and we for them, for as long as we stay away, hiding in communities that have never really welcomed us." Attempts at such reconciliation were no doubt complex for many people, but Hemphill's perspective grew out of the realization that the white gay world only had so much to offer.

In his essays, he offered critiques of the way that Black men were viewed by white gay men as hypermasculine and sexually charged, an age-old and fetishistic trope that served only to objectify. For meaningful connections to be made across racial differences, Hemphill argued, it would have to be about more than sex and sexuality. In both the family and the gay world, true connection involved parties seeing each other fully, in all their complexities, and leaving behind the singular or limiting lenses that often frame our encounters with people different from ourselves.

As I turned to the next item in the folder, I saw the same picture. There he was again, those searching eyes, that luminous smile. This time it was on a flyer for "Vital Signs," a memorial event that took place in Washington, DC, the following year, organized by a group of his friends who wanted to celebrate Hemphill as a bold figure of Black gay life, an aspect that had been conspicuously absent from the religious funeral ceremony. Similar celebrations of his life were held in other cities, including a reading and screening of *Tongues Untied* in London, where Hemphill had performed a number of readings in the late 1980s. His important legacy was felt widely, as was the grief at his passing. There were different ways to remember him.

What I felt in this moment was a genuine form of grief, for someone I never knew but felt attached to, as a writer and flamboyant hero from the past. But also, a sense of humility in the face of his archive, a certain caution about my affinity with him. There were of course aspects of Hemphill's lived experience that I could never understand fully, as a white gay man occupying a different material reality. As a reader, drawn toward the heat of his provocations, I had perhaps never paused to notice the softer quality that shone through from the portrait I now held in my hands.

Hemphill was, as his friends attested, fierce and uncompromising in his convictions, a fireball in a FAG CLUB tee. He was also generous and warmhearted, capable of great tenderness. A memorable performer of his work on stage and screen, and a fearless cruiser of the streets, he was also fond of evenings in, playing chess, or watching *Saturday Night Live.* Flaming was only one of the things, albeit a significant one, that made him Essex Hemphill.

Looking through his archive, I noticed how Hemphill often ended his letters to friends with the line "Take care of your blessings." This signature phrase was a simple but poignant reminder to nurture one's strengths in life. To protect whatever it is that brings you joy or makes you tick, the skills or qualities that are too easily misunderstood, or appropriated by others. Flamboyance is one such blessing, I reflected as I left the library that day. For those who have delivered it to the world like an unreciprocated gift, who acted with rage but also with love, in the face of death and injustice, it is important to remember them in their wholeness.

BURNING

PASSION & ECSTASY

“When your heart’s on fire [. . .]
smoke gets in your eyes.”

Jerome Kern and Otto Harbach, 1933

LOVING

OFTEN WHEN I catch the bus into central London, the journey takes me past the Shoreditch Fire Station, in the city's east. I turn up the music in my headphones at that point, to tune out the din of the Old Street roundabout, where traffic brings the bus to a standstill. Built in the Brutalist style—rather unflamboyant, as architectural styles go—the building is noticeable for the bright red banner displayed across the top. It features a small drawing of a stick figure in motion, and a simple statement, emblazoned in yellow text, all caps: LOVE IS THE RUNNING TOWARD.

The first time I saw this statement, I did not think much of it. It struck me as fairly banal, a vague mantra, one among the many you can find on social media. It took me a few sightings to spot the connection with firefighting, and clock that it was an homage to those who risk their own lives in the act of running toward danger. Later I discovered that this was a public art piece, unveiled during the London Design Festival, and devised as part of a wider campaign celebrating the London fire brigade. I looked this up online, on a day I was feeling particularly heartsick, as I wanted to know the origin of these words. I had previously written them off as vagary, but now they spoke to me like the purest of truths.

It feels wrong, of course, to suggest any kind of equivalence between the high-risk work of firefighters and what I was feeling. For firefighters and first responders, fire is no metaphor. Their everyday acts of heroism speak to love as a collective and social practice. The sign, I knew, was referring to something bigger than my own longings, the smaller flames of romantic love, the private aches and intimate pains.

But there are few people more dramatic than those with broken hearts. Few more likely to use the language of catastrophe and death to describe their own emotional landscapes. I would know, having spent much of my adult life in this mode, whether in the throes of an overwhelming crush, the raw and choked-up early days of a breakup, or even years hence, pining for memories that seem to be slipping out of view. Eventually I came to view this talisman of my commute as a sign, in more than just the literal sense, offering words that could tell me something about my own tendencies.

I had recently started regular therapy sessions for the first time, and began reflecting on what it might mean to love flamboyantly, which is itself is a running toward. Or at least not to run away from the dangers of love, from the risk of emotional harm, rejection, and the often overwhelming sensations of longing and need. I knew I had an instinct for running toward others in the hope of being loved, and of being consumed by the desire forged in those acts. In allowing ourselves to experience these things, and perhaps even seeking out the kinds of attachments that produce them in us, we are forced to face big feelings. The kind that fill arenas and set off fireworks, which make themselves known in the body as well as the mind. It is possible to enjoy these emotions, maybe even indulge them, or at least feel them out with a certain flair, even as they cause us pain. Don't be afraid to bleed.

Love, to me, is a flamboyant feeling. Is that definition compatible with something more grounded and lasting, an equitable partnership, rather than a flash in the pan? At the point I was reckoning with my own relationship to love, I was reading about the more enlightened models offered by some of its most inspiring theorists. There was love as an art, improved by practice and hard work (Eric Fromm); love as an investment in the spiritual growth of others (bell hooks), and love as a romantic ideal that we ask too much of, that requires rethinking in a capitalist society, particularly for those excluded by its heteronormative structures (Shon Faye). I felt moved by these ideas, which struck as their refrain a need to face reality, to think more realistically about love, beyond the romanticized ideals we are surrounded by from a young age. Reading these books, and speaking with my therapist, I felt like I was doing my homework. I was laying the groundwork for something sturdier to come.

But there was still something in me that would not come unstuck. It was hard to pinpoint, the product of an imagination that might be described, more generously, as "overactive," and, less generously, as "delusional." Love, at least as far as I understood it, was pure cinema, motivated by the kind of yearning that makes you fall on your own sword just to prove how much you are experiencing it. I never consciously sought out drama, but it always seemed to find me, and often it seemed, looking back, to have been at least partly of my own creation all along.

My entire twenties felt like riding the roller coaster of these desires. (I think another term for this is *anxious attachment.*) Although each new object of desire offered something particular, something distinctively lovable, I think I also craved the sensation of feeling love for someone, whoever that happened to be. When I was in that place, my emotions were raw and overwhelming, but I also felt connected to the world in a different way, as if my senses were heightened. Colors seemed brighter, skies more magnificent. Songs took on different meanings.

These romantic tendencies were most explosive during the year I lived on and off in America. I was twenty-five, and spent much of that time both roaming and retreating. I was challenging myself to be more adventurous, to seek out any kind of romantic connection I could. The wooziness of this way of life, the drinking and the fucking, felt like something to be embraced, a way of resisting heartbreak by diving headfirst into new experiences. I have thought and even written about this period of my life in idealized terms before. Looking back at it now, in a colder light, I can see how my cravings for intimacy were also leading me down destructive paths. I was sleeping with people at every opportunity. The unbridled time of night, spent in bars and dark rooms and other people's bedrooms, always gave way to the sweaty panic of mornings. I was learning, during my summer in New York, the place I had always dreamed of living, how easily those dreams could turn into nightmares, so feverish and hot.

It was melodrama as a way of life, perfectly set to the soundtrack of Lorde's record of the same name, which was released that summer, and remains one of my all-time favorites. I had never quite experienced such a synthesis of song to experience before. On this fraught and twisty record, replete with loud, anthemic choruses and introspective piano ballads, Lorde was singing about the ambivalence of getting high, on life, and love, and drugs, and being young in a city. Her brooding voice, beamed in through my headphones as I walked the streets and rode the subway hungover, affirmed how lonely life can feel even when surrounded by other people, among the mass of bodies of a crowded street or a lit-up dance floor. She sings from the perspective of one who lives and dies each night, who meets somebody and takes them home, in the hope that they might, just for a night, conjure up their own kind of perfect place together. "I'm nineteen and I'm on fire," she proclaims on one track. I was a few years older than that, and from the sound of things, I definitely wasn't going to the same parties as Lorde was, soirees filled with champagne glasses waiting to be smashed. But this line perfectly evoked the way I was burning up.

In the world of melodrama, as in life, feelings of love are heightened by the keening sense that things are moving too quickly, liable to slip through your fingers. When the relationship ends, and the beloved leaves, all you have are memories to reassemble in the ways you see fit. In the most lovelorn of tracks from *Melodrama*, Lorde calls this a "supercut," the endless ribbons of sepia-toned memories that play out in the mind, and in the dark, a monument to a relationship in all its cinematic glory. In this montage, even the messier memories—"Incontinence in cars" and the "violent overnight rush"—possess a mythic quality, a colorful hue. Captured through the lens of loss, the act of loving burns brightly; more brightly, even, than it seemed to at the time, when the petty conflicts and daily compromises threaten to take off the shine. Perhaps it is hallmark of young love, to experience it all not only in the present, but as an anticipated memory, one for the ages. "We were wild and fluorescent," says Lorde, in the act of looking back. To my ears, it is another way of saying flamboyant.

🔥

To be fair to my twenty-something self, we are surrounded by melodramatic stories of love's flamboyance from every angle, in songs, and novels, and films, and TV shows. (What stirs me, then and now, about Lorde's music is that it both inhabits and critiques the melodrama of it all, a moody yet winking message, delivered from inside the chaos.) From star-crossed lovers like Romeo and Juliet, to weepies and soap operas, love is frequently trailed by the shadow of doom, the suggestion that it is a force so powerful it can both sweep you off your feet and take your life. This is no less true when it comes to representations of queer love, which seemed relatively thin on the ground in my own memories of growing up. Gay love affairs on-screen are historically more likely to end in death and devastation, particularly when they are illicit. These stories are most often works of fiction, but for those of us still learning about romantic love, not yet in the position to receive or experience it ourselves, they become a vehicle for wider truths and unrealistic expectations about how good and how bad it can be, how earth-shattering and potentially destructive.

In the winter following my time in New York, I took up a study exchange program in Massachusetts. The primary purpose of the trip was to enroll in classes and make progress on my PhD, with the deadline looming. It also offered me an escape from the funk I had settled into back at home. I approached this particular adventure quite differently from my time in the city. It was more campus and cottage core, a snowy foil to the wild summer of the previous year, a time that I felt I had been eternally altered by somehow. I was drinking even more, that winter. While I adapted to the more studious rhythm of life in my temporary new home, I was also feeling pangs for a particular ex. Lorde was touring *Melodrama* around that time, and playing a show in Boston while I was there. It was inevitable I would go, and inevitable that it would all come flooding back, the recent past in all its wild fluorescence. It was a uniquely cathartic experience, to feel these feelings transformed into a flamboyant spectacle, expanded to stadium-sized proportions.

Toward the end of my stay in Massachusetts, I was speaking to a new friend about my love life. We were having a nightcap and a cigarette outside one of the dorm buildings after an evening poetry workshop. I brought her up to speed on my love life, and asked her whether she thought I should get back in touch with my ex. He had sent me a postcard just before I left for the US, which remained unanswered. In my mind, I had drawn a line in the sand and called it a boundary. I was protecting myself, and practicing the kind of care for my own feelings that had mostly been lacking in my behaviors up until that point. Her advice to me was, in some ways, exactly what I wanted to hear, but it also bore the sharp edge of wisdom and experience. She saw right through this performance of mine, and was even a little cynical about such narratives of individual agency and self-restraint, particularly when they make obscure to us the things we really want. What I wanted was to feel the force of the love again. She told me I should go for it. Reach out. So that's what I did.

When my stint in the US came to an end, and I moved back to the UK, we met up and decided to give the relationship another go. Things felt tentative between us, at first, but it wasn't long until we were all-in, and we stayed together for the next three years. I was still new to love in those years, struggling against the scale and intensity of my feelings, but I do not lament that I felt and acted upon them. Even now, when I reflect on how painful it was when we did eventually break up, and on some of my own naive mistakes, I would probably still give the same advice to myself. Send that text. Fuck it. What is there to lose? It is not inherently virtuous to remain on the even keel.

Love often begins in the running toward—it is saying a big flamboyant yes to something that has been imagined, romanticized, and yet to be known in its fullness. But love as I am coming to understand it—as something shared and complex, a flame kept alive through care and mutual understanding—all depends on what happens next. It will grow, as you grow, change, as you change, and it will not always work out. But to feel the force of love at its most flamboyant is to know that loss, however painful, becomes another opportunity to know ourselves in a new light, even transform ourselves in the process. There is always another song to meet such a moment.

TORCHING

WHEN ROMEO FIRST encounters his beloved Juliet, her beauty reminds him of a flame. "O, she doth teach the torches to burn bright!" he exclaims, in tribute to a beauty so luminous that real torches are lit from its source. "They've got their love torches burning," sang Elvis Presley in his 1966 cover of the aptly titled 1950s number "Fools Fall in Love," "when they should be playing it cool," a warning to overzealous lovers wreaking havoc with each other. Neither Romeo nor Juliet knew how to play it cool, famously, but Shakespeare's reference illuminates the origins of this distinctly modern metaphor, a prominent image in twentieth-century musical lore.

To carry a torch for someone is to love them, even, and often, without the expectation of reciprocity. From this idiom comes the torch song, the great art form of lost or unrequited love. Like lemons and lemonade, the torch song makes something flamboyant out of heartbreak. It may not be cool, but it can be pleasing and cathartic, even spectacular, in the hands of the right singer.

The most heartrending moment in a musical usually occurs in the second act torch song, when a character finally confesses her evident desires to the audience. It is Nancy in *Oliver!*, reassuring herself that her abusive partner, the villainous Bill Sikes, needs her in the same way she needs him. It is Éponine in *Les Misérables*, longing after Marius, who loves someone else, and falling deeper into the fantasy that he may one day walk beside her, that she will no longer be on her own. It is former showgirl Sally, in Stephen Sondheim's *Follies*, marking every moment of her day with thoughts of her former lover Ben, and beginning to lose her mind in the process. Sometimes, the torch song is meant to make something happen, to drive the action forward or achieve the desired outcome of a particular character. Like Effie, in *Dreamgirls*, who takes a more defiant approach, addressing her lover (and manager) directly, refusing to accept that he has ended the relationship, and affirming that she is not going. Other times, it comes from a place of acceptance, a last word in the face of loss. Like Whitney Houston, at the end of *The Bodyguard*, transforming the gentle and resigned melancholy of Dolly Parton's "I Will Always Love You" into something dignified but still defiant, scaled up to the size of a power ballad, maximalist and voice-defying.

I attribute much of my emotional education to the torch song, and there is a lot to learn from it. It is a genre with a particular history, a staple of the modern musical that first emerged out of the show tunes and jazz standards of the Great American Songbook, in the 1920s and 1930s. I also see it as a sensibility; a way of understanding ourselves, of making shareable what we are feeling. The torch song lights upon a space where we say the things we cannot always express in reality, face-to-face. It is a space of candor, of intense feeling and unwieldy desire. To listen to a torch song, to be ventriloquized by it, as if its lyrics were speaking to your situation, can be a form of retreat, sometimes, or wallowing, but also a way of facing your feelings head-on.

While the genre may easily fall into something schmaltzy, the feelings illuminated by the torch song are universal, their appeal hardly limited to a particular era. The record-breaking successes of Adele, who belts those distinctly defeated words *never mind* with the full power of her vocal range in "Someone Like You," suggests a need for pop divas who can set fire to the rain, using just their voice and a piano accompaniment.

In case it is not already clear, the particular yearning of the torch song could not be more up my street. I wear my sop badge with pride these days, happy to claim, without shame, my inclinations toward the sentimental. (Houston's version of "I Will Always Love You" is my chosen karaoke song, foolhardy as that may be.) I have called upon this genre countless times to soundtrack situations in my own life, the unrequited loves and messy breakups. Love in the torch song is often configured around this kind of formula, readymade for the brokenhearted. As historian Allan Forte notes, it usually takes one or two forms: "Individual A desperately loves Individual B, but Individual B is oblivious of the existence of Individual A or has loved but then abandoned Individual A." These are experiences that can make us feel vulnerable, and often like victims. But I see the torch song as a form whose sheer power resists victimhood, even if its lyrics, on the surface, might seem to affirm a sense of being wronged or rejected.

What the torch song gives voice to is longing, an emotion that Brené Brown defines as beyond "conscious wanting"; it is rather "an involuntary yearning for wholeness, for understanding." As she writes, "many of us feel we need to keep our longings to ourselves, for fear we will be misunderstood, perceived as engaging in magical or unrealistic thinking, or lacking in fortitude and resilience." This is the risk taken in any display of emotion, any display of our needs and vulnerabilities, of the unfulfilled fantasies of our inner lives. That we might be perceived as indulgent or even pathetic, opting to wallow in sadness, rejection, and existential uncertainty. But to me, there is a defiance in such candor. Sometimes the only way out is through. The torch song shows us the flamboyant power of owning your emotions—of feeling them, naming them, and allowing them to take up space, with a little flair thrown in.

To find flamboyance in torch songs might seem to go against the grain of how they have traditionally been viewed, as passive and melancholic, qualities that have also been imposed on the women who sing them. Although there have always been male torch singers, they have usually been categorized as "crooners" (like Frank Sinatra, Nat King Cole, or Tony Bennett), and the gay male performers who sing torch songs (like Marc Almond or Rufus Wainwright) are seen to be playing on the essential femininity of the form.

The close association of torch songs with women has involved ugly stereotypes about feminine passivity and desperation. These are sometimes reflected in the lyrics, many of them written by male songwriters, like the 1920 French piano ballad "Mon Homme," in which the singer narrates her life of despair, in love with a man who is not only unfaithful but emotionally and physically abusive. The song is considered, in some circles, to be the first torch song, and it has been widely performed in English, most famously by Fanny Brice, Barbra Streisand (playing Brice, in the musical *Funny Girl*), and Billie Holiday. And also, during his own moment in the spotlight, Jason Holliday. His tipsy rendition in Shirley Clarke's apartment nods to the queer potential contained in the torch song, and the way its feminized tropes inform the history of drag, as a subversive, though sometimes no less stereotypical, critique of them.

Queer icons are made here, at the intersection between mess and joy, pain and its parodies. Broadway stalwart Harvey Fierstein nodded to this when he named his three-act play about gay life *Torch Song Trilogy*, complete with musical interludes performed by the protagonist, who works as a drag queen, performing old torch songs in clubs and bars. One of the reasons that gay men have historically worshipped divas—many of whom, like

Judy Garland, and plenty of other torch singers—died in tragic circumstances, is that they are able to voice, from a woman's perspective, the intense loneliness of a life without love. They narrate what it is like to live in a world where your desires go unrecognized, as well as unreciprocated. Many torch singers have, in turn, subverted the identity markers forced upon them, and broken free.

In "Falling in Love Again," one of her signature numbers from the 1930s, German film star and queer icon Marlene Dietrich sang about the provocative allure of the female performer, the woman holding space in the spotlight. "Men cluster to me / Like moths around a flame," she sang, "And if their wings burn, / I know I'm not to blame." Born in Berlin in 1901, Dietrich worked as a chorus girl in the city's vaudeville shows during the flamboyant era of the Weimar Republic, and had small roles in silent films in the 1920s. Her breakthrough role was Lola in the 1930 German film *The Blue Angel,* a cabaret singer and femme fatale, who enters into a doomed marriage with an uptight professor, who descends into madness out of love for her, his wings burnt, as her trademark number had warned.

Dietrich's seductive appeal as a movie star, one of the qualities that made international audiences flock to her in this way, was an ability to embody different flamboyant fantasies—from the high-femme siren, dressed in furs and jewels, to a more androgynous and queer figure, done up in a tuxedo and a top hat. She went on to flourish in Hollywood in the early 1930s, before the introduction of the Hays Code in 1934. A moral crusade on the part of the Motion Picture Producers and Distributors of America, Hollywood's largest trade group, the code banned studios from making films with content deemed transgressive, which is to say anything queer or feminist, scandalous or sexual. The kinds of roles that first made Dietrich famous were curbed by this anti-flamboyant measure, although she continued to flourish in parts that were more glamorous than outright sexy, less transgressive, but also more nuanced. When Hollywood roles in general began to dry up for her in the 1950s, she revived her career by turning back to cabaret and performance and created a hugely successful solo show in which "Falling in Love Again" was an old favorite.

Many of the female stars of Old Hollywood—an era that spans the "It" girls of silent movies in the 1920s, through Marlene Dietrich and Rita Hayworth in the 1930s and 40s, to Marilyn Monroe in the 1960s—brought their considerable charisma to expand and enliven characters written by men. In this period, there was a close proximity between the torch singer and the femme fatale, the dangerously desirable woman found in the hard-boiled plots of film noir. Both of these archetypes were a product of the male gaze, and they would frequently coincide in a single character, like Dietrich's Lola, or Lauren Bacall's Marie in *To Have and Have Not* (1944), embroiled in dramas in which their agency and power, as women in a man's world, remained ambiguous.

It seems no accident that the songs these characters perform on-screen often refer to the question of blame, from Dietrich's Lola, absolving herself of responsibility for men's flocking toward her flame, to Rita Hayworth's Gilda, in the iconic 1946 film of the same, performing "Put the Blame on Mame," a song about women being blamed for natural disasters. The women in these films could be many things at once: fearless, promiscuous, and independent, but also fragile and manipulative, a threat to hapless men, but also to themselves. Through the flamboyant instrument of the torch song, they appear to have a direct channel to the melancholy of life, and the destructive side of love.

When she is not being viewed as sad or defenseless, the torch singer could seem dangerous, even otherworldly. In his 1947 short story "Torch Song," the American writer John Cheever created a character called Joan Harris (clearly an inspiration for her television namesake, the flame-haired office manager in *Mad Men*, played by Christina Hendricks). She is a woman in her thirties, living in New York but originally from Ohio, a friend of the story's male protagonist, Jack, and we quickly learn that she has terrible taste in men. Time and again, she seems drawn to those who will let her down and steal from her, who engage in self-destructive behaviors and commit crimes. When he thinks of Joan being evicted from her apartment because the neighbors believe she is "an immoral and drunken woman," Jack is reminded "of a torch song, of one of those forlorn and touching ballads," as he listens to Joan bemoaning her lot and "singing her wrongs."

By the end of the story, the narrative flips. What had seemed touching about Joan's sense of tragedy, her hip all-black outfits doubling up for mourning garbs, starts to look suspicious, even nefarious. Particularly when Joan shows up at his apartment at the moment he has hit his own rock bottom. Perhaps the men in Joan's life were not villains, Jack wonders, but instead clueless men whose evident penchant for madness and self-destruction placed them right in her path. Where her voice had "once before reminded him of a gentle and despairing song," it now made Jack uneasy. Although Joan herself remains oblivious of her instinct toward death and male vulnerability, Jack cannot help but see her as a harbinger of his own imminent demise. This unexpected conclusion to the story suggests there might be something supernatural afoot. Perhaps Joan is a modern-day Hecate, ancient queen of the underworld, a flamboyant goddess associated with the wilder aspects of human nature, who is frequently depicted holding torches.

The flamboyant torch singer challenges the regressive idea that there is something threatening about a woman owning her desires, owning her sexuality, and connecting with the loneliness and longing for love that is at the heart of all human experience. Beyond the fictions of Hollywood and literature, those who often pay the highest price for living and loving flamboyantly are female torch singers themselves, forced into the spotlight to keep the masses entertained, even in the face of prejudice and mistreatment. No story of the torch singer is complete without the story of one particular legend, a flamboyant prophet of love and loss whose career was shaped by such hardships. Still she kept the torch burning.

Lady Day knew how to set a stage alight, but there was nothing particularly loud or bombastic about her voice. She simply had a singular presence. Listen to any recording by Billie Holiday and you can hear how much happens in the hush, in the way she curves the words of a song to her will, and infuses them with the deepest feeling, both a sadness and a dark humor. Renowned as the consummate jazz singer of her era, Holiday is one of the most important figures in the history of music and popular culture, and particularly beloved among the flamboyant artists we have already encountered, who looked back and found inspiration in her legacy.

Alexis De Veaux, of the Flamboyant Ladies, explored Holiday's life and influence in her 1980 book *Don't Explain*, a biography in the form of written song. She paints an indelible image of the singer in her breakout moment in the mid-1930s, when her "reputation was growing" and she was hot stuff in Harlem, where she had moved with her mother in 1929, aged fourteen. The details of Holiday's early life in Baltimore, where she was largely raised by relatives while her mother worked on the railroads, are grim, and involve teenage prostitution, sexual assault, and a stint at a cruel and punitive Catholic reform school. The move to New York was a turning point, and she began singing in Harlem nightclubs as a teenager, while working as a cleaner by day.

It was in that period that Billie Holiday, who was born Eleanora Fagan, truly arrived, with a stage name to boot. By then, De Veaux writes, the young singer "knew how to style with her sequined / gowns / and slow time singing"; she was a "mesmerizing and witchful" presence. "Flamboyant. / Slicing words in untouchable patterns." The essence of Holiday's flamboyance was to find the eroticism in emotion, a sultry quality in the voicing of sadness, and to turn the pain of living into a musical force that can take your breath away.

One of Holiday's signature looks, on stage and in studio photographs printed on posters and album covers, was her gardenia hair. Arranged in ironed curls or tied back into a bun, Holiday added a large gardenia bloom above her ear. The Black hair historian Ayana Byrd has noted how the flower, "soft, delicate and beautiful," was a "reclaiming of this idea that Black women are also beautiful in this way." When this trademark look first appeared in 1939, however, it had come about by accident. Holiday was preparing for a show and "using a hot comb that was too hot and burned off a section of her hair near her left ear." Another female jazz singer, with whom Holiday was sharing a dressing room, ran out and bought a gardenia, so Holiday could cover up the burn. A flamboyant look that came about by accident, it seems a perfect metaphor for Holiday's artistry—a burn transformed, through flourish, into something beautiful.

Holiday voiced, through song, her experiences of being burnt—by her abusive husband Jimmy Monroe, whom she married in 1941, by her many lovers, male and female, and by her addictions to alcohol and heroin. But her torch songs also spoke to the realities of life in a racist society, which continued to segregate and oppress its Black citizens, no matter how famous and successful they became. When Essex Hemphill channeled Holiday's voice in his poem "Gardenias," he captured the indignities she faced as a traveling singer. Hemphill wrote, in

Holiday's voice, as a woman who sets herself "afire" singing for her man, with gardenias in her hair. Hemphill's poem also refers to the occasions when Holiday was made to wear blackface for shows in certain venues, because her skin was not deemed dark enough when performing with jazz bands. Blackface was rife among many of the white female torch singers of the days of the 1920s and 1930s, a cultural disgrace even Holiday was not spared as a Black artist. As she noted in her memoir, the "management never asked me to wear pink makeup to sing with a white band, but if they had I wouldn't have been surprised."

Holiday's most explicit commentary on the racist violence of a segregated America was heard in "Strange Fruit," a song about the lynchings of Black men in the South. Adapted from a poem written in the mid-1930s by Abel Meeropol, a schoolteacher and activist from the Bronx, the song does not hold back in its harrowing depiction of bodies swinging from the trees. Holiday first performed her spare and haunting rendition in 1939 at Café Society, an integrated nightclub in Manhattan, and recorded it the same year. Although her recording was banned from Southern radio stations, the attempts to suppress it were futile. "Strange Fruit" was soon taken up as a protest song, a spark in the burgeoning Civil Rights Movement.

Holiday mastered a broad range of genres as a performer, and brought her unique talents to jazz standards, show tunes, and old blues numbers. Later in her career, in 1955, she went to Los Angeles to record an album of torch songs, the musical mode in which she had long reigned. The mood of this record, as one blurb states, is "strictly after-hours: the party is long over but a few close friends remain for nightcaps." It evokes the scorched intimacy of the after-party, the sharing of deep feelings and difficult stories when the company is close, the sun is rising, and there are no fucks left to give in the room. But it also has the smooth and sultry quality that distinguishes Holiday's most-beloved vocal performances. The album's title, *Music for Torching,* gestures to some other valences in the metaphor of the torch song. Where the torch singer usually conjures up the image of the forlorn woman, wronged in love, the verb *torching* suggests an act of burning or destroying, or torching something to the ground. If anyone shows us how fine the line between these states can be, it is Billie Holiday.

In the final years of her life, Holiday's voice possessed a torched quality. Ravaged by years of drinking and drugs, the singer's "burnt-edged digressions" became louder, as the music historian Stacy Holman Jones puts it, but still nothing, "not age, not abuse, not being hushed or dismissed or labeled—*nothing* could silence her voice." Her final performance was a week-long residency in the Flamingo Lounge in New York, in mid-May 1959, just a few days before she was rushed to hospital, suffering symptoms caused by advanced cirrhosis of the liver. There she was accosted by police, who claimed they had found heroin in her room, and charged her with possession of drugs, although this claim was never substantiated, and many believe it was fabricated. She was placed under arrest and forced to stay on the ward, handcuffed to the bed, a scandal that was splayed across the national newspapers. She remained in the same hospital bed until her death from heart failure in July, aged forty-four.

Billie Holiday never got to see the richness of her legacy illuminated. She died, in the eyes of the state, as an addict and a criminal, who had escaped the difficulties of her upbringing only to be returned to the status of social outcast. In that sense, her life and death illustrate an age-old story about misogyny and racism, the way they have always been deployed to suppress flamboyant resistance. Although her "burnt, torched voice" at the end of her life seemed like evidence of her "destined decimation," as Holman Jones writes, it also contained the "promise of a new growth after the fire." Few other singers have been as influential, and Holiday's artistic achievements were testament to her multiplicity.

She was flamboyant, in her passion and fearlessness, but also cool, as Joel Dinerstein, historian of the concept of cool in postwar American culture, argues. Her performances gained power from a "stagecraft of economy," the way she "swayed subtly while singing, barely moving a muscle," and the way she "walked to the stage of every club and concert hall with the stately elegance of a trained dancer or born aristocrat," Lady Day. Coolness, Dinerstein argues, was a political and artistic strategy through which Black artists could resist the oppressive expectations projected onto them, and the "controlled emotional flow" of Holiday's delivery was an example of the way that passion could make itself known quietly. In this sense, flamboyance and cool do not seem as opposed as they first appear. Holiday's flamboyance contained a dash of the unexpected; more introspective than outrageous, less outright spectacle than bracing whisper.

Reviewing the film *Lady Sings the Blues,* in which Holiday is played by 1970s superstar Diana Ross, film critic Pauline Kael noted the obvious cinematic potential of the singer's story, a tragic arc ripe for the biopic treatment. "Who could be a more natural subject for a flamboyant downer than Billie Holiday," Kael asks, "whose singing can send even the cheeriest extroverts into a funk?" It reads as a little flippant, this question, but in that phrase "flamboyant downer," I also think Kael is onto something about feeling, and about torching. While flamboyance is traditionally considered the essence of extroverts, it is also to be found in the emotional depths of a self turned inside out, a torch song delivered from the heart. There is a value for everyone in following the path of flamboyance downward, even those otherwise cheery extroverts felled into silence by Holiday's songs. If only because it reminds us what it is to live, and what we stand to lose.

LOSING

AS A TEENAGER, there was one torch singer I loved the most. When she received the inevitable biopic treatment recently, to mixed results, the edges of her story softened, the magnetism of her talents honed away, I thought back to the first time I recalled seeing her on-screen. It was a TV advert for her debut album, and I remember that there was something about her that I could not place. We see her getting ready for a night out, doing her hair and makeup, and climbing into a taxi. She reminded me of girls I knew at school, confident, a little disruptive. But she was also very adult, a quality signalled by the jazzy, mature sounds playing in the background. Even her name sounded grown-up, and evoked the type of bar my mum might go to with friends. So when I first began to recognize this woman—who wore rollers in her hair, pink hoops, and a leopard-print dress, striding down a street in North London in her stilettos—as a singer called Amy Winehouse, I felt like I already knew her.

Looking back at this moment in her career, twenty years ago, it is hard not to imagine the alternative paths she could have taken, had things worked out differently. Amy Winehouse would become a megastar because of her music, but the things that made her even more famous—her incessantly documented struggles with drugs, alcohol, and an eating disorder, and her troubled, on-off relationship with Blake Fielder-Civil—were not yet in view. That first album, *Frank* has an aptly freewheeling outlook. It is a record sung by a carefree twenty-year-old–about-town, raised on jazz standards and the love stories of the Great American Songbook, but reaching toward the street-smart ethos of hip-hop.

Here is a girl who laughs at clichés about love while living inside them; who justifies infidelity because she heard that love is blind; who affectionately satirizes the vampy WAG-types she encounters out in the bars, women on the game who provide more fun on a night out than any of the men they are out to pull; who wonders, in quieter moments, if her loose relationship to monogamy is part of her "Freudian fate," paved by her father's infidelities and her parents' divorce.

By the next album, *Back to Black,* she had hardened into a slightly different character, a lovable antihero no longer young and sweet, though still only twenty-three, with several more years of living under her belt. She has experienced the peaks and troughs of relationships and the all-consuming wave of heartbreak. It is a logical extension, in some ways, but also a stark one. She brings that same wit to the skewering of romance, a signature blend of tenderness and misanthropy, but suddenly the stakes feel different. Why else make the lead single, and the album's first track, a song about refusing to go to rehab? The songs are scaled accordingly. Each is a work of high drama, the sound of introspection made loud.

On *Back to Black,* Winehouse emerges as a singer-songwriter who wears her influences, like her heart, on her sleeve. Roughly half the songs on the album still hark back to the same musical universe as *Frank*, inflected with jazz and Latin influences and peppered with the vernacular of hip-hop and reggae. But *Back to Black* is also a wholesale return to the sounds of the 1960s, and in particular the musical stylings of Motown and girl groups like

The Ronettes and The Shangri-Las, a backdrop that emerged from her sessions in New York with Mark Ronson and The Dap Kings. The pastiche is so expertly executed that it is little wonder why the album seemed to attain "instant classic" status as quickly it did. It sounded so much like the music already enshrined in those terms.

I hear *Back to Black* as a record that goes beyond pastiche. A concept album about what it means for young people to feel nostalgia for an era we never lived through, to find in its musical legacy a reflection of our own emotional landscape. But Winehouse's act of rediscovery also pulls from Black musical sources, an appropriation that places her in a longer history of white artists singing rhythm and blues, including Elvis Presley and Janis Joplin. Although *Back to Black* uses "1960s R&B forms" as a bridge to connect "Civil Rights aspiration with the dawning new millennial era," the scholar Daphne A. Brooks has noted, the album is more focused on the singer's individual crises, ranging from the "relatively mundane to the spectacularly tragic."

In the interviews where she speaks about her influences, Winehouse's face lights up with her evident love for the blues, and she is sanguine about what it means. "I know there are people in the world who have worse problems than falling in love and having it blow up in your face," she once said. "But I didn't want to just wake up drinking, and crying, and listening to The Shangri-Las. So I turned it into songs, and that's how I got through it." "Every bad situation is a blues song waiting to happen," she said another time. What the '60s music represented to her was not hope and change, political or personal. Compared to the more empowered "I don't need you" schtick of contemporary pop, she favored the yearning sentiment of older songs, whose messages were neither proper nor particularly progressive, more: "I don't care if you don't love me, I will lie down in the road, pull out my heart and show it to you."

Amy Winehouse showed us her heart, and when *Back to Black* landed she had already crafted an aesthetic to match this new status as a chanteuse of longing, her own punk take on vintage flamboyance. Inspired by the hairstyles fashionable in the 1950s and '60s, the beehive was the first thing you noticed, jet-black extensions piled together into a bulbous shape, held together with clips and hairspray. Her eye makeup had changed too, with kohl-black eyeliner dashed off at the sides into cat-eye wings. There were now a growing number of tattoos, retro symbols inscribed all over her body.

One of them, an image of a dark-haired pinup girl in a bright red blouse and black shorts, was a tribute to her beloved paternal grandmother Cynthia Winehouse. She inspired Winehouse's love of jazz, once dated Ronnie Scott, and was by all accounts a flamboyant figure in life and a personal style icon for her granddaughter. The look was a bold aesthetic statement. Tabloids were quick to pick up on her body art, as if there were still something risqué about a woman with tattoos, as well as her stark weight loss. The same thing that made people pay attention would eventually be used against her in the media's intrusive onslaught, and informed the grotesque parodies that followed, which turned Winehouse's look into the stuff of Halloween costumes.

The contrast between Winehouse's big hair and her slight frame seemed like a signifier of something ominous, an obvious vulnerability, as if she might topple over under the weight of her own persona. What here is authentic, and what is artifice? The look matched the music not only because the period details were historically appropriate, but because the component parts seemed like visual clues, nodding to the pain and insecurity that informed the record's lyrics.

Ronnie Spector, lead singer of The Ronettes, remembered gasping at the recognition of her own signature look when she saw the singer on TV for the first time, as well as the mental space it seemed to emerge from. "I knew that little girl lost look," she recalls, "and I saw it when nobody else probably could see it, because I went through it myself." Nor did Winehouse ever deny the association. Ever candid, she stated plainly in one interview that "I'm quite an insecure person, I'm very insecure about the way that I look. I'm a musician, not a model. I remember turning up at the BBC and places like that, and the more insecure I felt the more I'd drink." She would then ask her hair stylist to make the beehive bigger and bigger. "Like the more insecure I feel the bigger my hair has to be, I suppose."

Winehouse was once asked in an interview if she thought she was a sex symbol. "Only to gays," she replied, gruff and offhand. The joke is about not seeing herself as conventionally attractive, or appealing to straight men, but it is also an acknowledgment that she represented many of the things that have appealed to gay audiences: a prophet of longing, and singer of torch songs, with a heightened aesthetic persona. I am not sure if Winehouse was ever quite considered a gay icon during her lifetime, perhaps because the media's scrutiny of her struggles in the years after *Back to Black* was so relentless that it became difficult, even tasteless, to celebrate the melancholic aspects of her work.

But she was certainly an icon to me, a modern-day Judy Garland who held a mirror up to my own yearnings. I was deep in the closet when I first started listening to her as a teenager, but those songs stirred something in me that I could not yet recognize, as if they anticipated the pangs of desire to come, the impossible and unrequited feelings that would mark my first attractions to men. I listened to her music differently after she died, because how could we not, but also because by then, at nineteen, I had developed a taste for alcohol and a slightly new set of ears, attuned to the ways that love could be disorienting and destructive.

For all of its maturity, and its literacy in the musical past, it means something that Winehouse's entire body of work is that of a twentysomething. However much *Back to Black* sounds as if it is sung by a much older, jaded jazz singer who has seen it all, it is the testimony of a fairly new recruit in matters of the heart, a young person trying on different narratives for size. One of her close friends observed how they had a mutual understanding about their "kitchen sink drama mentality" toward life—following their "gut and emotions" above all else, and finding that "the 'star-crossed' lovers concept validated some undesirable relationships in our eyes, at least." You can hear this in the music. "It is, of course," she notes, "just a part of being young."

Winehouse's "vulnerability, coupled with a fearlessness," as one of the musicians from the recording of *Back to Black* put it, is what to me makes her a flamboyant artist. "She went straight into the fire." The song "Love Is a Losing Game" is a burnt-out message from that journey. "For you I was a flame," she sings. Does she mean a flame as in a flash or spark, something ephemeral? Or an old flame? Or is it flame as in hazard; a pleasing light source that will burn you if you get too close? Perhaps it is all of the above, but there is something else there too, a hidden adjective that conjures up a scene of devotion. It was for you that I was aflame. Desire spells catastrophe—there was a "five story fire as you came"—and everything is alight. Here are lovers who have burned each other, caught in a bind of sacrifice and pleasure, and a singer who is struggling to find her agency yet also seems remarkably in possession of it.

There were numerous live and acoustic performances of "Love Is a Losing Game," and it sounded like a slightly different song each time. This is partly because, as producer Mark Ronson has observed, Winehouse would never sing a melody the same way twice. In some versions it sounds like the sweetly melancholic mid-tempo ballad it is on the record, all schmaltzy minor chords and cinematic strings (to which Winehouse was initially opposed because they risked seeming artificial). In others it is pared back and raw, sung with just a guitar. She delivers certain lines—like the admission that love's game is one played "over futile odds"—

as a howl that travels up different registers and trips up the song's rhythm. The different ways she sings the line "Memories mar my mind" make that stain feel audible. These performances offer the illusion that she is realizing the song, and its emotional landscape, for the first time again. Sometimes it is delivered with a wry smile, others with a vacant, haunting stare. Her vocal ad libs are the sound of sparks flying.

Although there are many to be cherished and admired, live performances became a vexed part of Winehouse's legacy. Toward the end of her life, the bad gigs and public train wrecks were a central part of the media narrative. As Leslie Jamison writes, "her fans loved her as long as she gave them what they needed—as long as she broke down so they could watch, as long as she picked herself back up again so she could give them her voice."

The turmoil came to a head at what would be her final show in Belgrade in 2011. It was the first date in a planned European tour, following a long hiatus from performing. Winehouse was clearly not well enough to return to the stage, but boarded a plane, half asleep, and travelled to Belgrade to honor the commitment. When she appeared onstage an hour late, stumbling and slurring her words, and dropping the microphone, it seemed to confirm that the worst was true, that her musical gifts were no longer visible. The crowd seemed unwilling to show her grace, booing and hissing as she mumbled half-remembered snatches of her own lyrics. Footage from the show is chilling to watch, not only because of the crowd's behavior, but because "you could see a kind of reckless and unhappy wickedness begin to spread across her face," the critic Philippa Snow writes, "as if she'd realised that refusal was the one thing she had left."

It seemed like the end of the road, and the tour, which had taken months to prepare, was postponed indefinitely. Winehouse's close friend Naomi Parry had designed a whole wardrobe for the planned performances. Leafing through images of her brightly colored minidresses, the signature Amy aesthetic, I was stopped in my tracks by one that seemed to encapsulate what she was about. Printed on the dress was an image, of a midnight sky and shining palm fronds, and two bright pink flamingoes standing opposite one another, their necks curved to make the shape of a love heart. She had tried it on briefly during the fittings for the tour and helped come up with a punning nickname for the look: "Flamin' Go." I imagined her in it on stage, burning brightly, her outfit reflecting her art. A flamboyance of flamingoes that makes love visible, even if it is drawn from the darkness. The dress is a monument, but it also marks an absence. It was never worn.

🔥

When Amy Winehouse died a month after the Belgrade show, at the age of twenty-seven, from accidental alcohol poisoning, she joined a grimly defined club of other cultural figures who died at the same age. These include Jimi Hendrix, Jim Morrison, Janis Joplin, and Kurt Cobain. Spanning the 1960s to the 2010s, the "27 club" illuminates a history of high-risk lifestyles among those who became stars quickly, forced to grapple with the pressures of fame at a young age. But as a grouping it also begets other myths, from superstitious theories about the number 27, in some corners of the internet, to familiar ideas about the tortured artist. It is true that many artists dwell in life's darkest mental recesses, and in the process produce something glittering. This idea has become so culturally familiar, however, that it risks normalizing tragic outcomes, with the suggestion that flamboyance and self-destruction might be inherently linked.

"The light that burns twice as bright burns for half as long," goes a famous line from *Blade Runner*, often quoted in this context, "and you have burned so very, very brightly." When an artist dies, metaphors like these become a kind of soothing, as if there might be some consolation in the idea that a life lived so fully was worth it, even predestined. For the lyricist Bernie Taupin, the image of a candle in the wind was more resonant. He first heard the phrase used by the record producer Clive Davis, describing Janis Joplin, and decided to use it for his 1973 song with Elton John about Marilyn Monroe. The song is a cautionary tale about celebrity, the way a woman named Norma Jeane was made to perform as "Marilyn Monroe," a persona for public consumption, exploited by the system, and never "knowing who to cling to when the rain set in." As Taupin saw it, Monroe was an "inconsolably vulnerable" figure, so the candle was the "perfect metaphor for the song's title, a fragile flame flickering into immortality."

In addressing the human costs of making art, and the exploitative nature of the industry, these metaphors are neat, poignant, a little sentimental. They can also be disempowering. By reinforcing a portrait of the artist as a certain kind of flame—either blazing or flickering, self-sacrificial and vulnerable—they circle back to inevitable-seeming myths about an artist's agency. Made to serve, born to die. I had always been drawn toward these narratives, believing, as a teenager poring over gossip magazines and unauthorized biographies of singers in the throes of addiction, like Pete Doherty, that there was something romantic about suffering. That narrative reached its endpoint, for me, when Amy Winehouse died.

I was devastated by it. I remember hearing the news on TV during a family holiday and being completely overwhelmed with sorrow, unable to speak for hours afterward. It may have seemed like an excessive reaction, in the way that grief for someone you have never met often does, but her death spoke to something deep in me. For years afterward, I would regularly cry about Amy Winehouse when drunk, at ill-fitting moments, on nights out or at friend's parties. I still believed what bonded me to her as a listener was pain, and the ecstasy of drinking it away. Looking back now through the clearer lens of my own sobriety, I can also see that there was nothing ideal about those things, even if her music invites us to see the beauty in their expression.

Winehouse's legacy speaks for itself. It reminds us to remember her not merely as a victim of outside forces—even if there may have been serious lapses in care and judgment among those around her—but as an artist whose power lay in her craft. Her music inspired many artists who came before her and after her, elders and peers saw her as more than just her struggles, although they too would have recognized those experiences from their own lives. George Michael and Prince, two other legends also lost to addiction, both spoke about their admiration for her work and for "Love Is a Losing Game," a song they each covered in their own concert sets. She created that work in spite of her troubles, not because of them.

Of the newer artists explicitly influenced by her, a list that includes Billie Eilish, Adele, and Lady Gaga, to name just a few, Lana Del Rey is the perhaps the most obvious bearer of the torch. Del Rey also positions her songs squarely in the realm of mythology, in fatalistic narratives of love and torture, nostalgic for a cultural past that never quite existed. But some of her more recent work complicates the picture, and rejects the idea that she is always destined to be the persona she has sometimes adopted, fucked up and white-hot forever. Among her many lyrical motifs, which recur across different songs, she has added a newly defiant one, a variation on a familiar phrase: "No more candle in the wind."

The truth is that no one really makes their best work when they are in the throes of addiction, nor lives as their best self. When Lana Del Rey's career took off in 2012, just a year after Winehouse's death, she spoke publicly about being nine years sober from alcohol, a substance she described as "the first love of my life." Sobriety, and hindsight, hardly prevented Del Rey from being able to write vividly about self-destruction. If anything, they enabled her to. As Leslie Jamison, whose book *The Recovering* is a reflective critique of the myths around addiction and creativity, notes, "yearning is our most powerful narrative engine," and addiction is "one of its dialects," but only one. To tap into this yearning—for love and sex, booze or drugs—is a creative act that hardly requires active substance use. What it does require is living to tell the tale. As when Winehouse, as Jamison notes, "spent a sober week at her producer's condo in Miami, scribbling lyrics about booze that became the soundtrack to a million lives." Jamison likes to remember this scene from 2006, during the making of *Back to Black*, because it offers a glimpse of what could have been. "I would have loved to hear Amy Winehouse sing sober," Jamison writes, "not just two weeks sober, but three years sober, twenty years sober."

The story of Amy Winehouse shows us how flamboyance can be both a blessing and a curse. This gift is, at heart, a form of passion, a capacity to scale the heightened states of love and desire. And also, to find the words or melodies to express them, to create a spectacle of the unsayable that both inspires and soothes. These are risky talents to possess in an industry that seeks primarily to monetize them. When something precious is launched onto an unforgiving stage, in a culture that seems more capable of patronizing or neglecting its stars than protecting them, things can quickly go awry. Still, flamboyance depends most of all on vitality, not the risk of its own destruction. That's why Amy Winehouse's legacy impels us to better understand how art might come from pain, but also to get priorities straight. No artwork, however sublime, is more valuable than the person who made it.

I also like to think of Winehouse during that week at Salaam Remi's house in Miami, creatively on fire but safely distant, in that moment, from the coalface. She wrote the lyrics for "Tears Dry on Their Own" in the back garden one evening, sketching out from this Florida sunset a scene of personal change. In the song, the sky is "a blaze that only lovers see." This fiery spectacle is the final frame as the sun goes down. It is best viewed from the ground level, beneath a canopy of palm trees, the cool grass between your toes. She is still holding a torch, but in the "blue shade" of respite, a glimpse of recovery. Without which, there could be no light.

RECOVERING

ALCOHOL BURNS. NOT just throats when drunk, but through its own chemistry. Some of the earliest distilled spirits were known as "burning water," a strange combination of the elements. The discovery that alcohol is highly flammable gave rise to that appropriately showy method of cooking, the flambé, in which a dish—most commonly chicken, or a crepe, or bananas and cherries for desserts—is covered in alcohol while still in the pan and set alight. The flambé is not just for show (nor is it the sole penchant of gay men, whatever the guys in *The Sopranos* have to say about it). The burning actually changes the alcohol content of the spirit (evaporating around a quarter of it) and alters the chemical structure of the food as the sugars in the alcohol caramelize, introducing greater nuance to the dish's flavor. While the modern flambé has its origins in nineteenth-century European cooking, its heyday was in the first half of the twentieth, the theatrical flair a sign that you were in an upmarket restaurant.

Today the flambé's charms reside in its vintage status, an example of the way that past culinary trends can eventually come to seem tacky and endearing (even if they are legitimate cooking methods). The word has sometimes been used as a term for drunk (I was *flambéed* last night!), which certainly has technical appropriateness on its side. Neither *hammered* nor *wasted* nor any metaphor for intoxication conjures quite such a vivid image, of being soaked in alcohol and set on fire. But that metaphor never really caught on.

On the good nights, with the drink inside you, you might feel a bit like a flambé. You can convince yourself that you elicit the same reaction as a pan alight, its naked blue flame wielded by a table-side chef doing it for the hundredth time to the curious gasps of onlookers. Sometimes, drinking feels like blazing: tirades, cigarettes, whole sections of the dance floor. You are the definition of fun, not just a party animal but a soul in harmony with the night. It is like being on a first date with your oldest friend. Perhaps a wrong turn will school you in the risks you are taking, in your unthinking hubris, the lost possessions, and near misses. For many, the ashes of the morning after will bring sufficient pause, a simple lesson of age (that what goes up must come down). But you keep going. Suddenly your companions are no longer there, and this room, in which you are now alone, has no chandelier to swing from.

It is hard to write about drinking without entering the labyrinth of myths. Even the bad stories are seen to possess a certain worn glamour, the shimmer associated with hard living. Some of the most flamboyant historical eras go hand in hand with scenes of intoxication, from the spirited excesses of the roaring twenties to the coked-up boom of the 1980s. To indulge, collectively and individually, in the act of losing control is a hallmark of living outside the rules, or making the rules of capitalist time bend to the pursuit of pleasure. Flamboyant consumption appears as the antithesis of moderation.

When I consider some of the most appealing myths about what drinking has to offer, I often think of a scene from the play *People,*

Places and Things, by the British playwright Duncan Macmillan. It tells the story of Emma, an actress who enters a rehab facility for an addiction to drugs and alcohol. We watch her bristle against the efforts of family, friends, and therapists to help her get sober, clinging desperately to the coping mechanisms she has come to interpret as truths. "Drugs and alcohol have *never* let me down," she proclaims in one scene. "There are substances I can put into my bloodstream that make the world *perfect*," she continues, a world, as she puts it later in the scene, "that's *fucked*," full of injustice and pain and suffering. "Shouldn't we *feel good* for all those who can't?" she asks, not quite rhetorically. From the outside looking in, this seems like an improbable worldview, hardly an ethical code for living well. But it is extremely tempting. I believed something similar for a long time. That to give yourself over to substances is not a waste of life, but a more exalted form of living.

I too believed that drinking had never let me down. It was an instant path to heightened sensation. Feeling good, or celebrating something? Have a drink. Feeling sad, lonely, trapped in a state of uncertainty? Have two. My drinking began in a way that I think felt normal for many teenagers, from surreptitious glasses of wine at the family Christmas party, to house parties and end-of-night vomits and sprained ankles. These were all parts of the wear and tear of being young, and in the backdrop there was always the idea that one day you will learn your limits by testing them, and respond to your mistakes accordingly. But for some of us that learning does not come automatically. As you get older it can become harder, not easier, to refrain from taking it too far.

Everyone seemed to be drinking when I went to university, and even if I sometimes went further than others, the consequences did not quite form a problem, nor gather the momentum of a situation. As a student, my desires unmet by a series of unrequited crushes, I would sometimes forgo nights out and drink alone. I remember one particular evening, when I had been pining for a male friend, and my housemates were off doing something else, and I bought a bottle of gin from the supermarket and drank it neat, Amy playing in each ear from my iPod. Even at the time it seemed a bit silly, like I was looking for attention or cosplaying a tortured soul. But it is not really playing if you actually drink the whole bottle.

I often had a sense that my drinking was related to my sexuality, my difficulty accepting who I was, and that it offered a meaningful outlet for that. Drinking brought me out of my shell, made me more able to connect. The way I dressed on nights out changed over the course of my time at university, and I stopped feeling so self-conscious. As a student, alcohol offered a space for processing and letting out aspects of myself that seemed to have no other healthy outlet, and would have stayed inside otherwise, deep and festering. I had not, by the end of university, made peace with being gay yet, never mind taking pride in it. But flamboyance—in myself and in others—was no longer something I was afraid of. Drink, quite frankly, helped me get there.

The confidence offered by drinking, the charisma of lowered inhibitions, is often chalked up to what seems like a simple formula. Alcohol gives you the confidence to be your loudest, most ebullient self, and recoups its offerings the next day from your physical well-being. But what drinking can also do to your self-esteem throws this equation off balance. Is it really amplifying or liberating a version of who you are if it is also breaking you down in the background, whittling away at your capacity for fun and ease without it? To wake up and be told you were "on fire last night" is an affirmation of something that could easily have turned out differently.

I can recall plenty of times when the story of the night was triumphant, a tale of excesses kept just about in check, when even the more ridiculous aspects of drunk behavior are nothing more than a good punchline, a shared anecdote banked for the future. But I can remember many more occasions when the opposite was true. Blinkered memories of the night before, incomplete but no less forceful for it, filled with shame. All the actions that might have seemed funny and desirable become abject and embarrassing in the light of day.

That I needed alcohol to enjoy myself, to feel flamboyant, to feel like I was tapping into some inner reserve of authenticity, came to condition many of my behaviors in adult life. Not every social occasion would involve drinking, or heavy drinking, but I would always most look forward to the ones that did. If I drank only with other people, my habits may have seemed less problematic, confined to weekend binges or particular environments. But more and more frequently, the boundaries were beginning to blur; hangovers were not an endpoint but a momentary blip, easily fixed by a daytime hair of the dog. I could abstain without too much difficulty, but as soon as I had one drink, the cycle would start again. From that point onward, I never knew when this new session would burn itself out.

To be in recovery from alcohol addiction is also to be in recovery from the stories you tell yourself. This process is hard, but it is also beautiful, in its own way. In the place of the old stories, you write new ones. To do this, you have to let go of ideas that you hold dear, the notion that it has all been worth something. "I want to *live*," says Emma in *People, Places and Things*, "I want to live *vividly* and make huge, spectacular, heroic mistakes." To give up drinking can feel like trading in your exciting, chaotic, heroic existence for a drab and joyless one, discovered in its wake. "Because what else is there?" Emma asks, "This? Shame and boredom and orange fucking squash?" This is all another way of saying that recovery, for all of its wonders, has a PR problem in a culture centered around pleasure and excitement.

While the familiar images of intoxication seem to capture

life at its most intense and flamboyant, the familiar images of sobriety seem almost comically opposed. Exchange that flaming shot of absinthe for a mug of tea, the glimmer of a neon-lit bar for an Alcoholics Anonymous meeting in a carpeted church hall. Emma's own resistance to the wholesomeness of recovery is affirmed regularly in representations of drinking in film and TV, where group meetings are often used a set piece or a punchline. I am thinking of the start of *Rocketman*, the 2019 biopic about the life and career of Elton John. We see the musician (played by Taron Egerton) striding down a corridor in one of his signature outlandish outfits, all orange Lycra and glitter, shaped like the feathers of a flaming bird. It seems like he has just walked offstage, but as he struts closer to the camera, we see he is actually heading into a recovery group meeting, and takes his seat with a petulant scowl, the pain of acceptance clearly weighing on his chest.

It is a neat gag, this visual mismatch, about the contrast between the glamorous, excessive life of a famous rock star, flamboyant to the literal detail of his costume, and the quiet, benign mood of this nondescript room, its inhabitants assembled on fold-up chairs arranged in a circle, dressed in muted tones and ready to listen. In the context of this room, Elton's outfit seems ridiculous. That glamour is quickly shed as the reality of the situation becomes clear, that this self-professed alcoholic and cocaine addict is probably in the right place, however reluctantly.

I thought of this scene again when I went to see Elton John's headline set at Glastonbury a few summers ago. It was due to be his last ever UK show, and one of the final dates in his Farewell Yellow Brick Road tour, so I was primed for a bittersweet experience. There were well over a hundred thousand people gathered at the Pyramid Stage that night, and it had the feeling of something major. When the fireworks burst out, lighting up the sky a few songs before the end, as if they could not be contained any longer, I was already tearing up, moved by hearing that many people sing, in unison, the same tender words about a feeling inside. Although I had never thought of myself as a particularly attentive Elton John fan, the lyrics to his biggest songs came to me like second nature. I was connecting to them in a new way, as if coming to understand, in real time, what they meant to me. They had always been there, and so had he.

Elton John, I remembered, was one of the earliest reference points I had for a gay man. He was at the piano singing at Princess Diana's funeral, an emotional day I could distinctly remember, as a five-year-old, because my mum and her friends had gathered together to watch it. He was the man who wore a wig, which I remember my dad referring to as a "syrup" (Cockney rhyming slang for "syrup of figs"), and I wondered even then if there was something fruity about that. Later, he was the man who had a civil partnership with another man, who was the subject of bawdy innuendoes on British comedy shows. As far as flamboyance goes, he is one of pop culture's readiest examples, known for the extravagant stage outfits he began wearing in the 1970s, all feathers and diamonds, when his act shifted from bluesy piano man to glam-rock astronaut. When I saw him perform that night, I thought of the times he had lived through as a gay pop star: the homophobia that surrounded him growing up in 1950s suburbia, the loss of his friends to AIDS and his subsequent AIDS advocacy, and his well-documented struggles with addiction. He was still standing, over three decades sober, a survivor in a gold suit.

Now he was gilding his legacy before a field full of cheering fans and audiences watching the broadcast at home, thanking them for their love and support throughout his career. I felt close to him somehow. Not physically—the area around the Pyramid Stage is enormous, and my friend Astrid and I were way back on a hill—but close to what he has meant to people as an entertainer. The show ended with "Rocket Man," a climactic singalong that crescendoed with an elongated, almost frenzied piano riff, as fireworks lit up the sky. It was an appropriately flamboyant send-off for a flamboyant icon, a ritual display of passion and flair, but it also brought to my mind something that could not be seen on stage.

Here was a figure who had lived to enjoy his legacy written in light, performing a show that was, in part, a celebration of living long enough to have a say in how you bid farewell. There were poignant moments earlier in the set, when John sang two of his 1970s tracks: "Candle in the Wind," his signature tribute to Marilyn Monroe (and later Diana), and "Don't Let the Sun Go Down on Me," which he dedicated to George Michael, who sang it with him as a duet in the 1990s. This mini in memoriam section was a tribute to those whose lights had already burned out, and thus a reminder that what made this spectacle possible was a life that had also been sustained by quieter moments of resilience, care, and recovery. Joyful tears were running down my cheek as I looked up at the fireworks. I was just over a year into my own sobriety, at this point. What I heard, or perhaps chose to hear, in the montage of songs and years, was a call to reject the toxicity of self-hatred, to take care of myself. Although it seemed a world away from the rooms of recovery meetings, they had a part to play in this spectacle.

Long before I ever entered the rooms, I had also imagined an Alcoholics Anonymous meeting as a forum of misery. But then, by the time I went to my first meeting, I was pretty miserable myself. It was a period of flux in my life, as the world began opening up again after lockdown. I was entering into the final year of a temporary academic position, after which the future was unclear, and the publication of my first book was close on the horizon. My ex and I had broken up. Over a period of months, my drinking accelerated rapidly, and quickly lost its lustre, less jubilant than sad and compulsive. I was fortunate that I had held things together, so far, although it involved a fair amount of concealment from the people around me. I was drinking daily and surreptitiously, and even if to the outside world nothing appeared to be wrong, how I felt on the inside was another matter. In the early hours of the morning, during a solo bender, I found myself searching for local Alcoholics Anonymous meetings on my phone, aware that I needed help, and had nothing to lose.

The 12-step program is both simple and intricate, defined by its focus on spiritual recovery, and its nonhierarchical and, in theory, apolitical structure, which emphasizes collectivity and service. Since its founding in the 1930s in America, by a doctor and a stock broker, anonymity has been the foundation of the program's traditions, a core aspect of its communal ethics. For that reason, there is a certain dissonance in trying to write about it in much detail. What I can describe was the strange magic that came with the anonymous embrace of that first meeting. There was a sense of intimate familiarity with people I had never met, who received newcomers not as strangers but as one of their own, someone they may be able to help. Ironically enough, the closest reference point I had for this immediate sensation of closeness was the bar, those drunk nights out when you just click with a stranger, and decide to be best friends for an hour, maybe two, exchanging numbers before the taxi home, each promising you will call. (Neither ever does.) The ability to merge with people in this way had long been one of my favorite things about drinking, and I found it particularly useful during the summers I spent in my twenties stomping around in gay bars in unfamiliar cities, often on my own. I felt at my most flamboyant in these settings, precisely because I was at my most anonymous.

The anonymity of Alcoholics Anonymous is, naturally, of a

different sort. Although those rooms are, in the most basic sense, a space of reinvention, and lend people a floor to speak while free of identifying baggage, the program is intended as a long-term solution. A gradual and lifelong commitment to personal accountability, different in scope and tenor from the intensely transient bonds of pavement smoking areas. Its scriptural anonymity is about putting principles above personalities, about an investment in the collective mission of a group, rather than ladling attention upon individuals or allowing them to become focal, powerful, or publicly recognizable. That is not to say that meetings are impersonal spaces. If anything, they allow personality to shine in unexpected ways. It was, in other words, a pleasant surprise to discover that these church halls are not where flamboyance goes to die. Rather, they are a place where flamboyance and humility meet, an outlet for anger, about daily frustrations and resentments, but also gratitude.

Saying the words "I'm an alcoholic" forms a powerful speech act. This convention, which is not one of the program's official traditions, but a ritual handed down and now ubiquitous, is perhaps what makes it easily mockable, adjacent to the formality of confession or the angst of coming out. It has a theatrical quality, but that is not to imply anything is being fabricated or made up. The feelings and stories shared in those rooms are wholly real for the people living them. Nor are they intended as entertainment. Instead, the program's core practice of group sharing recalls a mode of oral tradition. Unlike group therapy, for example, in which people respond to and counsel each other, and establish dialogue, 12-step meetings guard against individuals speaking back to each other during the meeting (which is known as "cross-sharing.") A share, in essence, is a monologue, an act of live storytelling intended to impart strength and hope among its listeners.

In that opening scene from *Rocketman*, Elton John goes on to tell his life story to the group, revealing the meeting as a narrative framing device for the entire film. Despite the glum image surrounding recovery groups, shares and stories can be funny, running the gamut of gallows humor and self-deprecation. It is perhaps no accident that people who have been in the rooms for a long time, the old-timers, are often adept sharers, able to distil their insights and experience into a story that can help its listeners. I have even heard such storytellers share about the way they share, about the need sometimes to check themselves and their ego, to make sure they are not approaching their share as if it were a headline stand-up set.

Egos could easily run wild in a 12-step meeting, but the program is about looking beyond ego to see yourself as a community-minded member of a group, and the limits on how long people can share for are there to rein in dominant personalities. The program's reservations around ego, its emphasis upon acknowledging your defects of character and surrendering to the program and a higher power (of your own definition), have proven divisive. Common critiques, as writer Virginia Heffernan notes, point to the fact that, for people with trauma, focusing masochistically on your own culpability can be a form of "victim blaming," in a way that seems out of step with contemporary values.

While 12-step recovery begins with admitting that you are "powerless over alcohol" (Step 1), the face of contemporary sobriety, and the new sober culture, is largely about empowerment. Today's sobriety movement is effective because it responds to popular trends. The "quit lit" genre has refashioned the ethos of self-help to speak to the immense benefits of sobriety, and encourage readers to pursue pleasure and self-affirmation, while online sober influencers celebrate and amplify the richness of life without alcohol. Other figures look at sobriety from a social justice perspective, and comment on all of the ways alcohol use can repress and disenfranchise, taking people further away from their sense of purpose.

Often designed in opposition to 12-step programs, the new sober culture is no less divisive. Heffernan identifies three dominant strands among sober influencers—"Mystical gurus who ground their sobriety in rococo superstitions; professional habit-breakers who regard sobriety as a happiness hack, and reps from the managerial class who advocate for medical interventions and cognitive science." No sobriety system is perfect, but the new sober culture is certainly more comfortable than the old way with making sobriety flamboyant. As the authors of *The Sober Lush* affirm, it is possible to live "a giant, dirty, wild, glamorous life without consequences of numbness or regret." I totally agree. However you get sober, you will eventually have to redefine what living flamboyantly looks like, and it is a great comfort to discover that much is still there for the taking. But I first learned about this the old-fashioned way, in those fateful church halls.

The American poet Eileen Myles, who stopped drinking in the early 1980s, remembers the story they told themselves in early sobriety. "I was really just fine," they thought, "and the only thing that had been wrong with me was that I drank a lot, and now I wanted to be the same great person, only sober." Their commitment to the pose meant that they "would still be suavely leaning over a bar," or "at some fabulous dinner with cool people, a total nervous wreck, maybe in a nice jacket, drinking gallons of Perrier, girlfriend by my side, pretty speechless but sober." In that era, "looking good was good enough." But later, fifteen or so years into sobriety, they realized that "if I'm writing the score to this film, I have to be in it. Even like how it feels," even if that means refusing invitations to bars and dinners, and only sticking to the company of "really good friends."

The film of my early sobriety has involved scenes I could never have imagined at the beginning—of wedding dance floors and music festivals, powered only by diet cola, of leaving nightclubs in the early hours, and not until closing time. This film has had its fair share of flamboyance, of rituals and heightened emotions. During the series of firsts (first house party, first pub and club trip), it was almost a point of personal pride to do certain things, to say I have done them, a completist attitude that may have been energizing at the time but is better left behind. Over time, that sense of endurance has been replaced by gratitude, for the capacity to enjoy the largesse of these experiences in a way that feels healthy. I like how it feels to be there. But there is no saying, as yet, how this might change. What feels affirming now may feel merely tempting, and anxiety inducing, later. Embracing sobriety in this way means still embracing the flamboyance of certain activities, and past pleasures, but also working out when space is sometimes needed, and when they might pose the risk of relapse. It is a calculation you can only perform if you remain in touch with what you are feeling.

Flamboyance comes in many forms. Only sometimes is it loud and bombastic. It can be quiet too. I find it in the account Eileen Myles shares of sobriety as a form of creative renewal, the transition they describe from being "wine poet" to a "water poet—a reluctant lover of clarity." Sobriety made them alive to the fact that there is a "whole world" and "it's all out there waiting for you, in a way it never was before." Instead of going to parties, Myles looked at the sky through their telescope, finding in the skyline of New York, where they had lived for many years, "something wonderful and new about the way light clustered at the tips of buildings, and the buildings themselves had an articulate quality that was riveting." Or they considered water, the"way it moves and all the colors it holds at once." Sober creativity, like all creativity, arises from our capacity to notice, to receive the world around us. To spot a sunrise, a quality of the day's light, or the orange of a poppy on a deserted shoreline.

As I understand it, recovery involves building a life in which you can find fulfillment without the aid of intoxication. It is not about leaving exciting exteriors behind, or replacing them with their opposites, but acknowledging that flamboyance does not begin or end on life's surfaces. For those of us who struggle with addiction or addictive tendencies, the spiritual or personal practices fostered in recovery are often helpful, even vital, for illuminating this other path. In a way I never could have predicted, sobriety has only intensified my belief in flamboyance as a life-affirming force. It has allowed me to see what Harriet Monroe noted over a hundred years ago, in the midst of a blazing and hedonistic era. That where flamboyance begins, its place of origin, is within.

THE ART

FIRE HAS LONG been a way to make ourselves known, in all its wild and manmade varieties. A bonfire, lit on a beach, lets passing ships know the land is inhabited. A flare is launched into the sky by those at sea, lighting up the dark for a moment, before fizzling out. Flamboyance can be another of these human lifelines, a signal, for whoever sees it, that there are other ways of being.

I wrote a poem on this subject some years ago, during my winter in Boston, when I was feeling a little stranded myself. It was for submission to a zine, published in conjunction with Flare, London's annual queer film festival at the British Film Institute. Taking stock of the flamboyant figures and images from the films I had been watching, in the spirit of exploration, I was hoping to account for the ubiquity of flamboyance among even a small sample of films, and a makeshift canon of stars that included Judy Garland, Jason Holliday, Derek Jarman and the queens of *Paris Is Burning.* I called the poem "A Flare," a nod to the name of film festival, but also to the power of these figures, how they embody the flair of flamboyance, the sheer brightness of its craft, rather like a flare, illuminated across a great distance, through screens and moving images.

There was another image I had in mind, a scene at the end of Jarman's 1990 film *The Garden*, which depicts him fast asleep in a double bed on the Dungeness shore while the tide is out. As he sleeps, a group of five robed figures circle him with lit flares. The trailing smoke around them gives the impression of a ritual, and the light is captured and reflected back on the surface of the wet sand. They are ethereal, angelic figures, protecting our hero from changing tides, or dancing in solidarity with him. It reads as a dream sequence, although perhaps the dream being reflected is not exclusively that of the sleeping artist, but also our own, the viewers, a primal wish for someone to watch over us. To tend our dreams as we sleep, much like Jarman tends his gardens, flaming flowers vulnerable to the wind, and the difficult conditions of the soil, yet still bursting forth.

The deeper I have delved into flamboyance and its history, the longer this montage has grown in my mind, made up of artists, writers, singers, dancers, filmmakers, and individuals who simply make flamboyance their daily practice, living boldly and without apology. Like so many lit flares, or angels of my dreams, I have found myself looking to these figures for solace and inspiration, at low points, and been faced at every turn with my own memories and desires. Looking back across these pages now, I find in them a map of my own experiences, and of the artworks that have helped me through those experiences over the last fifteen years of my life, ever since I went to university and began, slowly, through studying and sex and self-fashioning, to emerge from hiding.

The history of flamboyance, when I began writing this book, seemed to me important and interesting in its own right. I approached my research, at first, with a critical eye, hoping to do the concept justice, to make a clear case for it as something unique, distinct from camp and richer than its regular definitions. A memoir was not what I intended to write, but I quickly learned that I had skin in the game. The more time I spent with flamboyance, tracing its linguistic origins and the stories of some of its brightest stars, the more I realized that I was seeking an understanding about myself. Still uncomfortable in my own skin, unsure of myself and the way I walked and talked and felt and loved, chasing after flamboyance brought me up short, and showed me what I felt I had always lacked.

Flamboyance, it turns out, has always been there, a guiding force behind my interests and entanglements, from early on and still today. The rebellious boy dancing to Michael Jackson in the playground. The bad jumpers and loud shirts. Crying loudly about boys in smoking areas. Drinking alone with Amy Winehouse. Sticky-floored bars and bright lights. A recovery meeting. The first page of a notebook, blank but for an unfinished sentence, still to be completed, and the idle doodle of a flame.

Flamboyance is the beginning of art, and I think the reverse is also true. Art is the beginning of flamboyance, a blueprint for a way of being in the world, where we do not suppress our vibrancy, out of fear or shame, but let it show. Flamboyant figures can act as role models, in this regard. In them we find vestiges of our own fantasies, and unlived potential. Freud understood the crucial role that fantasy plays in our inner lives, as a container for our unfulfilled wishes. From the games of role-play and invention that characterize childhood, to the daydreams that occupy our adult lives, fantasies can reveal our unconscious desires. Only an "unsatisfied" person fantasizes, he argued in his lecture on fantasy and creative writing, and our "unsatisfied wishes" are the motors of fantasy, which is always in some sense "the fulfillment of a wish, a correction of unsatisfying reality." While an active fantasy life can lead, in certain cases, toward delusion, it is not always, Freud notes, a pathological trait. In fact, it is the basis of creativity, a way of giving form to an artist's own inner life. What art gives us, in return, as an audience, is permission. Aesthetic pleasure, in Freud's book, is the "liberation of tensions in our minds," something that enables us "to enjoy our own day-dreams without self-reproach or shame."

In seeking to inhabit flamboyance myself, to learn from its artists, I have needed to reassess my own fantasies, to better understand the roles I assign them, consciously and unconsciously. Recovery has asked this of me, and therapy. Getting older does it too. I am thirty-three as I write this, but some days I still feel like a teenager, staring up adoringly at a poster of a pop star, wondering what my adult future will hold. Other days I feel older, jaded but a little wiser, looking back upon a wanton past. In reality, what I have at my fingertips is neither naivety or wisdom, but experience, and a story I have to tell. I have learnt that I want to be bigger, because I have spent so long feeling small. I want to take up more space because, as I can now see in the clearer light of sobriety, without the artificial confidence of substances, how often I have wanted to shrink myself, to avoid friction in my encounters with the world and with others. To keep hiding yourself, in the name of an easier ride, gets exhausting after a while. The opposite of flamboyance is inhibition.

In the end, art is only the beginning. To use it as a model for living offers pleasures that are real and significant, but also vicarious. At this stage of my life, I want to do more than just enjoy my own daydreams. I want to bring them closer to reality, in the knowledge that this process is messy, and rarely easy. I am picking up strategies, the things that work for me, making space to queen out more, to apologize less, to enjoy the natural high of live music, which is my happy place, the closest I can get the sensations I used to chase. Standing in a crowd, in the force field of energy created by others, screaming words I know by heart, everything can feel, for a moment, more expansive, ecstatic. These may be temporary thrills, but they fill the cup, and can be relived in tranquility.

Flamboyance, I am learning, is not a permanent state of being we achieve, but something we move closer toward in increments, through particular acts and outlets. Nor does flamboyant transformation take place overnight, other than in fantasy versions of this story. What precedes the spectacle, the grand reveal of a new and more confident self, is the sometimes laborious work we do behind the scenes. It is about facing, rather than avoiding, certain truths. It is the life's work of self-love, a process of trial and error, with its own fair share of risks and failures. It is about building a life that feels secure enough to contain those risks, and, in our politically darkening era, about building communities in which people are free to express their flamboyance, without censure or hostility, as is their right.

I am still learning how to put these ideas into practice, to better shape my daily life around them, to find in them a mode of connecting with, and learning from, others. And while there is no one right way to do this, there are ways that are best avoided. Approaches that are less honest, more perilous, where flamboyance functions as a mask, concealing the truth, or a cosmetic change, a temporary fix, a potentially dangerous aspiration. This is a tale as old as time, and many of Western culture's founding narratives offer cautions against flamboyant wanting. The overstepping Icarus flies too close to the sun. Joseph is attacked by his jealous brothers for his coat of many colors. In Shakespeare, there are flamboyant fools, witty and subversive, and flamboyant kings, power hungry and doomed by their bids for grandeur. One of my favorite variations on this narrative arc, which I share here as a final example, is found in a different kind of classic.

The 1994 Australian comedy *Muriel's Wedding* is a comic and tragic tale of transformation, leavened with an offbeat humor and a pop sensibility. It tells the story of Muriel Heslop (played by the brilliant Toni Colette), a young woman living in the fictional dead-end seaside town Porpoise Spit. She longs to escape her family home, presided over by her domineering father, a crooked local politician, and her put-upon mother, who is repeatedly belittled by her husband. Muriel is socially awkward, and the ugly duckling among her mean-spirited group of friends, but she is not dowdy, which is the usual cinematic signifier for life's losers. In fact, she dresses loudly, wearing leopard-print blouses and bright red lipstick. This aesthetic has class associations, but in bristling against the banality of Muriel's existence it also hints at something deeper, the colorful visions that illuminate her inner world.

Muriel possesses a keen imagination, fueled by optimism and fantasy. Her biggest dream is to get married, to be the center of attention at a glamorous wedding, a shorthand for her desire for a dramatically different life. It figures that she is also the world's biggest ABBA fan. Much of her life seems to be spent inside the joyful fantasies of their music, imagining herself in the flamboyant, sparkling costumes of the band's 1970s heyday.

As the film plays out, we watch Muriel's dreams start to come true. She sees an opportunity to escape Porpoise Spit and tricks her mother into signing a blank check, so she can use the money to go on holiday, in pursuit of her friends, who neglected to invite her on their trip. While at the holiday resort she meets Rhonda, a flamboyant misfit (played by Rachel Griffiths), who is rebellious and free-spirited, and teaches Muriel to reject the way that others see her. It is a transformative friendship from the start, full of play and abandon, as when the pair take to the stage during the resort's open-mic karaoke, and perform "Waterloo" together, dressed up as Agnetha and Anni-Frid from ABBA.

They decide to run away to pursue a new life together in Sydney, where they work odd jobs, go dancing most nights, and bring men back to the apartment they share. Muriel renames herself Mariel, and reinvents herself in the process. "When I lived in Porpoise Spit, I used to sit in my room for hours and listen to ABBA songs," she tells Rhonda. "But since I've met you and moved to Sydney, I haven't listened to one ABBA song. That's because my life is as good as an ABBA song."

Before long, however, the foundations of Muriel's fairy tale start to crumble. Within the space of about fifteen minutes, in the middle of the film, *Muriel's Wedding* goes from being a joyful and flamboyant comedy about female friendship, to something much darker and sadder. First, Rhonda is diagnosed with a tumor on her spine, which leaves her paralyzed. While Muriel offers her friend support initially, as she adjusts to life in a wheelchair, she gets distracted when an opportunity to get married, her biggest dream of all, lands in her lap. She enters into a sham marriage with a South African swimmer who needs an Australian visa so he can compete in the Olympics, arranged through her father's political contacts. Although the relationship is purely transactional, and evidently loveless, Muriel retreats back into the world of fantasy as she organizes her dream wedding. In the process, she forgets about Rhonda, but also about her mother, whose fragile mental state is deteriorating rapidly.

Shortly after her fake wedding, Muriel is called home when she learns of her mother's death by suicide. She is forced to face up to the fact that her initial act of deceit, tricking her mother with the blank check and bringing her family to financial ruin, set these events in motion. The scorched earth of the back garden, which her mother set fire to just before her death, perhaps accidentally, or perhaps as a final cry for help, is a potent symbol of the consequences of Muriel's naivety. The film acts as a cautionary tale about pursuing one's dreams through dishonest means.

To dream, like Muriel, of a better life—according to the familiar metrics of wealth or beauty, of style or effortless charisma—is to imagine the acceptable flamboyance of an optimized self, the luminous quality of standing out in a capitalist world. Capitalism teaches us to want things that are, for the most part, unattainable, although the fact of this hardly kills or quells those fantasies. As the late theorist Lauren Berlant observed, there is something cruel about this optimism, the idea that we cannot help but strive for "the good life," even, or especially, when all of the evidence points to the contrary. Muriel dreams of getting married, even though her model for marriage, the relationship between her parents, is toxic and unequal. She dreams of being popular, an "It" girl, even though the queen bees of Porpoise Spit are cruel and shallow. The values of benign success, and the imperative to belong in particular ways, are so ingrained that it can be difficult to see the alternatives.

"Why do people stay attached to conventional good-life fantasies" of couples and families, of social status and institutions, Berlant wondered, "when the evidence of their instability, fragility and dear cost abounds?" Optimism is a powerful force, and we often remain attached to things that do not serve us because being attached, as Berlant puts it, is inherently optimistic; it "moves you out of yourself and into the world, in order to bring closer the satisfying *something* that you cannot generate on your own." We can find that something, Berlant continues, "in the wake of a person, a way of life, an object, project, concept, or scene," all of which can instill and inspire the fantasies that there is something better in store for us. *Muriel's Wedding* is about what happens when those fantasies fray and come apart. What emerges in their wake can be tragic, or depressing, or alternatively, an opportunity for renewal, a desire to change the system or the role you play within or outside of it.

Somehow, the film does end up feeling like an ABBA song, with a final tableau of hope and friendship and a hard-won joie de vivre. I remember watching the film for the first time with my friend Charlotte, who introduced it to me, one lazy Sunday afternoon, and it leaving us both in tears. It is a moment that never fails to move me, if only because it feels so full of possibility.

Following her mother's funeral, Muriel resolves to leave Porpoise Spit once again to pursue her new life, having learned the difficult lessons of her first attempt. On her way out of town, she swings by Rhonda's house to save her from the clutches of her own overbearing mother and their nasty group of friends. Rhonda is reticent, for a moment, but her frown quickly turns into a conspiratorial grin. As Muriel grabs the handlebars of Rhonda's wheelchair and takes her out to the taxi, the intro of ABBA's "Dancing Queen" kicks in, the unmistakable piano line and shimmering "aahs." As the taxi drives away, the two friends bid farewell to the streets and the malls and the beaches they once called home, and onward to Sydney.

Its potential cheesiness, as an ending, is mitigated by what has come before. This moment invites us to walk a middle path, where neither reality nor fantasy are disowned. Instead, they sit side by side, through difficult moments. The undertow of tension and sadness has not disappeared entirely. We see something of it in Muriel's face as she looks out the taxi window, her smile an indication of a difficult past, but also an exciting, if still unknown, future.

This elliptical moment also leaves us enough room, as viewers, to find in it what we might be seeking ourselves, the conventions we hope to flee, or the boldness we observe from afar, like a flare. Queer readings have been plentiful. Film critic Andy Medhurst once argued for *Muriel's Wedding* as "one of the great lesbian love stories of film history," crowned by this moment when Muriel arrives to "save the princess from the evil tower," to escape, once again, the "hyper-hetero constraints" of Porpoise Spit. Rachel Griffiths, who plays Rhonda, remembered once meeting a gay man who offered a "whole thesis" about the film as a "metaphor for LGBTQ+ people growing up in small-minded places" and also the AIDS crisis, when people got sick and were "dragged back to the judgmental place where you're not seen or loved."

This, at last, is what makes this ending feel more authentically like an ABBA song, the sense of joy shadowed by melancholy, the combination of euphoria and yearning that is so key to their music's potency. The flamboyance of this moment of transformation, as the hum of the everyday gives way to the bright tinkling of the disco piano, tells us that there is always more to see. It offers a simple message, one I would convey to my younger self, and one found, I believe, in all things flamboyant. You are not alone.

A FLARE

is peachy Oliver dancing to The Psychedelic Furs in short
shorts or Adèle Exarchopoulos dancing to Lykke Li and
  Annette Bening
singing to Joni Mitchell or Julianne Moore dancing and
  singing to
Etta James and it's Chipper Corey dancing and syncing to
Patti's LaBelle's 'Somewhere Over the Rainbow' in a
  Harlem ballroom
it's Judy Garland and her lineage, it's life as a cabaret and
  it's sitting alone
in your room watching Cate Blanchett watch Rooney
  Mara sipping
a martini and it's friends and comrades marching in Paris
  in 1991
and Mya Taylor marching down Santa Monica Boulevard
  in 2015
it's not just high camp or down-low-masc it's being taught
  to swim by

Mahershala Ali and it's a cigarette shared through a prison glory-hole

it's the way Jason smokes to Shirley Clarke's camera in furs and smiles

it's Tilda Swinton in everything and it's Derek Jarman's everything

it's being busy thinking about boys and beautiful movements queer

cinematic sexiness because what else is flamboyance but the flame

that lights a screen or steals a heart, projections you hold a torch for

because with them you feel found and less alone and in 'times of great

crisis', Frank O'Hara said, "we must all decide again and again whom

we love," and what else is fandom but deciding who loves us back across

the barrier, as when a train departs like the end of *Weekend* and we wait

for another star, one we haven't met yet, knowing we'll be the better for it—

it's that after years of watching we never call off the search

A PLAYLIST

A playlist of songs mentioned in the book.
Scan below to listen along.

ACKNOWLEDGMENTS

John Glynn, Eden Railsback, and the team at Hanover Square Press, Jason Arthur, Lamorna Elmer at Granta, Jane Finigan and the team at Lutyens and Rubinstein, David Forrer at Inkwell Management, for making it happen, and bringing this book into the world. Toby Bull, Sophie Harrold, Alex Hawkins for the moral support in the final push. Amelia Abraham, Cal Revely-Calder, Benedict Welch, for reading. Jeffrey, Jackson, Suzanne Bronski, Celine Lowenthal, Tom MacNeil, Robyn Massey, for New York. For the conversations, Cloud Downey, Mirela Ivanova, Joe Moshenska, Eli Zuzovsky, and Temi Wilkey, for exploring flamboyance together. Gisel, for the genesis. Michael Bronski, for our chats, and your encyclopedic knowledge. My friends, my family, Mum, Dad, Hannah, for everything else.

To Matthew, my therapist, thank you.

NOTES

THE SECRET

1 “confidence, stylishness . . .”: “flamboyant (adjective),” Oxford English Dictionary, 3rd ed. (Oxford: Oxford University Press, 2010).

5 “You’re not going to go . . .”: Bruce Handy, “He Called Me Ellen Degenerate?” TIME, April 14, 1997: https://time.com/3484943/he-called-me-ellen-degenerate. [Accessed August 1, 2025.]

8 “The secret . . .”: Clark Coolidge, “FO’H Notes,” in Homage to Frank O’Hara, eds. Bill Berkson and Joe LeSueur (California: Big Sky Books, 1978), p. 183.

THE WORD: A BRIEF TOUR

CHURCHES

13 “happy expression” (“expression si heureuse”) [translation my own]: Eustache de La Quérière, “Eglise Saint-Vincent de Rouen,” *Revue de Rouen et de Normandie* (France: Au bureau de le Revue de Rouen, 1843), p.259.

14 “components formed . . . (“compartiments en form de flammes”)” [translation my own]: Arcisse de Caumont, *Essai sur L’Architecture Religieuse du Moyen Age, Principalement en Normandie* (France: Memoires de la Société des Antiquaries de Normandie, 1825), p.72.

14 "alluding to the wave": Thomas Rickman, "Four Letters on the Ecclesiastical Architecture of France," *Archaeologia, or, Miscellaneous Tracts Relating to Antiquity*, 25 (London: Society of Antiquaries of London, 1833), p.179.

14 "strange fear and melancholy": John Ruskin, "The Flamboyant Architecture of the Valley of the Somme" (1869), in *The Works of John Ruskin,* ed. E.T. Cook and Alexander Wedderburn (London: George Allen, 1905), pp.260–61.

15 "would have lived . . .": Ruskin, *The Seven Lamps of Architecture* (New York: John Wiley, 1849), p.138.

15 "becoming too florid . . .": Ruskin, "The Flamboyant Architecture of the Valley of the Somme," p.262.

15 "dilettantes and aesthetes . . .": Marcel Proust, "Preface to *La Bible d'Amiens*," in *On Reading Ruskin,* translated and edited by Jean Autret, William Burford and Philip J. Wolfe (New Haven: Yale University Press, 1987), p.33.

16 "sparkling bunch . . .": Proust, *Swann's Way*, translated by Lydia Davis (East Rutherford: Penguin, 2004), p.141.

17 "lesbian desire": See Hannah Freed Thall, *Modernism at the Beach: Queer Ecologies and the Coastal Commons* (New York: Columbia University Press, 2023), p.61.

17 "brilliant luminescence": Proust, *Sodom and Gomorrah*, translated by John Sturrock (New York: Penguin Books, 2005), p.27.

21 "*les folles*": James Baldwin, *Giovanni's Room* (London: Penguin, 2001), p.30.

22 "made one feel . . .": Ibid., p.41.

22 "I fear that you . . .": Ibid., p.42.

22 "flaming, away . . .": Ibid., p.43.

22 "scarcely seen . . .": Ibid., p.29.

23 "I have never seen . . .": Baldwin, "Down at the Cross: Letter from a Region of My Mind," *The Fire Next Time* (New York: Random House, 2009), p.33.

23 "my sexuality . . .": Baldwin, "To Crush a Serpent," *The Cross of Redemption: Uncollected Writings* (New York: Vintage, 2010), p.197

25 "I've been trying to deviate": Owen Myers, "Lil Nas X: No Limits," *CR Men* 11 (Fall 2020), p.16.

25 "In the mix . . .": Ibid.

25 "flows through . . .": Sasha Geffen, "Male musicians have a rich history of using flamboyance as armour," *GQ*, June 27, 2020, https://www.gq-magazine.co.uk/fashion/article/male-singers-performance [accessed January 18, 2024].

26 "I went from being . . .": *Lil Nas X: Long Live Montero* (dir. Carlos López Estrada and Zac Manuel, 2023).

26 "fight for the soul . . .": Quoted in Carrie Battan, "The Unexpected Introspection of Lil Nas X," *The New Yorker*, September 24, 2021, https://www.newyorker.com/magazine/2021/10/04/the-unexpected-introspection-of-lil-nas-x [accessed February 8, 2025].

26 "devil's interval": The Mystery of Montero AKA Lil Nas X (feat. "Take a Daytrip," *Switched On Pop*, podcast, April 27, 2021, Spotify.

27 "Historians similarly pored . . .": See Andrew R. Chow, "Historians Decode the Religious Symbolism and Queer Iconography of Lil Nas X's 'Montero" Video,' March 30, 2021, https://time.com/5951024/lil-nas-x-montero-video-symbolism-explained [accessed February 8, 2025].

FLAMENCO

31 "*fellamenghu*": Wall text, The Flamenco Museum, Seville, Spain [accessed October 2024].

32 "To them, I would always . . .": RuPaul, *The House of Hidden Meanings* (London: 4th Estate, 2024), p.78.

34 "his own masterpiece . . .": Quoted in Jaime Manrique, *Eminent Maricones: Arenas, Lorca, Puig, and Me* (Madison: University of Wisconsin Press, 1999), p.76.

34 "torn like a medieval . . .": Federico García Lorca, "Play and Theory of the Duende," *In Search of Duende*, ed. and trans. Christopher Maura (New York: New Directions, 1998), p.53.

FLAMINGOS

41 "Many things in the world . . .": Susan Sontag, 'Notes on "Camp,"' *Against Interpretation and Other Essays* (London: Eyre & Spottiswoode, 1967), p.275.

42 "playful" (p.288), "apolitical" (p.277), "the love of the exaggerated" (p.279.): Ibid.

42 "favourite colour . . .": Mark Booth, *Camp* (London: Quartet Books, 1983), p.183.

42 "a complicated colour": Zandra Rhodes, *Iconic: My Life in Fashion in 50 Objects* (Bantam: London 2024), p.244.

43 "The old-style dandy . . ." Sontag, "Notes on 'Camp,'" p.289.

43 "themes which are . . .": Sontag, "Jack Smith's *Flaming Creatures*," *Against Interpretation*, p.229.

44 "strongly drawn . . .": Sontag, "Notes on 'Camp,'" p.276.

44 "the movie was so . . .": Quoted in Emanuel Levy, *Gay Directors, Gay Films?: Pedro Almodóvar, Terence Davies, Todd Haynes, Gus Van Sant, John Waters* (New York: Columbia University Press, 2015), p.283.

44 "trapped in the 1950s": Danny Fields and Fran Lebowitz, "*Pink Flamingos* & The Filthiest People Alive?" (1973), in *John Waters: Interviews*, ed. James Egan (Jackson: University Press of Mississippi, 2011), p.27.

45 "in John's films": Cookie Mueller, "John Waters and the Blessed Profession—1969," in *Walking through Clear Water in a Pool Painted Black* (South Pasadena, CA: Semiotext(e), 2022), p.61.

46 "wearing a wig . . .": Michael Moon and Eve Kosofsky Sedgwick, "Divinity: A Dossier, A Performance Piece, A Little-Understood Emotion," in *Tendencies* (London: Routledge, 1994), p.216.

46 "Divine exaggerated": quoted in *I Am Divine* (dir. Jeffrey Schwarz, 2013).

46 "Tracy's flamboyant flip": *Hairspray* (dir. John Waters, 1988).

47 "I don't remember . . .": Quoted in Levy, p.283.

47 "posture of amused . . .": Simon Doonan, *The Camp 100: Glorious*

flamboyance, from Louis XIV to Lil Nas X (London: White Lion Publishing, 2024), p.6.

47 "a bit dismissive . . .": Mark Allen, "Bruce LaBruce's New Take on Susan Sontag's 1964 Essay 'Notes on "Camp,"'" *HuffPost*, May 13, 2013, https://www.huffpost.com/entry/bruce-labruce camp_b_3230251 [accessed November 20, 2025].

47 "conservative camp . . .": Bruce LaBruce, "Notes on Camp/Anti-Camp," *Nat. Brut* 3 (April 2013), http:/www.natbrutarchive.com/essay-notes-on-campanti-camp-by-bruce-labruce.html [accessed November 20, 2025].

49 "an aesthetic that requires . . .": madison moore, *Fabulous: The Rise of the Beautiful Eccentric* (New Haven: Yale University Press, 2018), p.8.

49 "art created . . .": Ibid., p.19.

50 "failed seriousness": Sontag, "Notes on 'Camp,'" p.283.

50 "I'm a risk taker . . .": "Fergie: Sorry About the Anthem . . . But I Tried My Best!!," *TMZ*, February 19, 2018, https://www.tmz.com/2018/02/19/fergie-apologizes-for-nba-all-star-game-national-anthem/ [accessed November 20, 2025].

50 "it's good . . .": Sontag, "Notes on 'Camp,'" p.292.

51 "It's always been . . .": Danyel Smith, "When Whitney Hit The High Note," *ESPN Magazine*, February 1, 2016, http://www.espn.com/espn/feature/story/_/id/14673003/the-story-whitney-houston-epic-national-anthem-performance-1991-super-bowl. [accessed November 26, 2025]

51 "diamonds and furs . . .": "The Lasting Power of Whitney Houston's National Anthem," NPR, https://www.npr.org/transcripts/963595598 [accessed November 20, 2025].

FLOWERS

54 "Flamboyant trees are lovely . . .": Jean Rhys, *Voyage in the Dark* (London: Andre Deutsch, 1976), p.78.

54 "fire and sunset . . .": Rhys, *Wide Sargasso Sea* (London: World Books, 1967), p.183.

54 "If you are buried . . .": Ibid.

55 "ugliness of life . . .": February 11, 1946, *The Letters of Jean Rhys* (New York: Viking, 1984), p.43.

55 "Just as flamboyancy in art . . .": Oakes Ames, "Observations on the Capacity of Orchids to Survive in the Struggle for Existence," *Orchid Review* 30 (1922), p.231.

56 "In the world of flora and fauna": I am grateful to Mike McCarthy for our email correspondence (7 June 2024) about the role of flamboyance in the natural world.

56 "fist on his hip . . .": Proust, *Sodom and Gomorrah*, translated by John Sturrock (New York: Penguin Books, 2005), p.27.

57 "strategic use of flowers . . .": Dominic Janes, *British Dandies: Engendering Scandal and Fashioning a Nation* (Oxford: Bodleian Library, 2022), p.100.

57 "pansy": George Chauncey, *Gay New York: Gender, Urban Culture and the Makings of the Gay Male World, 1890–1940* (New York: Basic Books, 1994), p.15.

57 "Pansy Craze": Ibid., p.301.

57 "Was the pansy pinned . . .": Derek Jarman, *Modern Nature: The Journals of Derek Jarman* (London: Vintage, 2018), p.30.

59 "whole being has changed": Ibid., p.25.

59 "the seventies were . . .": Ibid., p.95.

60 "Can there be . . .": Derek Jarman, *The Last of England* (London: Constable, 1987), p.225.

60 "Jarman is an outsider . . .": Philip Hoare, "Tarry, Tarry Night: The Queer Nature of Derek Jarman," *Derek Jarman: Protest!*, ed. Sean Kissane (London: Thames and Hudson, 2020), p.286.

60 "short-lived, spring-flowering . . .": Jonny Bruce, "Wallflower," *On the Necessity of Gardening: An ABC of Art, Botany and Cultivation*, ed. Laurie Cluitmans (Amsterdam: Valiz, 2021), p.177.

60 "the introvert . . .": Ibid., p.178.

61 "interesting rather . . .": Zandra Rhodes, *Iconic: My Life in Fashion in 50 Objects* (Bantam: London, 2024), p.78.

61 "fabulously sunny": Ibid., p.31.

LIGHTING UP: CREATIVITY & CHARISMA

CREATING

65 "*flamelike* . . .": Richard Ellman, "Oscar at Oxford," *New York Review of Books,* March 29, 1984, https://www.nybooks.com/articles/1984/03/29/oscar-at-oxford [accessed November 20, 2025].

65 "success in life . . .": Walter Pater, *The Renaissance: Studies in Art and Poetry* (London: Macmillan, 1912), p.236.

66 "dandyism, effeminacy . . .": Alan Sinfield, *The Wilde Century: Effeminacy, Oscar Wilde and the Queer Moment* (New York: Columbia University Press, 1994), p.2.

66 "playing down . . .': Ibid, p.3.

66 "it tended toward . . .": Brigid Brophy, *Prancing Novelist: A Defence of Fiction in the Form of a Critical Biography in Praise of Ronald Firbank* (Dallas: Dalkey Archive Press, 2016), p.244.

68 "be happy to give up . . .": Harriet Monroe, *A Poet's Life: Seventy Years in a Changing World* (New York: The Macmillan Company, 1938), p.55.

68 "lively and interesting people": Ibid., p.37.

69 "trapeze-performer hurtling": Monroe, "Flamboyance," *POETRY: A Magazine of Verse,* 21 (November 1922), p.89.

69 "skimming the clouds": Ibid., p.90.

69 "exemplary . . .": Ibid., p.89.

70 "The imagination . . .": Ibid., p.90.

71 "blazing a tirade": Frank O'Hara, "For Grace, After a Party," in *Collected Poems*, ed. Donald Allen (Berkeley: University of California Press, 1995), p.214.

72 "You spent six months . . .": *A Bigger Splash* (dir. Jack Hazan, 1973).

73 "Picture a ceramist": This description is an account of the film *Showing Up* (dir. Kelly Reichardt, 2022).

DECORATING

77 "human life . . .": G.K. Chesterton, "William Morris and His School," in *Twelve Types: A Book of Essays* (London: Arthur L. Humphreys, 1910), p.30.

77 "great reformer": Ibid., p.28.

78 "some pleasure for the eyes . . .": William Morris, "The Lesser Arts," *Hopes and Fears for Arts: Five Lectures Delivered in Birmingham, London and Nottingham, 1878–1881* (London: Ellis & White), p.34.

79 "decorative value . . .": Oscar Wilde to A.S. Benson, May 16, 1885, in *The Letters of Oscar Wilde*, ed. Rupert Hart-Davis (New York: Harcourt, Brace & World Inc., 1962), p.174.

79 "beautiful objects . . .": Florence Nightingale, *Notes on Nursing: What It Is and What It Is Not* (New York: D. Appleton and Company, 1860), p.58.

80 "The child sees . . .": Baudelaire, "The Painter of Modern Life," in *The Painter of Modern Life and Other Essays,* trans. and ed. Jonathan Mayne (London: Phaidon Press, 1965), p.8.

81 "burly, corpulent . . .": March 10, 1869, *The Letters of Henry James*, vol. 1, ed. Percy Lubbock (New York: Charles Scribner's Sons, 1920), p.18.

82 "effeminate gay decorator . . .": Stephen Vider, *The Queerness of Home: Gender, Sexuality & The Politics of Domesticity after World War II* (Chicago: University of Chicago Press, 2021), p.69.

83 "gay creativity gene . . .": Alan Downs, *The Velvet Rage: Overcoming the Pain of Growing Up Gay in a Straight Man's World* (New York: Hachette, 2012), p.20.

83 "to hide behind . . .': Ibid, p.21.

83 "decorate the world . . .": Ibid., p.20.

83 "extremely flamboyant . . .": Jo-Ellan Dimitrius and Mark Mazzarella, *Reading People: How to Understand People and Predict Their Behavior—Anytime, Anyplace* (London: Vermillion, 1999), p.262.

84 "flamboyant heterosexual": "Rylan: How to Be A Man: Laurence Llewelyn-Bowen," June 8, 2023, BBC Studios, https://www.bbc.co.uk/sounds/play/p0fldh5h [podcast accessed August 24, 2025].

86 "Anglo-American art . . .": David Batchelor, *Chromophobia* (London: Reaktion Books, 2000), pp.9–10.

86 "colour has been . . .": Ibid., p.22.

86 "been systematically . . .": Ibid., p.22.

87 "typical of prejudices . . .": Ibid., p.23.

87 "The color is repellent . . .": Charlotte Perkins Gilman, *The Yellow Wall Paper* (Boston: Small Maynard, 1901), p.8.

TRYING

89 "Their placement . . .": Charlie Porter, *Bring No Clothes: Bloomsbury and the Philosophy of Fashion* (London: Particular Books, 2023), p.88.

93 "It's fantasy": Olivia Anderson, "Loewe's William De Morgan-Inspired Capsule Will Top Your Christmas List," *British Vogue*, November 11, 2019, https://www.vogue.co.uk/news/article/jonathan-anderson-william-de-morgan-collection [accessed 21 November, 2025].

94 "newly fledged and High-art . . .": Quoted in Rob Higgins and Christopher Stolbert Robertson, *William De Morgan: Arts and Crafts Potter* (Oxford: Shire Books, 2017), p.20.

96 "courage to face . . .": G.K. Chesterton, "William Morris and His School," in *Twelve Types: A Book of Essays* (London: Arthur L. Humphreys, 1910), p.28.

96 "If you put one of . . .": Jack Moss, "'Clothing Is Theatre': Jonathan Anderson on His Latest Loewe Collection," *An Other*, June 28, 2021, https://www.anothermag.com/another-man/13418/clothing-is-theater-jonathan-anderson-on-his-ss22-loewe-collection-david-sims [accessed November 21, 2025].

97 "You must decide": Quentin Crisp, "Having Style," *Crisperanto*, http://www.crisperanto.org/writings/HavingStyle.html [accessed February 11, 2025].

98 "Modesty, propriety . . .": Sting, "Englishman in New York," . . . *Nothing Like the Sun* (A&M, 1987).

99 "People have always": Quentin Crisp, *The Naked Civil Servant, How To Become A Virgin and Resident Alien* (New York: Triangle Classics, 2000). pp.414–15.

99 "foolishly attentive . . .": Monica L. Miller, "Fresh-Dressed Like a Million Bucks," in *Artist, Rebel, Dandy: Men of Fashion* (New Haven: Yale University Press, 2013), p.168.

99 "does not take . . .": moore, *Fabulous: The Rise of the Beautiful Eccentric* (New Haven: Yale University Press, 2018), p.8.

99 "parading financial status . . .": Ibid., pp.22–23.

STYLING

104 "I look handsome . . .": Tim Rice and Andrew Lloyd Webber, "Jacob & Sons," from *Joseph and His Amazing Technicolor Dreamcoat,* Tim Rice and Andrew Lloyd Webber (Polydor, 1991).

105 "that celebrity magazine": "Jamaica Kincaid: "Don't get me started on the New Testament, that celebrity magazine," *The Guardian*, August 9, 2024, https://www.theguardian.com/books/article/2024/aug/09/jamaica-kincaid-dont-get-me-started-on-the-new-testament-that-celebrity-magazine [accessed 21 November, 2025].

105 "One should either . . .": Oscar Wilde, *Phrases and Philosophies for the Use of the Young* (London: privately printed, 1894), p.8.

105 "studied by religious scholars . . .": For the queerness of Joseph, see Wendy Zierler, "Joseph(ine), the Singer: The Queer Joseph and Modern Jewish Writers," *Nashim: A Journal of Jewish Women's Studies & Gender Issues*, 24 (Spring 2013), pp.97–119; and Lori Hope Lefkovitz "Passing as a Man: Narratives of Jewish Gender Performance," *Narrative*, 10.1 (January 2002), pp.91–103.

106 "site upon which . . .": Alan Sinfield, *The Wilde Century*, p.74.

107 "mounts a critique . . .": Monica L. Miller, *Slaves to Fashion: Black Dandyism and the Styling of Black Diasporic Identity* (Durham: Duke University Press, 2009), p.10.

107 "negotiation of . . .": Ibid., p.6.

107 "Afro-Caribbean . . .": Miller, "Fresh-Dressed Like a Million Bucks," in *Artist, Rebel, Dandy: Men of Fashion* (New Haven: Yale University Press, 2013), p.168.

108 "elegant, well-appointed . . .": Ibid., p.159.

108 "scared to death": Quoted in Elias Leight, "Big L is 'Rap Royalty.' Why Is His Legacy in Disarray?" *Rolling Stone*, May 18, 2021, https://www.rollingstone.com/music/music-features/big-l-legacy-estate-1170642/ [accessed 21 November, 2025].

108 "flamboyant for life": Big L, "Flamboyant," *The Big Picture* (D&D Studios, 2000).

108 "Afro-Caribbean cultures . . .": Jeffrey Boakye, *Hold Tight: Black Masculinity, Millennials and the Meaning of Grime* (London: Influx Press, 2017), pp.384–5.

109 "communication of . . .": Miller, "Fresh-Dressed Like a Million Bucks," p.159.

109 "want you to be . . ." Alex Nagshineh, "Big L Interview," *Bonafide* (2015), https://www.bonafidemag.com/big-l-interview-2/ [accessed 21 November, 2025].

110 "sole employment": Pet Shop Boys, "Flamboyant," *PopArt: The Hits* (Parlophone, 2003).

110 "about the importance . . .": Neil Tennant in a radio interview, quoted in *Literally*, 28 (2005), p.2, https://petshopboys.net/literally/literally-20-to-30/literally-28-page1/literally-28-page-2 [accessed 21 November, 2025].

113 "derogatory term . . .": Ben Beaumont-Thomas, "Pop sensation Dorian Electra: 'I'm not a woman dressing as a man. It's more complex,'" *The Guardian*, July 12, 2019, https://www.theguardian.com/music/2019/jul/12/pop-sensation-dorian-electra-im-not-a-woman-dressing-as-a-man-its-more-complex [accessed 21 November, 2025].

114 "Electra had an extensive list": See Brendan Wetmore, "Dorian Electra's Top 5 Flamboyant Icons, *PAPER Magazine*, April 26, 2019, https://www.papermag.com/dorian-electra-flamboyant#rebelltitem1 [accessed 21 November, 2025].

114 "the whole joke . . .": Ibid.

114 "I'm a very flaming . . .": Dorian Electra, "Flamboyant," *Flamboyant* (Self-released, 2019).

EMPOWERING

117 "if there's one . . .": Dolly Parton, *Behind the Seams: My Life in Rhinestones* (London: Ebury, 2023), p.7.

118 "love / my momma . . .": Dolly Parton, "Coat of Many Colors," *Coat of Many Colors* (RCA Victor, 1971).

118 "It costs a lot . . .": Dolly Parton, *Dolly: My Life and Other Unfinished Business* (New York: HarperCollins, 1994), p.2.

118 "town tramp": Dolly Parton, *Behind the Seams,* p.23.

119 "I have my own idea . . .": Ibid., p,37.

120 "has embraced all . . .": "Chappell Roan: 'The Giver' & Country Music," Apple Music, March 14, 2025, https://youtu.be/I5eNUIgfq5Y?si=bub2cVJbbW4dGGRJ [accessed 15th August 2025].

120 "plastic bag": Katy Perry, "Firework," *Teenage Dream* (Capitol, 2010).

121 "came from me wanting . . .": Sonya Ribner, "Slumber Party Pop: A New Authenticity with Chappell Roan," *Cherwell*, August 12, 2022, https://cherwell.org/2022/08/12/slumber-party-pop-a-new-authenticity-with-chappell-roan [accessed 21 November, 2025].

122 "I was scared of flamboyantly gay . . .": Brittany Spanos, "Chappell Roan Is a Pop Supernova: Nothing About It Has Been Easy," *Rolling Stone*, September 10, 2024, https://www.rollingstone.com/music/music-features/chappell-roan-good-luck-babe-fame-fans-1235094314 [accessed 21 November, 2025].

122 "so loud . . ." "Faces of Music: Chappell Roan," January 24, 2025, https://youtu.be/AgabfySQ0rA?si=3ZQ36NB7KUJJZy7j [accessed August 15, 2025].

122 "sex worker drag": Ibid.

122 "Everything I do . . .": Ibid.

124 "Give me your tired . . .": Quoted in Jon Blistein, "Chappell Roan on Why She Turned Down White House Invite: 'I Won't Be A Monkey For Pride,'" *Rolling Stone*, September 10, 2024, https: www.rollingstone.com/music/music-news/chappell-roan-explain-turned-down-white-housepride-invite-1235098090/ [accessed 30 November, 2025].

124 "We want liberty . . .": Ibid.

FLAMING: PERFORMANCE & PROTEST

PERFORMING

129 "He would sometimes . . .": Reported by Shirley Clarke in "Choreography of Cinema: An Interview with Shirley Clarke," *Afterimage*, December 1983, p.10.

130 "fabulous people": *Portrait of Jason* (dir. Shirley Clarke, 1966).

131 "I was going to let Jason . . .": "Choreography of Cinema," p.11.

133 "borrowed from the theater . . .": Jonas Barish, *The Antitheatrical Prejudice* (Berkeley: University of California Press, 1981), p.1.

135 "strangest and gaudiest . . .": Langston Hughes, "Spectacles in Color," in *The Big Sea: An Autobiography* (New York: Hill and Wang, 1963), p.273.

135 "bastion of standards . . ." Essex Hemphill, "To Be Real," *Ceremonies: Prose and Poetry* (Plume: New York, 1992), p.113.

136 "well enough . . ." Ricky Tucker, *And The Category Is . . . Inside New York's Vogue, House and Ballroom Community* (Boston: Beacon Press, 2021), p.73.

137 "You've got to be real": Cheryl Lynn, "Got to Be Real," *Cheryl Lynn* (Columbia, 1978).

137 "The late bell hooks . . .": See bell hooks, "Is Paris Burning?," *Black Looks: Race and Representation* (Boston: South End Press, 1992), pp.145–57.

138 "Gender theorist Judith Butler": See Judith Butler, "Gender is Burning: Questions of Appropriation and Subversion," *Bodies That Matter: On the Discursive Limits of "Sex"* (New York: Routledge, 1993), p.121–140.

138 "the runway . . ." Kate Bornstein, "Foreword," *RuPaul's Drag Race and Philosophy: Sissy That Thought*, ed. Hendrik Kempt and Megan Volpert (Chicago: Open Court, 2015), p.1.

139 "I thought . . .": "Madonna Talks Her Rise to the Top, Dating Tupac, and Her Infamous VMAs Performance During Her First Interview with Howard," *Howard Stern Show,* March 11, 2015, https://soundcloud.com/howardstern/madonna [accessed 21 November, 2025].

140 "Black aesthetics . . .": Lauren Michele Jackson, *White Negroes: When*

Cornrows Were in Vogue . . . And Other Thoughts on Cultural Appropriation (Boston: Beacon Press, 2019).

141 "I'll put on something . . .": Hamish Bowles, "Playtime with Harry Styles," *Vogue,* November 13, 2020 https://www.vogue.com/article/harry-styles-cover-december-2020 [accessed 21 November 2025].

WALKING

145 "Washington, DC, the late 1980s . . .": This account reenacts the encounter described in Essex Hemphill, "If I Simply Wanted Status, I'd Wear Calvin Klein," *Ceremonies: Prose and Poetry* (Plume: New York, 1992), pp.109–11.

146 "I had to carefully . . .": Hemphill, "Ceremonies," *Ceremonies,* ibid., p.95.

147 "I didn't want to strike . . .": Hemphill, "The *Other* Invisible Man," *Boys Like Us: Gay Writers Tell Their Coming Out Stories*, ed. Patrick Merla (New York: Avon Books, 1996), p.184.

148 "the director asked him . . .": Reported in Martin Duberman, *Hold Tight Gently: Michael Callen, Essex Hemphill and the Battlefield of AIDS* (New York: The New Press, 2014), p.117.

149 "*If I simply wanted* . . .": Hemphill, "If I Simply Wanted Status," *Ceremonies,* p.110.

150 "He pointed out . . .": Hemphill, "The *Other* Invisible Man," *Boys Like Us*, p.184.

150 "truly voguing": Hemphill, "If I Simply Wanted Status," *Ceremonies,* p.109.

150 "I remember Frank O'Hara's . . .": Joe Brainard, *I Remember* (New York: Granary Books, 2001), p.20.

150 "Girl, you walk . . .": Charli xcx and Lorde, "Girl, so confusing featuring lorde," *Brat and It's Completely Different but Also Still Brat* (Atlantic, 2024).

151 "Everybody is quite peculiar . . .": Edwin Denby, "Dancers, Buildings and People in the Streets," *Dancers, Buildings and People in the Streets* (New York: Curtis Books, 1965), p.165.

151 "pretty movements . . .": Ibid., p,155.

151 "American young men . . .": Ibid.

152 "the peculiar way . . .": Ibid., p.156.

154 "the performance art . . .": Zadie Smith, "Mark Bradford's *Niagara*," *Feel Free: Essays* (New York: Penguin Press, 2018), p.186.

155 "Think about a man . . .": Mark Bradford, "Lisa Tan Mark Bradford at Laxart" (2008), YouTube, https://www.youtube.com/watch?v=rI6dIbI6iH0 [accessed 21 November, 2025].

155 "fearless embodiment . . .": Mark Bradford, quoted in Victoria Wynne-Jones, *Choreographing Intersubjectivity in Performance Art* (Basingstoke: Palgrave Macmillan, 2021), p.186.

156 "nuclear option . . .": Zadie Smith, "Mark Bradford's *Niagara*," p.181.

156 "political urgency . . .": Ibid., p.186.

RESISTING

157 "The time for flamboyance . . .": David B. Goodstein, "Opening Space," *The Advocate*, November 16, 1977, p.5.

159 "vaguely disturbed . . .": Quoted in Larry P. Gross, *Up from Invisibility: Lesbians, Gay Men, and the Media in America.* (New York: Columbia University Press, 2001), p.46.

161 "fabulous, original . . .": The Lesbian Avengers Handbook, ACT UP Historical Archive https://actupny.org/documents/Avengers.html [accessed February 15, 2025].

161 "transform the image . . .": Kelly Cogswell, *Eating Fire: My Life as A Lesbian Avenger* (Minneapolis: University of Minnesota Press, 2014), p.21.

162 "circus trick . . .": Ibid., p.23.

162 "The bodies that say . . .": Judith Butler, *The Force of Nonviolence: An Ethico-Political Bind* (London: Verso, 2020), p.196.

162 "It was the old handcuffing . . .": "Seven things we learned from Liz Carr's Desert Island Discs," BBC Radio 4: https://www.bbc.co.uk/programmes/articles/4sdKjsj6XkfKWSxcL0ShYMX/seven-things-we-learned-from-liz-carrs-desert-island-discs [accessed February 15, 2025].

164 "gratuitous desire . . .": *Born in Flames* (dir. Lizzie Borden, 1983).

165 "in an obscure way . . .": Lucas Hilderbrand, "In the heat of the moment:

Notes on the past, present and future of *Born in Flames*," *Women & Performance*, 23.1 (2013), 13.

165 "For women . . .": Audre Lorde, "The Master's Tools Will Never Dismantle the Master's House," in *Sister Outsider: Essays and Speeches* (Trumansburg, NY: Crossing Press, 1984), p.111.

166 "Images of women . . .": Audre Lorde, *Zami; Sister Outsider; Undersong* (New York: Quality Paperback Book Club, 1993), p.3.

167 "not elaborately . . .": Kate Davy, *Lady Dicks and Lesbian Brothers: Staging the Unimaginable at the WOW Cafe Theater* (Ann Arbor: University of Michigan Press, 2010), p.73.

167 "outrageousness . . .": Alexis De Veaux, quoted in ibid., p.73.

168 "Contrary to other trees . . .": Quoted in Chandra Frank, "Flamboyant: Wildness, Loss, and Possibility in Feminist Organizing in the Netherlands," *Meridians*, 22.1 (April 2023), 35.

RECLAIMING

169 "Maybe you're a *flambé*": "Live Free or Die" (dir. Tim Van Patten, 2006), *The Sopranos,* Season 6, Episode 6, HBO.

170 "ROY COHN . . .": Albin Krebs, "Roy Cohn, Aide to McCarthy and Fiery Lawyer, Dies at 59," *The New York Times,* August 3, 1986, p.1.

170 "finds the flamboyant . . .": Harriet Monroe, "Flamboyance," *POETRY: A Magazine of Verse,* 21 (November 1922), p.89.

171 "Taking meetings . . .": *The Apprentice* (dir. Ali Abbasi, 2024).

171 "Why not say . . .": Eve Kosofsky Sedgwick, *The Epistemology of the Closet* (Berkeley: University of California Press, 1990), p.243.

171 "sexually expert": "flamer (noun)," *Green's Dictionary of Slang*, https://greensdictofslang.com/entry/mvv5vwi [accessed 16 Feb, 2025].

173 "masculine *character* . . .": Erich Fromm, *The Art of Loving* (London: Thorsons, 1995), p.29.

174 "conservative camp . . .": LaBruce, "Notes on Camp/Anti-Camp," *Nat. Brut*, 3 (April 2013), http://www.natbrutarchive.com/essay-notes-on-campanti-camp-by-bruce-labruce.html [accessed 20 November, 2025].

176 "brazenly calling . . .": *Fag Rag*, 2 (Fall 1971), p.2. LG MS 007, 15, 277, Lesbian, Gay, Bisexual, Transgender, Queer+ Collection, Special Collections, University of Southern Maine Libraries, Portland, ME.

176 "when a straight man . . .": Ibid.

176 "we are faggots . . .": Quoted with the permission of Michael Bronski.

179 "to mark a flamboyant . . .": Robert McRuer, "Crip," in *Keywords for Radicals: The Contested Vocabulary of Late-Capitalist Struggle*, ed. Kelly Fritsch, Clare O'Connor, AK Thompson (Chico, CA: AK Press, 2016), p.119.

179 "flamboyantly identitarian . . .": Ibid., p.122.

179 "Flamboyant was a word . . .": Ashley C. Ford, "Becoming Billy Porter," *Allure*, January 9, 2020.

REMEMBERING

181 "I've always been called . . .": Charles Michael Smith, "Bruce Nugent: Bohemian of the Harlem Renaissance," in *In the Life: A Black Gay Anthology* (Boston: Alyson Publications, 1986), p.209.

181 "burn up . . .": Langston Hughes, *The Big Sea: An Autobiography*, (New York: Hill and Wang, 1963), p.235.

182 "his bohemianism . . .": Charles Michael Smith, "Bruce Nugent," p.209.

182 "I must mold . . .": Joseph Beam, "Brother to Brother: Words from the Heart," *In the Life*, p.233.

183 "Anger unvented . . .": Quoted in *Tongues Untied* (dir. Marlon Riggs, 1989).

184 "I remember thinking . . .": Michele Wallace, "A Fierce Flame," *Dark Designs and Visual Culture* (Durham: Duke University Press, 2004), p.379.

184 "If you hadn't known . . .": Ibid., p.380.

184 "illusion of safe . . .": Marlon Riggs, "Unleash the Queen," *Black Popular Culture: A Project by Michele Wallace*, ed. Gina Dent (Seattle: Bay Press, 1992), p.105.

184 "crit queens": Ibid., p.102.

184 "Can she . . .": Ibid, p.103.

184 "rhetorical gender-fuck . . .": Ibid., p.99.

185 "I fell in love . . .": Wallace, "A Fierce Flame," p.380.

186 "lucent flames . . .": Essex Hemphill, "Vital Signs," *Life Sentences: Writers, Artists and AIDS*, ed. Thomas Avena (San Francisco: Mercury House, 1994), p.50.

188 "our mothers . . .": Hemphill, "Does Your Mama Know About Me?," *Ceremonies*, p.42.

BURNING: PASSION & ECSTASY

LOVING

195 "its most inspiring theorists": See Erich Fromm, *The Art of Loving* (London: Thorsons, 1995); bell hooks, *All About Love* (New York: William Morrow, 2018); and Shon Faye, *Love in Exile* (London: Allen Lane, 2025).

196 "I'm nineteen . . .": Lorde, "Perfect Places," *Melodrama* (Lava, Republic Records, 2017).

197 "supercut": Lorde, "Supercut," Ibid.

TORCHING

201 "O, she doth . . .": William Shakespeare, *Romeo and Juliet*, Act I, Scene V.

201 "They've got their . . .": Elvis Presley, "Fools Fall in Love" (RCA Victor, 1966).

203 "Individual A . . .": Allen Forte, *Listening to Classic American Popular Songs* (New Haven: Yale University Press, 2001), p.203.

203 "conscious wanting": Brené Brown, *Atlas of the Heart: Mapping Meaningful Connection and the Language of Human Experience* (Vermillion: London, 2021), p.11.

205 "Men cluster . . .": Marlene Dietrich, "Falling in Love Again," performed in *The Blue Angel* (dir. Josef von Sternberg, 1930).

207 "an immoral . . .": John Cheever, "Torch Song," in *Collected Stories and Other Writings* (New York: Library of America, 2009), p.117.

207 "once before reminded . . .": Ibid., p.123.

208 "reputation was growing . . .": Alexis De Veaux, *Don't Explain: A Song of Billie Holiday* (New York: Harper & Row, 1980), p.20.

209 "knew how to style . . ." Ibid.

209 "soft, delicate . . .": Quoted in Lauren Valentin, "The Story Behind Billie Holiday's Iconic Gardenia Hair," *Vogue*, February 26, 2021, online: https://www.vogue.com/article/billie-holiday-gardenia-flower-hair-history [accessed February 22, 2025].

210 "afire": Essex Hemphill, "Gardenias," *Ceremonies Prose and Poetry* (Plume: New York, 1992), p.133.

210 "management never . . .": Billie Holiday (with William Duffy), *Lady Sings the Blues* (New York: Harlem Moon, 2006), p.87.

210 "strictly after-hours . . .": Music for Torching, The Billie Holiday Estate, https://billieholiday.com/album/music-for-torching [accessed February 22, 2025].

211 "burnt-edged digressions . . .": Stacy Holman Jones, "Burnt: Writing Torch Singers and Torch Singing," *Cultural Studies ↔ Critical Methodologies*, 10.4 (2010), p.289.

211 "her burnt . . .": Ibid.

212 "stagecraft of economy": Joel Dinerstein, *The Origins of Cool in Postwar America* (Chicago: University of Chicago Press, 2017), p.166.

212 "walked to the stage . . .": Ibid., p.165.

212 "controlled emotional . . .": Ibid., p.168.

212 "Who could be . . .": Pauline Kael, "Lady Sings the Blues: Pop Versus Jazz," in *For Keeps: 30 Years at the Movies* (New York: Dutton, 1994), p.457.

LOSING

214 "Freudian fate": Amy Winehouse, "What Is It About Men?," *Frank* (Island Records, 2003).

215 "1960s R&B . . .": Daphne A. Brooks, "'This voice which is not one': Amy Winehouse sings the ballad of sonic blue(s)face culture," *Women & Performance*, 20:1 (2010), p.44.

215 "I know there are people . . .": *Amy Winehouse* Back to Black*: The Real Story Behind the Modern Classic* (dir. Jeremy Mare, 2018).

216 "I knew that little girl . . .": Ronnie Spector, in Ibid.

217 "Like the more insecure . . .": Ibid.

218 "kitchen sink drama . . .": Naomi Parry, *Amy Winehouse: Beyond Black* (London: Thames & Hudson, 2021), p.98

218 "vulnerability, coupled . . .": *Amy Winehouse* Back to Black.

218 "For you I was . . .": Amy Winehouse, "Love Is a Losing Game," *Back to Black* (Island Records, 2006).

218 "Winehouse would never sing . . .": *Amy Winehouse* Back to Black.

219 "her fans loved her . . .": Leslie Jamison, "Confessions of an Unredeemed Fan," *Longreads,* July 23, 2018, https://longreads.com/2018/07/23/confessions-of-an-unredeemed-fan/ [accessed February 24, 2025].

219 "you could see . . .": Philippa Snow, *It's Terrible the Things I Have to Do to Be Me: On Fame and Femininity* (London: Virago, 2025), p.268.

220 "two bright pink flamingos . . .": Naomi Parry, *Amy Winehouse: Beyond Black*, p.271.

220 "The light that burns . . .": *Blade Runner* (dir. Ridley Scott, 1982).

221 "knowing who to cling . . .": Elton John, "Candle in the Wind," *Goodbye Yellow Brick Road* (DJM, 1973).

221 "inconsolably vulnerable": Bernie Taupin, *Scattershot: Life, Music, Elton and Me* (London: Monoray, 2023), p.201.

222 "No more candle . . .": Lana Del Rey, "Mariners' Apartment Complex," *Norman Fucking Rockwell!* (Interscope and Polydor Records, 2019).

222 "first love . . .": Jonathan Sheaf, "Lana Del Rey: 'I never wanted to lead a normal life,'" *GQ*, 1 October 2012, https://www.gq-magazine.co.uk/article/woman-of-the-year-lana-del-rey [accessed 21 November, 2025].

223 "yearning is . . .": Leslie Jamison, *The Recovering: Intoxication and its Aftermath* (London: Granta Books, 2019), p.425.

223 "I would have loved . . .": ibid., p.399.

224 "a blaze . . .": Amy Winehouse, "Tears Dry on Their Own," *Back to Black*.

RECOVERING

227 "Drugs and alcohol have . . .": Duncan Macmillan, *People, Places and Things* (London: Methuen, 2021), p.52.

227 "that's *fucked*": Ibid., p.89.

229 "I want to *live* . . .": Ibid.

230 "We see the musician . . .": *Rocketman* (dir. Dexter Fletcher, 2019).

235 "victim blaming": Virginia Heffernan, "The End of Alcohol," *WIRED*, April 19, 2022, https://www.wired.com/story/the-end-of-alcohol [accessed February 23, 2025].

236 "Mystical gurus . . .": Ibid.

236 "a giant, dirty, wild . . .": Amanda Eyre Ward and Jardine Libaire, *The Sober Lush: A Hedonist's Guide to Living a Decadent, Adventurous, Soulful Life—Alcohol Free* (London: TarcherPerigree, 2020), p.5.

236 "I was really just . . .": Eileen Myles, "Coming Clear," *OUT*, February 1999, September 15, 2017, https://www.out.com/vaults/2017/9/15/eileen-myles-reflects-sobriety-coming-clear#toggle-gdpr [accessed February 23, 2025].

237 "wine poet": Eileen Myles, Ibid.

THE ART

241 "unsatisfied wishes . . .": Sigmund Freud, "Creative Writers and Day-Dreaming" (1908), in *The Standard Edition of the Complete Psychological Works of Sigmund Freud,* vol. 9, ed. James Strachey (London: Vintage, 2001), p.146.

241 "liberation of tensions . . .": Ibid., p.153.

244 "When I lived . . .": *Muriel's Wedding* (dir. PJ Hogan, 1994).

246 "Why do people . . ." Lauren Berlant, *Cruel Optimism* (Durham: Duke University Press, 2011), p.2.

246 "moves you out . . .": Ibid., pp.1–2.

246 "in the wake of . . .": Ibid., p.2.

247 "one of the great . . .": Andy Medhurst, "Muriel's Wedding: The greatest film of all time?" April 3, 2025 (originally published 2002), *Sight and Sound* https://www.bfi.org.uk/sight-andsound/features/muriels-wedding-greatest-film-all-time [accessed August 15, 2025].

247 "whole thesis . . .": Rachel Griffiths, quoted in "How we made Muriel's Wedding," *The Guardian*, April 14, 2025 https://www.theguardian.com/culture/2025/apr/14/plus- sized-thief-liar-muriels-wedding-toni-collette [accessed August 15, 2025].

INDEX